MW01010452

Directing
CHRISTIAN
EDUCATION

Directing

CHRISTIAN

EDUCATION

The Changing Role of
The Christian Education Specialist

Michael S. Lawson ▪ Robert J. Choun, Jr.

MOODY PRESS
CHICAGO

© 1992 by
MICHAEL S. LAWSON and ROBERT J. CHOUN, JR.

The author of chapter 8, Lynn Gannett,
is director of Christian Education
at Chelton Baptist Church, Dresher, Pennsylvania.

All rights reserved. No part of this book may be
reproduced in any form without permission in writing
from the publishers, except in the case of brief quotations
embodied in critical articles or reviews.

All scripture quotations, unless noted otherwise, are from
the *New American Standard Bible*, ©1960, 1962, 1963, 1968, 1971,
1972, 1973, 1975, and 1977 by The Lockman Foundation.

ISBN: 0-8024-1702-7

3 5 7 9 11 10 8 6 4 2

Printed in the United States of America

To
Tish Lawson and Jane Choun,
special wives,
gifts from God.
You are allies, friends, and confidantes,
reasons for our success,
and "helpmeets" in life and ministry.

Contents

Introduction

More people than ever are directing Christian education in the church, but the term "director of Christian education" no longer describes the average church educator. *Minister* and *pastor of Christian education* have emerged as popular titles for this position in the church. In larger churches, those responsible for Christian education often supervise specific groups, such as adults, youth, children, or early childhood, which require even more specific title designations. At times, churches subdivide adults into senior adults, young couples, singles, career, and college in order to provide specialized attention. Youth typically is segmented into senior high and junior high.

Each of these groupings may need the undivided efforts of a professional staff member, but each involves Christian education. Therefore the authors have developed the term *Christian education specialist* (CES) to describe the varying duties and differing titles of the C.E. professional. In some cases, a church will have only one CES. In others, many will work in concert to develop a comprehensive approach to Christian education. We include both types in this study of the roles and relationships of the C.E. specialist.

This book describes that part of Christian education that occurs within the local church. We ignore the parts related to Christian schools, parachurch organizations, or individual "discipleship" efforts. Although we see possibilities for the field to expand into entrepreneurial multichurch efforts, neither of us has any personal experience with this creative approach and omit this discussion. We want to define more clearly a job we both enjoyed for a combined total of twenty-seven years. We explain what succeeded for us. We tried many things—a few really worked!

We could not produce a definitive work on Christian education in the church from our own substantial experiences, as conditions and expectations vary from church to church. Therefore we have asked three CESs to respond to each chapter. Their "Principles in Practice" contain responses to chapter ideas, personal insights, and practical suggestions. The job titles of our responders range widely and describe the varying roles in the Christian education effort of their churches. They typically represent the small, medium, and large church, come from a cross-section of denominational backgrounds, and possess varied training and tenure in the field. Some, like the children's ministers, write from a very focused perspective. But because they give more time and thought to one area, they can help other CESs to understand key elements in educational ministry.

Of course, the size of church and denominational affiliation of our responders will color their perspectives on Christian education. Their critiques of our ideas and practical applications vary and should provoke the reader's thinking. No doubt you will find some principles immediately useful. Others would never work in your situation, or you might feel uncomfortable implementing them. Still others would serve your church best if adapted. You are the expert in your church. Use the thinking of your fellow practitioners as written consultations to enrich your ministry.

Chapter 1 lays a biblical and philosophical base for the specialist, and our responders are the coauthors of *Christian Education: Its History and Philosophy.* Kenneth O. Gangel gives enormous leadership to the field with his prolific writing. Warren S. Benson combines twelve years of experience in the church as a CES with his thoughtful approach to the issues facing Christian education. We asked them to be candid, feeling free to disagree where necessary. They did. You may not agree with either them or us. But at least you have our perspectives to consider.

From the beginning, competent women have helped shape both the theory and the practice of Christian education. Henrietta Mears, Ethel Barrett, and Mary and Lois LeBar head a long list of women who have influenced Christian education. Only a woman should describe the female experience, and Lynn Gannett evaluates the role and reception of women CESs in chapter 8. Gannett has served as a CES for more than fifteen years and earned an Ed.D. from Memphis State University. She brings a practitioner's eye to the chapter "The Female Education Specialist."

In the American church, the field of Christian education continues to develop and expand. In a survey of CESs, the Professional Association of Christian Educators (PACE) found thirty-five different ministry areas for the CES (see chap. 2). Rarely is any individual CES asked to be an expert in all these; however, movement from church to church can dramatically alter the job requirements. Therefore we have included eight different job descriptions as samples in Appendix A. In Appendix B we offer a sample schedule planner as a guide to organized planning by the Christian education specialist. The planner also reminds CESs that their duties are diverse and many.

Because of the dynamic nature of Christian education, we chose to survey current practitioners, and 113 CESs participated in the survey. The survey results are found in Appendix D. The data provide a basis from which to work, and confirm what we expected. The survey results appear throughout the book, clarifying the problems and, in some cases, suggesting solutions.

The survey participants are also members of PACE, formerly known as the National Association of Directors of Christian Education (NADCE). Formed in 1960 to provide a fellowship for the growing number of men and women employed by churches to supervise their education programs, the NADCE was renamed the Professional Association of Christian Educators in 1990 to reflect the changing titles and growing international focus of the organization. PACE has about 500 active members (5,000 on its mailing list). PACE is the only evangelical association for church education professionals that crosses denominational lines.

We applaud those front-line experts, who implement Christian education in their church week after week. What they do fulfills Ephesians 4:12, "to prepare God's people for works of service, so that the body of Christ may be built up." They recruit, train, and coordinate armies of volunteers in the service of the King. If we make their efforts easier by clarifying their task and addressing a few of the tougher problems, we rejoice.

The National Association of Professors of Christian Education represents those who teach Christian education in Bible colleges and seminaries. Perhaps this book will serve as a benchmark against which they can test the training and experiences of those preparing to enter the profession.

We also write to help the increasing number of men and women who enter the profession directly from their own congregations with no formal training. They face an enormous task, but they usually benefit from strong relationships with and confidence from their congregations.

The Third World church desperately needs the insights gained by Christian education practitioners in the United States. In addition to books and materials, the American church should share its professionally trained and experienced human resources. In 1989 and 1991, PACE pioneered such an effort in Mexico City. More than 1,000 people representing twelve denominations attended each of the four-day training efforts. The fifteen-member faculty included both Mexican and American church educators. PACE plans to sponsor similar events both in Mexico and elsewhere. We hope the ideas in this book stimulate international exchanges like this, as they directly and immediately impact the local church.

Christian education faces a bright future. American churches and foreign mission agencies heavily recruit Christian education specialists. May God multiply their enabling and encouraging ministry.

A Biblical and Philosophical Perspective

In order to understand the relationship of a Christian education specialist to the modern church, we must answer two questions: (1) What is the nature of the educational task facing the church? (2) Does the church need specialized help to achieve the task? These two questions, and their interdependent answers, form the overall outline for this chapter. Each question has two answers, and those answers will provide a fourfold biblical and philosophical justification for someone to supervise and coordinate the Christian education ministry in the church.

Our rationale builds from an assumption that many of the New Testament imperatives for Christian education resemble God's directive in Genesis to replenish the earth. God has explained exactly the results He expects, but He does not discuss the specific procedures necessary to accomplish the task. He leaves many details for the church to determine in concert with clear biblical instructions, human wisdom, and prayerful consideration. With this in mind, let us examine the first question.

THE NATURE OF THE CHURCH'S EDUCATIONAL TASK

Educational implications permeate the New Testament. Beginning with Jesus as a teacher, the movement known as Christianity sits squarely on an educational foundation. Consider these references from sixteen different New Testament books:

Acts 2:42-47	The believers devote themselves to the apostles' teaching.
Rom. 12:7	The gift of teaching is given for the benefit of others.
1 Cor. 12:28	God appoints teachers third after apostles and prophets.
Gal. 6:6	Recipients of teaching/instruction are reminded to share material blessings with the teacher.
Eph. 4:11	God gives pastors and teachers to build up the church.
Phil. 4:9	Paul reminds the Philippians to practice what they had learned from him.
Col. 1:28	Paul informs the Colossians that, among other things, he teaches everyone with all wisdom.
1 Thess. 4:1	Paul recalls that he instructed them how to live.
2 Thess. 3:6	Paul instructs them to separate from idle brothers who ignore his teaching.
1 Tim. 4:11	Paul urges Timothy to command and teach the things in this epistle.
2 Tim. 2:2	Timothy is instructed to train qualified men who will teach others.
Titus 1:10	Elders must hold firmly what they have been taught.
Heb. 5:12	Many should have become teachers already.
2 Pet. 2:1	Peter predicts that false teachers will exist among Christians.
2 John	The lady is reminded that those who do not continue in the teaching of Christ do not have God.

Jude   Readers are reminded to contend for the "faith," or teaching, entrusted to the saints.

The church surely should take these educational implications seriously. More than mere implication, the New Testament provides an educational guide, as Jesus outlines an educational vision unparalleled in human history. Following His departure, the Holy Spirit empowered the church described in the book of Acts and the epistles to implement Christ's vision. Both Christ's outline and the early church's implementation clarify the church's educational responsibilities.

The Great Commission

If Matthew 28 is more than the "Great Suggestion," an enormous and complex project lies before the church. The Great Commission envisions a unique quality and scope for education. To borrow a phrase from the children's gospel song, the task appears both deep and wide.

First, Jesus instructs the apostles to "make disciples" (Matt. 28:19a). Disciples do not make themselves. Leaders must make and teach them. In fact, Jesus Himself trained those twelve leaders to assume that responsibility. Jesus expects the results of their efforts to be "disciples" or, better still, "learners."

Matheteusate (make disciples) appears in the imperative mood, carrying the force of a command. It is the primary verb, upon which all the other verbs depend.[1] Making learners is the focus of the Great Commission.

Developing students hardly qualifies as a novel idea. The unusual educational expectations on Jesus' students and those who teach them is surprising. Two tasks lay before these new followers. Clearly, Jesus expected them to both know and observe all that He commanded. These students would develop beyond creedal recitation. His disciples must "observe" His teaching. The proof of observing lay in obeying the teaching of Jesus. His followers must blend the cognitive recognition of facts with obedience.

In modern educational terms, His truth will govern the cognitive, affective, and psycho-motor domains. The Great Commission anticipates an educational depth that permeates the very core of life. Christ's disciples examine every thought, word, and deed in light of His teaching.

The church faces a unique and demanding task of bringing people beyond understanding to obedience. Successful disciple making remains incomplete without application of truth to life. The living proof of the church's success or failure parades through each culture for everyone to see.

Christian education in simple terms is the disciple-making ministry of the church. Christian education does more than combine public education principles found in modern research with the Bible. Properly done, Christian education at the local church level focuses on spiritual development, life change, and values education in ways fundamentally different from general education. For instance, public education completely ignores the student's spiritual dimension. No Scholastic Aptitude Test questions whether a student applies mathematics or English to his/her life. Modern educational relativism rejects Christianity's set of core values as an educational standard.

True, Christian education does lean on modern educational research even as biblical studies use modern archaeology and other disciplines. Unfortunately, modern educational research largely belongs to secular scholars. Most Christian educators depend on secular research to explain how students learn ordinary information. Then they draw implications about how people assimilate spiritual truth.[2] Everyone's understanding about the learning process remains somewhat fuzzy. Important areas still need correlating with other pieces of information. In spite of these limitations, Jesus clearly called for knowledgeable and obedient learners.

Second, the educational task is easily as wide as it is deep. Jesus envisioned a universal dimension to His education program when He challenged the apostles to move beyond the borders of Israel to "all the nations" (Matt. 28:19). Whether this phrase is a geographic, political, or linguistic designation, Jesus clearly does not limit the obligation for disciple makers. No exemptions exist for language, culture, education, wealth, sex, age, or religious background. In training disciples, the only implied limit appears self-imposed by those who decline discipleship.

Consider the prospect of teaching *everything* Jesus taught to *everyone*. Perhaps no one has ever been in the education business to the extent the church has. What school system, public or private, ever envisioned so ambitious an undertaking as Jesus describes in the Great Commission?

Whatever else may be true, the church ought to be a gathering of Jesus' students. The church ought to be a learning community. This learning community must enable her children, youth, and adults to grow in the faith. All must become Jesus' disciples.

The Early Church

Beginning with Acts 2, the Holy Spirit begins to help the church fulfill the Great Commission. The remainder of Acts and the epistles clarifies the church's mission. The same components exist: (1) All become learners. (2) They must learn everything the Lord commanded. (3) They must obey what they learn. The experiences recorded in Acts, Hebrews, and Ephesians hint at how the church tackled new problems while implementing Christ's command.

Acts 11:19-30 and 13:1-5. Although many churches may have sprung up later, Luke describes the gathering at Antioch in singular terms as "the church" (11:26). Phrases such as "a large number" in 11:21 and "considerable numbers" in 11:26 describe a sizable congregation. In this one very large church, Luke names five prophets and teachers who apparently constituted the leadership (13:1). To some extent, this church found multiple prophets and teachers necessary to implement the disciple-making process.

Their educational strategy required some creativity. For the first time, a church confronted the problem of educating a large pagan constituency. The Antioch church had to provide different levels of instruction as they integrated the Gentile community. The Jewish believers possessed the rich symbolic background of the Old Testaament sacrificial system upon which to build the truth concerning the good news. However, the Gentiles brought their polytheistic background into the church. They were ignorant of Old Testament teaching. Almost everything was novel in their newfound faith.

The strategy in Antioch focused on education. In Acts 11:22-26 Barnabas became the first educational consultant when he evaluated the needs of the Antioch church, determined that their education efforts were deficient, and decided on a remedial education program. He recruited a controversial but brilliant teacher from Tarsus and implemented the teaching along with Paul for one year. Interestingly, Paul did not lead the group at that time. Almost everyone agrees that Barnabas directed the ministry team since his name precedes Paul's until Acts 13:42. Even the list in 13:1 places Paul last.

The fledgling Gentile believers of Antioch needed training in the Old Testament. No wonder Barnabas recruited Paul. As an Old Testament scholar, Paul could explain how the good news of Jesus Christ fit with the ancient promises of God. Those converts responded by distinguishing themselves with the label of "Christian."

All kinds of questions surface about the inner organization, the exact curriculum, the division of responsibilities, and so much more. Did one teacher cover basics while another taught advanced courses? Did one teach adults, while another one taught children and youth? Is the large church model in Antioch superior to the house church model seemingly described in the early experience in Jerusalem?

Some conclusions seem obvious. The church at Antioch was large enough to require multiple teachers. Barnabas functioned like many modern church educators. The church adopted an educational strategy to accommodate the unprecedented developments in Antioch.

Hebrews 5:11-14. Unlike Acts 11 and 13, this letter is not localized. The recipients were not in one church. But the unnamed author of this epistle scolds everyone because they were slow learners and ought to have been *teachers.* The *whole group* should have been teachers! There must have been enough classes and students for them to teach. Otherwise, why scold them?

This passage suggests that two classifications of educational material existed. The author calls the first "milk" (5:12), which equals basic food for beginners. Although crucial to early development, "milk" should soon give way to something the author calls "solid food" (5:12). Surely the early church coordinated teaching materials and assigned specific teachers to each group. This dual curriculum makes sense. New converts continually entered the church, and each new wave needed basic orientation and information. Meanwhile, older believers needed to build on and practice what they already knew.

Even more intriguing, the author concludes that the educational progress had been interrupted. He suggests a remedial program beginning again with the "elementary truths." The readers actually required "milk" again since they had not grown into teachers.

More questions than answers arise from this passage. Did these teachers normally go about their business in an autonomous fashion without supervision or accountability? Who decided what should be included in the "milk" diet and the "solid food" diet? Was the teaching random or systematic? If systematic, who planned it? Obviously this passage does not specify.

Here again, the idea of multiple teachers appears normative rather than exceptional. The need to coordinate the efforts of a corps of teachers looks obvious. Developing curriculum on multiple levels implies something more sophisticated in structure and planning than merely hoping everybody gets what they need when they come to church. These activities reflect the heart and soul of Christian education that seeks to systematically consolidate the products of evangelism by developing learners who love learning about and obeying Jesus.

Ephesians 4:7-16. Although God's purpose for an individual church cannot rest exclusively on one pastor's abilities, the pastor does have a crucial part to play in the development of Christians within the church. This passage states that God gave pastors and teachers to prepare Christians for works of service. If teaching provides the heart and soul of Christian education, then service provides the feet. The obedience part of discipleship requires Christians to minister to each other and their world.

These works of service may involve isolated acts of mercy, but they might also require complex coordinated efforts. To achieve larger objectives, the effort must be organized. Church members may be biblically knowledgeable and willing to serve by virtue of the pastor's preaching, teaching, and exhorting. But their efforts in ministry may fail until each person's job is small enough for busy people to manage. In the Old Testament, Nehemiah provides an excellent example for churches to follow in coordinated planning of large projects. It is not enough to merely exhort people from the pulpit to do something. Leaders must explain specifically what portion of the overall task each Christian is called upon to do.

The church languished educationally during the Middle Ages, when priests and pastors did the work of the ministry instead of preparing others. Paul insists that the Body of Christ functions best when everyone contributes (1 Cor. 12:7). Peter agrees that this should be the norm (1 Pet. 4:10). Coordinated efforts avoid duplication and oversight of significant ministries.

In the late twentieth century, pastor Frank Tillapaugh has implemented this biblical model at the Bear Valley Baptist Church in Denver, Colorado. The ministry has steadily gained momentum, and Tillapaugh describes his church's journey in his book *Unleashing the Church.* His fundamental premise appears in the subtitle, "Getting People Out of the Fortress and Into the Ministry." As he elaborates, "I do not mean to imply that ministries taking place inside church buildings are wrong. Persons teaching Sunday School or singing in the choir meet the needs of the body. Their ministries are very important. It's just that they are not enough if we are to fulfill the Great Commission completely."[3] Although the Bear Valley church leaders systematically plan to meet the needs of the body, they encourage a huge diversity of ministries outside the church fueled by individual motivation and vision. Meanwhile, the church leadership coordinates both areas to avoid duplication or even competition.

The educational strategy from Ephesians 4 presents yet another perspective. While challenging and coordinating mature believers' services, the church must simultaneously provide nurture and a different selection of ministries to the young believers. Clearly, some church ministries are off limits to the novice (1 Tim. 3:6). Designing experiences that account for all the variables can get confusing. Chronological age, biblical information, and spiritual age all affect a believer's capabilities and needs.

Some might be chronologically young and yet possess a great deal of biblical data they have not yet integrated into their experience. On the other hand, someone might be chronologically old and possess very little biblical data. How can the church account for the development of these diverse experiences unless someone addresses their specific needs? A full-time job exists for someone to provide multiple opportunities to study and serve. This raises the second major question: Does the church need specialized help to achieve the task?

THE NEED FOR A SPECIALIST

The church can hardly escape education as a major part of her mission. Through her leaders the church must provide Christian education for the next generation. But does the church need a Christian education specialist (CES)?

For a number of years, modern churches have employed individuals who carry titles such as director, minister, or pastor of Christian education. No specific biblical mandate exists for a CES as does the call for the pastor, deacon, elder, and bishop. Is there an adequate biblical rationale for a specific individual to devote exclusive time to develop educational strategies?

Theologians commonly use deduction to develop their sophisticated understanding of doctrines such as the Trinity or the hypostatic union. Churches justify buildings, organs, hymnals, and pew Bibles because these items assist the church's mission. Thinking the same way about the nature of God and the nature of modern societies helps explain why churches need a CES.

Reason #1: The Nature of God

One attribute of God points specifically toward a CES in the church. God is organized. His creation reflects incredible organization. Who can comprehend the myriad details God ordained in just one of the following areas—human anatomy; language, memory, and thinking; or the stars in the heavens? Countless details puzzle the mind.

In theology, the eternal plan of God is just that, a plan with countless details. More than generating vague ideas, God specializes in detailed planning. The following verses remind us how the interests of God extend to minutiae.

Matthew 10:30   He numbers the hairs of our heads.
Matthew 10:29   He remembers the fate of common sparrows.
Romans 8:28   He works all things for the good of those who love Him.
Ephesians 4:10 He prepares good works for every Christian to walk in.

Since God is no stranger to organization and detailed planning, the educational program designed to teach people about Him should not reflect less. Sure, churches can be organized without being godly, but can they be godly without being organized?

Churches normally do not permit just anyone to preach or perform music. Some level of proficiency and training is expected. Why should the church allow just anyone, or worse, no one, to coordinate the educational program of the church? If the church must do everything "decently and in order" (1 Cor. 14:40), that requirement should also apply to one of the main functions of the church, its educational program.

Even the earliest history of the church (Acts 6:1-7) demonstrates that when something must be done, someone must be assigned to supervise and coordinate. In Acts 6, the church appointed deacons because no one watched out for the widows of Grecian Jews. No doubt those early deacons were called upon to do many things not specifically detailed in the account. What else did deacons do? Were deacons ever expected to think about the educational needs of the church?

In 1 Timothy 3:5, Paul requires elders to manage their own households as evidence of their ability to "take care" of God's church.

The word "take care" also occurs in the story of the Good Samaritan. Jesus describes what the Samaritan does with the wounded Jew upon arriving at the inn. He "takes care" of him. Jesus covers many unnamed but necessary details with that simple phrase. What exactly did elders "take care" of in the church since the deacons took care of the widows? Perhaps God intended elders to give specific oversight to the educational program of the church. Would God give such a clear mandate without expecting some organized attempt to accomplish the task?

The job of organizing and planning Christian education must receive systematic and orderly attention. In this way the church can reflect the nature of God.

Christian education will not spontaneously occur just because everyone is sincere. Although the educational task looms complicated and vast, the church must make the effort.

Reason #2: The Nature of Modern Society

Societies exist only by God's permission. Babel, Sodom, Nineveh, Babylon, and even Israel provide grim reminders that God controls the destiny of each culture. God calls the church to carry on its mission in the midst of diverse and ever changing cultural conditions. The letters to the churches in Revelation suggest that God understands when limitations exist. Where there is an open door, He has opened it. Where there is conflict and persecution, He has permitted it.

God calls the church to make disciples in today's culture, not to the culture of a generation ago or even the first century. The society where one Sunday sermon met the educational requirements for every Christian in a church does not exist today. Perhaps it never did.

Long ago societies changed little from generation to generation. Information needs may have been less. Presently, decades bring quantum leaps that alter and threaten life. Drug abuse, international terrorism, sexual promiscuity, air pollution, and nuclear waste clutter a long list of complex problems plaguing the world community and this society. As distasteful as these problems are, the church cannot ignore them.

Unfortunately, in early generations the church addressed her worship and education primarily to adults.[4] Why? Did the church assume that parents would trickle down crucial information to youth and children in the home? Did stable rural cultures allow this procedure more opportunity to succeed? Was it an oversight?

Whatever the reason, leaders in the Reformation finally recognized the need to educate children and youth. However, Calvin's educational system relied on schools as separate institutions from the church to educate the young.[5] Eventually those public schools became secular, and the church made no immediate adjustment. Only later under the visionary leadership of Robert Raikes and Charles Wesley did the church formally undertake education as a part of a child's overall church experience.[6] More recently, in the latter twentieth century, churches have begun to seriously challenge the prevailing educational systems of children and youth.

The Home as a Christian Education Leader

Based on Deuteronomy 6, the family also bears responsibility for spiritually discipling the next generation. The family and the church carry the burden jointly. Ideally, neither one would relinquish its separate role to the other. In reality, the church may need to carry the bulk of the responsibility. Protestant educators have hesitated to say this clearly. The modern collapse of the family puts the church squarely in the position of needing to strengthen both the family unit and the individuals within it.

The home was once the center of Christian nurture. Now child abuse, working mothers, and single-parent families lead a long list of stresses that presently sap the strength of this fundamental Christian education agency. By the time repairs occur in the home, the nurturing years for children have too often slipped silently away. Without question the Bible makes the home responsible for Christian education. Yet in their present condition, families may be unable to fulfill the call to Christian education. If the home fails, either the church fills the void or the task remains undone.

The Community and Schools as Christian Educators

If the church does not lead in Christian education, who will? In Puritan New England, the community, home, and school functioned in concert with the church to support Christian education. Today, those conditions exist only in remote pockets of America.

The typical bedroom community, much less the inner city, provides little consistent support for Christian values. Local governments struggle to cope with substance abuse, pornography, rape, and deviant behavior of every sort. The church serves as a lighthouse to modern communities, not an expression of their shared values.

Some families remain strong and have a profound influence on the Christian education of children. But these constitute a dwindling, not an expanding, percentage of the population.

The private Christian school is important to the overall advancement of Christian education. However, Christian schools could not accommodate all the students if every Christian child suddenly shifted to the private sector. Only a small percentage of the overall population will ever attend Christian schools due to cost and availability. Home schooling, although effective, is not possible for single parents or the uneducated.

The church cannot relinquish its leadership role in Christian education to the public or private school. The church has broader responsibilities than a school. In fact, some argue that Christian schools (or any schools for that matter) should function as elitist educational institutions.[7] Proponents recommend that those who can learn do so and those who cannot find something else to pursue. Even if unintentional, private schools cannot avoid the elitist problem to some extent. Almost all private schools select students by their ability to pay, parental agreement with a doctrinal position, cooperation by the student, or other criteria.

The church must continually extend itself without restriction into the community. The church that provides education for one member should provide it for every member. If a church offers discipleship classes to challenge adults, why not appropriate classes to challenge children? A church should not provide less for one group of people than another.

Christians find themselves in all levels of government agencies and multinational corporations making crucial decisions about these and other issues. Do they have a Christian perspective? Where did they get it? Must they rely on their own thinking? Do they have the benefit of thinking with the whole Christian community and especially their own local church? The church must prepare these disciples to live as Christians.

A FUTURE FOCUS

In *Learning for Tomorrow*, Alvin Toffler sets forth the premise that education should focus on the future.[8] In other words, education should anticipate world developments and prepare young and old for the anticipated changes. Should the church look to the future as well? Can Christian education afford to wait and then react? The Bible's eternal message suggests answers for today and tomorrow. Educational programs in the church need to reflect this timeless attitude.

Kirschenbaum and Simon suggest how a focus on the future affects the goal of public education: "More recently, we have realized that, in a world in which the amount of knowledge increases geometrically, and in which no one can keep pace with it, we need to change our emphasis from what to learn to how to learn."[9]

Applied to Christian education, disciples would learn how to think and integrate their biblical faith in new and unfamiliar settings. A comprehensive educational program linking the Bible with current and future issues requires thinking, planning, organizing, recruiting, training, and evaluation. Who will do this in the church? Overworked pastors should not face the task.

The church cannot change its message. It must, however, organize itself creatively to meet the barrage of changing needs in the local setting. Modern missiologists stress the need for contextualization of the message in developing countries. However, only a few brave pioneers have applied it here in America.

Gene Getz argues cogently for distinguishing between form

and function in the church.[10] Functions always remain the same whereas forms may vary. Following his reasoning, the function of Christian education has always been fundamental to the church. One modern form that facilitates that function is a Christian education specialist.[11] Certainly the function could be accomplished in other ways, but this seems to be a good way.

How should church forms adapt to urban settings, modern technology, and compressed schedules? Urban settings require more sophisticated educational offerings because of the diverse population. "One size fits all" is an inadequate strategy for the twenty-first century. A single church may need to develop educational strategies to minister to the illiterate on one hand, while challenging highly trained college graduates on the other. A simple declaration of truth may have met the preaching requirements of the New Testament era. But nothing short of enabling the student to discover truth for himself from the Bible will meet the requirements of teaching today.

Organizing discovery experiences for different ages and levels of spiritual development requires considerable thought and effort. The church may be able to meet the challenge only through specialized help, namely, the CES.

Prior to the printing press, the church could do only limited things with written material. Modern tools of education include high-speed copiers, computers, graphics, and projection capabilities. As a result, new educational procedures can help Christians learn more quickly, retain information longer, and apply the truth more systematically. A specialist familiar with such procedures can help the church take advantage of the technological revolution.

A specialist also may help the church evaluate something as simple as the typical Sunday schedule. Why does the worship service meet at 11:00 A.M. and the Sunday school at 9:45? Didn't that choice of time revolve around morning farm chores? For most Americans, there are no farm chores. Early morning hours are needlessly lost for educational purposes. Feasibility studies to streamline educational programs require time, energy, and creativity. Who will implement needed changes in the church?

Today, more than ever, the church faces a staggering educational task. Many churches still limp along without giving serious consideration to an overall, in-depth, educational strategy. Some seem unaware that this critical need exists. Others understand the objective but feel helpless to attack the overwhelming task.

FINAL CONSIDERATIONS

The job seems too big to add to the typical pastor's already crowded list of responsibilities. How could a pastor, in addition to counseling, studying, board planning, visiting the sick, and evangelism, expect to be an educational strategist as well? We doubt God ever intended one person to do it all. In light of the staggering challenge, justifying someone full-time to coordinate the church's educational efforts hardly seems necessary. Christian education should receive the attention of a specific person in addition to the pastor. The size and the significance of the educational task facing the church should cause it to think and act more aggressively in developing the Christian education program. The church needs specially trained leaders to formulate and execute educational strategies that impact peoples lives.

If the church must take the lead, then leaders must be trained. Where? Many seminaries still provide only minimal training in Christian education for their pastoral ministry majors. Some do not provide any.[12] Seminaries, Bible colleges, and Christian universities need more carefully researched Christian education strategies for the church. Pastoral trainees must receive more help in this area. Until pastors receive more training, the church might use periodically a C.E. consultant. This option becomes attractive when the church budget is limited or if the denomination provides help in this area. For a fuller discussion of the C.E. consultant, see Appendix C.

We disagree with thinkers such as Gordon Clark. In *A Christian Philosophy of Education* he declares: "The conclusion is that schools of education with their uneducated faculties should be abolished. . . . Somewhere a place could be provided for a one semester course on pedagogical tricks to amuse children and catch their attention."[13]

The serious study of educational strategies for the Christian community demands more than mastering a bag of tricks! It even requires more than mastering modern educational theory and practice.

When the church fails to effectively educate the next generation, the consequences involve starting over completely. In spite of the Reformation, many mission agencies classify Europe as a mission field today. We wonder whether the lack of Christian education within the church caused this disastrous consequence. One young European shared this enlightening observation about his experience with the church, "Oh, I didn't grow up in the church. You have to remember, it doesn't have anything for young people." Chilling words indeed!

The next generation must receive godly training specifically designed for them. The church must lead with a comprehensive educational strategy to fulfill the Lord's command to "make disciples." How Christian education specialists can develop such a strategy, both in theory and in practice, is the subject of the remaining chapters of *Directing Christian Education.*

— NOTES —

1. Ron Blue, "Go, Missions," *Bibliotheca Sacra*, Oct.-Dec., 1984, pp. 341-53.
2. James Fowler utilizes Lawrence Kohlberg's work in moral development to build a similar model for faith development. Marlene LeFever utilizes the work of Gregorc to write her article on learning styles.
3. Frank Tillapaugh, *Unleashing the Church* (Glendale, Calif.: Regal, 1985), p. 19.
4. James J. DeBoy, Jr., *Getting Started in Adult Religious Education* (New York: Paulist, 1979), p. 64.
5. Ivan L. Zabilka, "Calvin's Contribution to Universal Education," J. I. Packer, ed., *The Best in Theology*, vol. 4 (Carol Stream, Ill.: Christianity Today, 1990), pp. 337-55.
6. Wesley R. Willis, *Two Hundred Years and Still Counting* (Wheaton, Ill.: Victor, 1974), pp. 35-47.
7. Gordon H. Clark. *A Christian Philosophy of Education* (Jefferson, Md.: The Trinity Foundation, 1988), p. 176. Normally, we would not cite a work originally copyrighted in 1946. However, the author claims to have updated the work. We commend his vigorous treatment of philosophy from a Christian perspective. His handling of education must be challenged as rather provincial and uninformed.

8. Alvin Toffler, ed., *Learning for Tomorrow* (New York: Random House, 1974), p. xxiv.
9. Ibid., p. 267.
10. Gene Getz, *Sharpening the Focus of the Church,* (Wheaton, Ill.: Victor, 1984), pp. 32-46.
11. Vernon Kraft traces the origin of the office of director of Christian education in the church to early in the 20th century. Vernon Kraft, *The Director of Christian Education in the Local Church* (Chicago: Moody, 1957), p. 14.
12. A simple survey of seminary catalogs reveals: (1) Many schools have extremely limited course offerings; (2) some schools do not require any C.E. courses, and (3) a few prominent schools do not have a C.E. department.
13. Clark, *A Christian Philosophy,* p. 141.

Response

JESUS CHRIST AND PAUL AS
CHRISTIAN EDUCATION SPECIALISTS

by Warren S. Benson

Asbury Seminary professor H. W. Byrne has written, "Most everyone is willing to admit the superiority of Jesus Christ as teacher. Jesus knew Christian education as no other. His methods have motivated countless efforts since His day. He was a Director of Christian Education."[1]

In twelve years as a DCE, I found these words a source of sustenance when I was misunderstood in this role. You see, people wondered if I would finally "get my own church" when I "grew up." After all, why would you go to college for four years and seminary for five years and then be a director of Christian education?

A month ago when my wife, Lenore, was asked what our older son does, she replied that he is a pastor to high school youth at a large West Coast church. The woman in our denominational home office (who should have known better) said, "Well, that's a good place to start!" Lenore spoke passionately to her about the importance of this ministry and that it isn't just a "good place to start."

The woman's statement demonstrates a common misperception of the role of people in Christian education/youth ministry. Even our best friends in theological circles sometimes share in this misunderstanding. Admittedly we have an identification problem, but a basic ignorance is all too common. Why is this?

First, we evangelicals talk a good game regarding spiritual gifts, but we frequently come up short when thinking them through in a coherent scheme. Is there not a place for a church staff person who possesses the gift of teaching (Eph. 4:11-12) and/or administration (1 Cor. 12:28) to be a model servant leader and a trainer of teachers? In chapter 1, Lawson and Choun stated categorically that senior pastors do not have the luxury to invest more time in educational matters, or, interestingly enough, sometimes do not have the educational background pedagogically to be trainers of teachers. Our pastors are taught theology and Bible, and few if any courses in the educational process are required in their three- or four-year seminary programs. Yes, there is some distortion here. And that is written with sadness rather than sarcasm on this author's part.

Second, as H. W. Byrne has pricked our thinking, Jesus did spend large blocks of time as a teacher, educator, trainer, discipler, administrator/supervisor, shepherd of workers, and as a recruiter. Let's probe this idea of Jesus Christ as a DCE in light of the roles/responsibilities of the minister of education. A teacher of teachers? Yes! A master of managers? That, you say, is going too far. Note, then, the areas of concern that our Savior had as the ultimate educator.

Christ was without peer in the assessment of both Christians and non-Christians alike. He was the personification of the truth He taught, the Savior who fully understood His students. Jesus employed methodology perfectly without robbing His students of their autonomy. The Master and the DCE share a common goal: effecting change in lives.

JESUS AS A TRAINER AND DISCIPLER

A major role of Christ's ministry was that of being with His disciples (Mark 3:14). But the methods He used were never stereotypical. He, too, did not always see immediate results. Patiently He worked with the disciples, practicing repetition with variety. The concept of the kingdom's being spiritual and not political was difficult for them to grasp. He slowly wove it into the curriculum (Matt. 15:32–17:23) and trained them for service in view of His departure. He spent an amazing amount of time with individuals and a small band of men.

The wise CES, like the Master, invests time with a nucleus of leaders and potential leaders. One of the obvious breakdowns in the comparison is this: the CES needs to stay longer than 3½ years in discipling and training within the local church. Michael Lawson remained in one church for seventeen years. Sherwood

Strodel served at Park Street Church, Boston, for fifteen years, as did Allyn Sloat at the Wheaton Bible Church. Bill Stewart was at First Baptist, Modesto, for twenty-four years. The CES must not expect rapid growth. It is a strategy of deliberate and intentional preparation of others.

JESUS AS ADMINISTRATOR AND SUPERVISOR

The Savior was concerned with His people holistically. His desire was to see them grow in every dimension of life so that they in turn could discern the needs of others. He left a leadership team that had watched Him do ministry. Christ not only told them but demonstrated in minute detail how to do His work. Further, He left the Holy Spirit to guide them (and us) into truth. As a supervisor/coach He worked gently with inept and fearful students. He never lost sight of what they could become. He did not forget that they needed careful instructions, which were provided in the gospels and Acts.

The minister of education should strive for excellence in organizational and management concerns, but he/she must remember that it is the investment in leaders' lives that brings the payoff, rather than devising charts or doing long-range planning, as valuable as they may be. Christ constantly showed them by His life and equipped them with His power. He always encouraged initiative, creativity, and self-reliance (Mark 6:7-13, 30-34). He refused to say, "Do it My way or else!" The CES is to place greater emphasis on the oil of the Holy Spirit than on the oiling of church management machinery.

JESUS AS A SHEPHERD, RECRUITER, AND MOTIVATOR

Jesus Christ was a shepherd to the three, the twelve, and the seventy. He counseled them regarding personal problems as well as ministry conundrums. On occasion He was in their homes and always worked in reality contexts. He was an indefatigable encourager, a winsome instructor, and a caring colleague. He did not shrink from needed confrontation but dealt sensitively and tenderly with His people. He called unflinchingly and unapologetically for a clear commitment to His and, in time, their mission. Their commitment had to be total. The call by the DCE should be no different.

A LOOK AT THE APOSTLE PAUL

Without question, Paul was the greatest theologian and master strategist of the Christian mission other than the Son of God. And although his epistles provide the cognitive base for our evangelical theology, Paul should always be seen as a praxis theologian. His words are pragmatic, for he was involved in ministry. His heartbeat was for the people in the churches. His theology was born in mission, oriented in experience, and relevant to the culture. His teaching was more a declaration of faith than propositional theory. He thought in more functional and relational terms than in static or speculative forms. What does Paul's ministry say to the CES/minister of education?

Dean S. Gilliland describes Paul as a praxis theologian and points out four principal constructs, which we can summarize as follows.[2]

First, Paul's theology was one of practice because of the nature of his ministry. His method was to preach, press the claims of Christ at every point, appoint leaders, ground the leaders in the truth, and move on. Paul's calling demanded that he not remain in one place unless there was need, such as Ephesus where he remained for three years.

Second, Paul was the first to communicate Christian truth in a non-Jewish context. The Jerusalem Council (Acts 15) opened the door to the Gentile world. As he went to the Gentiles, Paul related to them culturally without prostituting Christian theology. The cross-cultural impact required new approaches, new forms, and a precise definition of the essential gospel.

Third, he modeled a theology of practice that was committed to authentic churches rising out of each town or area that he touched. "Paul did not plant copies of the Jerusalem church, or even of the Antioch church."[3] Unity centered on Christ, and each church was allowed to develop its life and witness with its own local forms and flavors. The indigenous principle is reflective of Christ's strategy of freedom in methodology.

Fourth, as a theology of practice Paul's theology was reliant on the Holy Spirit. Paul is often caricatured as a proponent of a rigid system. His theology was strongly based in doctrinal convictions given to him by the Holy Spirit and that continued the theological presuppositions of the Savior. Theologically speaking, then, there was a firmness and even an unbending quality to it because of the divine origins of the material. But his modus operandi was flexible and resilient. The spiritual gifts were allowed to flow as the Spirit dictated. Rules that would "contradict the voice of the Spirit" were shunned. "The reliance of Paul on the Holy Spirit and the authentic ways in which he taught this same reliance to the converts of Asia and Europe was the first principle of his ministry."[4] This freedom spurred the church on to continuous evangelism and edification.

Paul was a praxis theologian, a competent manager, and yes, a minister of education. As a remarkably capable servant-leader, he was a Spirit-led visionary and a wise and winsome strategist for building the church of Jesus Christ. His involvement models several essential tasks of the CES/minister of education.[5] Consider these four examples:

1. Paul worked continually to build unity and cohesiveness around the Person of Jesus Christ as the uncommon common theme or value. (See 2 Cor. 13:11; Eph. 4:1-6; Phil. 2:1-11; and Col. 3:16-17.)
2. Paul knew the importance of caring for people and expressing open affection for them. He addressed them by name in his correspondence. (See 1 Cor. 1:4-8; Phil. 1:3-6; 4:2-3; Col. 4:7-18; 1 Thess. 2:7-12; and 2 Tim. 4:19-21.)
3. Paul intentionally was a model; he was not hesitant to associate with or be involved with people. (See Acts 20:18-31; 1 Cor. 4:16; 11:1; Phil. 4:9-13; 1 Thess. 1:6-7; 2 Thess. 3:7-9.)
4. Paul was more concerned about the quality and develop-

ment of individual leaders than he was about organizational patterns and structures. (See 1 Tim. 3; 2 Tim. 1:12–2:7; Titus 2.)

Paul was a master educator and manager. He never diminished the value of planning, organizing, staffing, and directing, but he always remembered that the discipling of people was his primary role—reaching, evangelizing through preaching and teaching, and training people to do the work of the ministry (Eph. 4:11-12).

Lawson and Choun have most adequately laid down the foundation stones for the justification and establishment of the role of the Christian education specialist/minister of education. The demands of evangelical churches now exceed the number of men and women our schools are producing. Seminary and Bible college teachers/equippers must continue to bow to Scripture for guidance to train more people who have the marks of Jesus Christ and Paul in their educational philosophies of ministry. As long as they do so, the role of the CES will remain legitimate and worthwhile.

THE GREAT TEACHING COMMISSION

by Kenneth O. Gangel

The authors have done well to build their work upon the foundation of pedagogical ecclesiology. During the past two decades student enrollment in church education programs has declined 34 percent, while the number of church members involved in educational ministries has dropped from 31 percent to 18 percent. Multiple reasons circulate to account for this negative scenario, but I share the view that posits an inadequate understanding of the Great Commission as the primary problem. In short, we must attack the figless tree at its roots.

Matthew 28:16-20 offers New Testament readers a commission narrative much like those found in Genesis 12, Exodus 3, and Isaiah 6. But Matthew alone records this mountain meeting and has already noted two references to it by the Lord (26:32; 28:10) and one by the resurrection angel (28:7). Mainline orthodoxy, particularly as evidenced by the twentieth-century evangelical movement, holds a traditional and somewhat normative interpretation of these five dramatic verses, namely, that this paragraph lays the foundation stone for the modern missionary movement. Indeed, so strong is our commitment to that concept that we gravitate to this text during missionary conferences and missionary Sundays while failing to see two crucial dimensions of the passage:

1. The passage mandates both evangelism and teaching, with the latter being at least equal to and quite possibly greater in emphasis.
2. The Commission has been given neither for apostles nor for missionaries alone, but to the church. The entire universal Body of Christ stands under the requirement of this great teaching commission.

Choun and Lawson draw our attention precisely to this dramatic point, which stands foundational to any further considerations about organizing or staffing church education programs.

Everywhere I go pastors and church educational leaders struggle with inadequate quality and commitment to the church's educational ministry. In some places teachers serve such short tenures that they must be replaced sometimes quarter by quarter or even week by week. Perhaps the problem can be at least partly explained by a breakdown in the church's obedience to the Great Teaching Commission.

Central also to this passage (and to this book) is the issue of authority in the church. Jesus proclaimed to the gathered believers at this mountain meeting that there would be no further dispute regarding who is in charge—there is one Lord of the church. Yet these are days in which we wonder who runs the church. Does the congregation best govern itself? Should we have elders, and, if so, how do we get them, what must they do, and how long do we keep them? How much leadership should we accept from the pastor and how much from the people?

One of my colleagues at Dallas Theological Seminary recently observed in print, "It has been my experience that the churches the Savior is using to reach people are these kinds of churches (where the pastor is 'a biblically qualified, experienced, gifted leader to whom others would look for direction and vision'); whereas, those in which several men are trying to lead are most often small and struggling." Granted, the church growth movement literature amply supports that notion. But where does that leave us with respect to staff relations? Are we indeed talking about a single leader or a leadership team?

It matters little whether that leadership team is composed of professional paid staff or lay leaders—at stake here is a philosophy of ministry, not size of church and payroll. I have growing fears, however, that many seminary leaders have been improperly and overly impressed with the recent rash of secular literature on entrepreneurial, visionary, and charismatic leadership. We can learn much from that style, but only if it can be positively blended with what we know about servanthood and humility. Doubtless we are all after the same goal here, but I suspect our differences may be more than just semantic.

In a practical sense, the abominable short tenure of CESs relates precisely to this problem of pastoral leadership. I have participated in several surveys in the sixties and early seventies regarding tenure and, though I have no statistics from the eighties, I suspect the problem has not abated. The national tenure remains approximately a year and a half for associate staff, including the Christian education specialist.

Does that come about because pastoral leadership is insufficiently entrepreneurial? I doubt it. More likely the short tenure occurs because both senior pastors and associate staff have been inadequately trained for the cooperative give and take of team leadership. Our Lord's words regarding His dominance over the Body serve to warn papal pastors, entrepreneurial elders, and imperial deacons that there is only one Authority in the church. The only biblical spirit at the human level must be a mutual yielding and submission.

Like the authors, I also feel drawn to Antioch for demonstration of that team leadership. Unlike the authors, however, I see Barnabas as the senior pastor and Paul as the first director of Christian education. The former was sent by the church at Jerusalem to "head up" the work in Antioch; the latter recruited by Barnabas to take charge of the educational ministry. Indeed, the secure, nonthreatened vulnerability of Pastor Barnabas set a first-century standard for leadership that can be found only rarely at the end of the twentieth.

As the authors point out, standing center stage in the Commission we find that lonely imperative "Make disciples." *How we understand the meaning of that command determines what we do with Christian education in the local church.* Many have taken it to mean communicating the gospel and have thereby limited the Great Commission to evangelism at home and abroad. But disciples, biblically understood, are those who hear, understand, and obey Jesus' teaching. The Master emphasized life change, not content transmission; He highlighted multiplication of the Body in the world, not addition of members on the roll. In the spirit of the Great Commission, a DCE, or CES, is a leader of leaders, a teacher of teachers, and discipler of disciplers.

In full awareness that the authors may have developed these

themes other places in the book (I have seen only the manuscript for one chapter), I wish they would explore further some areas that are mentioned briefly in "Biblical and Philosophical Perspective." For one thing, the authors have referred fleetingly to two dominant theorists with respect to ministry philosophy—Gene Getz and Frank Tillapaugh. Without dealing with structures, organization, or methodology advanced by these two pastors, it would have been interesting to compare their approaches and delve a bit further into foundational considerations they advance regarding lay involvement, lay education, and lay ministry. Second, the few brief paragraphs at the end of the chapter, which treat multiple church educational leadership, touch upon what I consider to be a major and very positive option for the future, one I would like to see developed in some detail in this book.

All things considered, we may thank the authors for reminding us that the central focus of any educational ministry is *teaching*—not bureaucracy, board meetings, buildings, or budgets. If Christian education is not distinct in what happens in classrooms and informal study groups, if the evangelical church does not cherish and nourish its teaching ministry, then we have fallen into heteropraxy, a false practice, and may very well be headed for heterodoxy.

— NOTES —

1. H. W. Byrne, *Christian Education for the Local Church* (Grand Rapids: Zondervan, 1963), p. 103.
2. Dean S. Gilliland, "The Apostle Paul As a Praxis Theologian," in *Theology, News, and Notes,* Fuller Theological Seminary, October 1981, p. 9.
3. Ibid., p. 10.
4. Ibid.
5. Edwin H. Robinson, "In Search of Excellence . . . A Message for Church Leadership?" A paper submitted in the doctoral course entitled A Biblical Philosophy of Management and Leadership, December 1984, Trinity Evangelical Divinity School.

An Ever-Expanding Role

Christian education specialists are directing educational ministries in thousands of churches, yet CES job descriptions lack uniformity. Each church contains a unique combination of strengths, weaknesses, and priorities, and the differing job descriptions often reflect this diversity.

The field of Christian education continues to expand as practitioners meet varying job requirements (see Appendix A). In fact, in a 1987 annual survey of its members, the Professional Association of Christian Educators (PACE) distinguished thirty-five different categories of ministry.[1] Of course, no one can do all of these well. In fact, members were asked to specify only their "three best areas" in the survey. On the following page is the list of duties spanning thirty-five categories.

Designations such as Sunday school, children's church, and club activities end up under other headings, such as administration or training. This list reflects the most common expectations of the job and is, of course, subject to change. For instance, the 1991

Duties of Christian Educators

Administration	Counseling	Music
Adult ministry	Creative teaching	Nursery
Audio/visual	Curriculum	Recruiting
Bible studies	Discipleship	Retreats
Budget	Education (misc.)	Schools
Buildings/facilities	Evangelism	Seminars
Camping	Family ministry	Small groups
Children's ministry	Leadership	Staff relationships
Church life	Marriage counseling	Summer ministries
Computers	and classes	Training of volunteers
Conferences	Missions	Vacation Bible school
Consulting	Multiple services	Youth ministries

Source: *The Ministry Idea Network*, PACE, 1987

edition of *The Ministry Idea Network* distinguished two more categories, college ministries and writing. These additions exemplify the ever-expanding role of the C.E. specialist.

Through this network, CESs share information and contact each other for expert counsel. Often they have developed creative new ministries in the field before journal articles or books can record their beginnings. In many cases, ministry experts are in the church.

Essentially, the CES recruits, trains, and supervises a corps of volunteers who carry out the church's educational objectives. Sometimes the church leadership have no clearly stated educational objective. In such churches, the CES should help the leaders articulate and publish them. Otherwise, misunderstanding, confusion, and a patchwork approach to education result. The CES who wants to create clear objectives must balance two agendas. He must recognize and answer the felt needs of the congregation as well as the needs he/she perceives as an education specialist.

The C.E. specialist's main responsibility is to assist church leaders in preparing people for the work of the ministry—making disciples of all nations. As shown in the following chart, the main focus of the CES's ministry is to bring people to maturity in Christ,

THE CYCLE OF ROLES AND RESPONSIBILITIES FOR THE CES

Chart developed by Lin McLaughlin, pastor of Christian education,
Plano Bible Chapel, Plano, Texas. Used by permission.

ready to serve others. The chart delineates the ongoing roles of the CES to do this—supervision, administration, control, leadership, and management—as well as the objectives and programs needed to bring people to Christian maturity. We suggest that the CES adapt this chart for local church ministry, adding or deleting specific programming from year to year.

EIGHT SPECIALTIES

A bit of everything creeps into the job description over a period of time. The wise CES will develop flexibility and a general comprehension of how everything works. Some churches request concentrated time devoted to developing crippled or underdeveloped areas of ministry. The church may even specify how much time to give to the area of specialization. Our survey of CESs currently in the field revealed that eight popular specialties were often combined with overall educational supervision. They are: (1) children, (2) youth, (3) adult, (4) evangelism/outreach, (5) business management, (6) music, (7) missions, and (8) activities/recreation.

Note that the first three specialties are generic to Christian education. Actually they form subcategories. Large churches often hire specialists to devote exclusive attention to one age group's need. Smaller churches usually need more general coverage.

The next specialty, evangelism/outreach, normally works in tandem with Christian education at almost every level. For instance, Sunday schools stress evangelism in building classes of all ages, vacation Bible school stresses evangelism among children of the community, and youth retreats stress evangelism among the friends of the church's young people. Evangelism normally feeds the education programs of the church. Without evangelism, the church slowly dies. Using a manufacturing model, evangelism provides the raw material that Christian education uses in developing disciples.

The last four specialties reflect more unusual combinations and often require special training, gifts, or experiences.

Business managers appear more frequently on church staffs than in previous decades. In fact, the National Association of Church Business Administrators represents this particular staff position in a professional national organization.[2] Some churches have replaced CESs with business administrators, believing they get more responsible management of funds. Although responsible money management certainly is essential, the church's overall educational effort may suffer.

Business administrators untrained in education have difficulty in evaluating, prioritizing, and supervising an educational program governed by a concise philosophy. To understand how challenging the task is, simply reverse the roles and have an untrained Christian educator furnish complicated financial reports and discuss sound fiscal policy. If a church chooses a business administrator to supervise educational programs, it should require training in church-related educational philosophy and ministry.

Combining music (specialty #3) with Christian education obviously requires at least some aptitude or skill in music. CESs who develop this area along with educational training offer an extremely desirable package for a church. Music is one of the most profound educational tools available. Unfortunately, most pastors and CESs receive absolutely no training in this God-ordained medium of communication.

Slowly, churches have learned that vocational leadership can raise the sensitivity of the church to missions more effectively than lay leadership. The attitude of a church rarely changes with a single annual emphasis. Churches need continued high profiles for missions and missionaries, and a CES focused on missions can give the amount of time necessary to organize, publicize, and promote mission projects and giving throughout the year. With this educational duty, the CES can plan for the church to stay informed. One promising development in this area is the National Association of Church Mission Committees, which acts as a clearinghouse for promotional information and interesting mission programs.[3]

Only recently have churches looked for someone to develop recreational activities that specifically promote relationships and fellowship. The loss of the extended family in our society has emphasized the need for fellowship bonds to enrich life. Recreation increases in importance as our stress-filled society makes increasing demands on each person. Many families must learn to play together. Single parents (there are almost seven million of them in our country) especially need help formulating fun experiences for their children and with other families.[4] This legitimate educational specialty can help churches address the needs of this largely untapped group, resulting in rapid growth in attendance. The key will be the church's ministry for children and the help they provide single parents in scheduling wholesome activities.

In addition to these fairly normal responsibilities, the CES may face even more diverse and perhaps unexpected tasks. These occur for three basic reasons: (1) The CES occupies a church staff position. (2) Church ministry creates unique expectations in dealing with people. (3) Christian education involves certain ancillary ministries. The remainder of this chapter surveys the tasks that arise for one of these three reasons.

TASKS RELATED TO CHURCH STAFF POSITION

The CES As Role Model

Churches usually discover this unwritten expectation only when a failure occurs. Everyone on a church staff and their families live in a fishbowl. For better or worse, the nature of the job means scrutiny and sometimes criticism from the congregation. Because everyone is watching, the CES has several unique opportunities to positively influence people's values.

First, the CES must spend a great deal of time in the office where the telephone functions like a lifeline connecting aggressive education programs. Being in the office, the CES is more available for drop-in visitors. Rarely can the senior pastor of a medium-to-large church be quite so available while balancing study, counseling, visitation, and planning. For the CES who meets these guests, the impromptu meetings provide strategic informal learning opportunities. In addition, each encounter gives the CES an opportunity to communicate another piece of information about Christian living or the church's philosophy of education.

Some of these informal meetings serve purely social purposes. Others occur because the individual wants to discuss something specific but not in formal counseling; some occur because people do not have enough to do with their time. All of them strengthen relationships, which facilitate staffing a volunteer educational program.

Church leaders frequently have difficulty understanding the

time drain or the vital importance of this phenomenon. Any given church member may drop by only two or three times a year. But multiply three or four unplanned visits by all the members and the load becomes considerable indeed. Yet the visits are beneficial in at least four ways for the CES. First, these spontaneous encounters communicate in a tangible way that people are more important than programs. They should be treated as planned interruptions in a weekly schedule.

Second, the nature of directing a Christian education program demands enlisting countless numbers of volunteers. Meetings for planning, training, and evaluating create tremendous visibility for the CES with a great number of people. These workers see the CES in action and under pressure. Because of the working relationship, people often feel more at ease and casually discuss personal concerns in hallways and other unusual spots.

Third, the CES by virtue of age may appear more approachable. Often younger than the senior pastor, the CES may seem less threatening and easier to talk to. True, this may be only a perceived difference, but perceptions influence choices. Young people almost always prefer someone closer to their age, who may vaguely remember the kinds of problems they face.

Fourth, no individual staff member relates equally well to everyone in a congregation. Some people will relate more strongly and identify more personally with the CES for a variety of reasons. Unfortunately, this sometimes creates jealousy in a senior pastor who is unaccustomed to sharing people's loyalty. Some pastors feel threatened when another staff member receives preferential treatment by a church member. This personal insecurity can create such a serious problem that the CES may end up looking for another position.

The CES may prevent such tension with the pastor through a proper response to adulation, a response of gratitude and yet humility. Under no circumstance should the CES encourage comparison between the pastor and himself. Instead, he should reaffirm his loyalty to the pastor and his ministry while acknowledging differences in their styles or personalities. When appropriate, the CES can personally affirm the pastor. The day the CES cannot support the pastor or his ministry should be the day he quietly begins looking for another ministry.

The CES can help a church by being a strong role model. People emulate areas such as devotional life, treatment of spouse, care for children, concern for the lost, compassion for the hurting, interest in Bible study, patience under pressure, and flexibility under stressful circumstances. They watch the CES work, play, and worship. The impact of life on life can hardly be overestimated in educational value.

The CES As Interim Pastor

One ever-present threat to the tenure of the CES revolves around the staying power of the senior pastor.[5] Some denominations expect all associates to resign with the senior pastor. Others allow them to stay until the new pastor arrives to see if a working relationship develops. Usually, the CES, along with other associates, moves on.

When the pastor resigns, the associate with the most tenure frequently functions as an interim pastor. Seldom does he receive the title, almost never does he receive a pay increase, and always the work multiplies. Few people really appreciate the burden caused by these circumstances. New responsibilities complicate the life of the CES who adds to his job the role of interim pastor. As such, the CES typically will need to devote time to preaching, visitation, counseling, administration, pastoral tasks, and even job hunting. When the CES accepts—or is automatically bestowed—the title of interim pastor, each task will consume his time and distract from his primary function. Consider the issues in just three of these tasks: preaching, counseling, and job hunting.

Preaching. Seminary students are often taught that a Sunday morning message requires between fifteen and twenty hours of preparation. Even half of that becomes a significant addition to a weekly schedule. Sometimes the church charitably allows a guest to preach one or two Sundays a month during the interval without a pastor. If the CES does not possess skills in preaching, the additional stress can be disproportionate to the task. In addition, the CES may have to coordinate the preaching schedule by dividing time between other staff members (if available), guest speakers (where allowed), and candidating senior pastors. This complicated but unappreciated task sometimes requires hours of telephoning, scheduling, and rescheduling.

Counseling. At a church where the CES has built relationships, many church members will seek counsel whether or not the CES received the official interim pastor job. Counseling produces so much stress that even professional psychologists burn out and move into other areas. Counseling can consume four or five hours a week or more. After particularly stressful sessions, time to debrief and wind down is essential. Moving immediately into some other project is almost impossible. Counselors share the human suffering. Recovery time may add thirty minutes to the schedule. In addition, anticipated problems may require preparation time. Thinking, praying, and reading on certain issues in light of a particular problem all consume time.

Job Hunting. Whether the CES assumes the role of interim pastor or remains "just" the CES, he or she must consider a new job in anticipation of the coming new pastor. However, only veterans begin to look immediately upon the departure of the senior pastor. Although not desirable, eventually seeking a new Christian education position is advisable and often necessary due to a general lack of loyalty toward associates on the part of church leadership and new senior pastors. Horror stories abound where the associates stepped in to give stable interim leadership only to find themselves dispensable when the new pastor arrived. They thought they had earned a measure of commitment for themselves, but church leadership failed to reciprocate. Leaving the job hunting task until later could prove very foolish.

Allocation of Time

The CES can anticipate a certain amount of family tension created by the uncertainties of additional pastoral responsibilities, regular CE duties, and job hunting. Managing the family's instability with the incessant time demands requires sensitivity and personal discipline.

Last, because of the ethical crisis in the church, the interim's motto must be "Put It in Writing." Board members may never understand the actual demands on time and energy. The board should write on one sheet of paper the new responsibilities. This should be signed and dated by everyone, including the supervising board. Immediately beginning a daily log of your work time may protect the CES from unnecessary criticism. List in half-hour intervals your activity and area. In a column designated "Activity," include notations such as phone calls, committee meetings, study, staff meetings, crisis intervention, and so on. In the column designated "Area," put down whether the task related to Christian education or interim pastoral activity. Omit from the record specific names of people involved in sensitive counseling appointments or phone calls.

The governing board should assign a three-member task force to evaluate weekly time usage. The task force should have the authority to prioritize responsibilities. When the church needs two people to carry on the jobs of pastor and CES, one person obviously cannot cover both areas completely. Which ones will be, should be, can be ignored? The task force relieves the CES from making judgment calls that others may question.

Even these changes require documentation. The task force members should sign and date the notation. Everyone will not be happy with their choices or priorites, but the CES will be protected. Remember, only written documentation counts. Conversations and verbal instructions, no matter how clear at the time, will be fuzzy to those recalling them in a meeting charged with emotional differences. Put it in writing!

PEOPLE SKILLS IN EDUCATIONAL MINISTRY

In church minstry, the CES faces unique expectations in dealing with people. Churches are not businesses, but businesspeople dominate the middle-class American church. Consequently, business value systems often spill over into the church. Some of these help, but many are counterproductive. Movers and shakers in business often expect the church to operate similarly. A business might identify its task as moving from point A to point B as efficiently and profitably as possible. A church with the same task must make sure *everyone* gets from point A to point B at the same time. Shepherding the flock means not leaving anybody behind in the process.

Business concerns itself with "the bottom line" profit. Churches focus on people, not profit. When these two completely different objectives clash, the CES needs such people skills as negotiating, conflict management, and small group processes to keep the C.E. program on track.

Negotiating

Negotiating, a skill commonly used in business, frequently is overlooked as necessary to church ministry. Yet churches create negotiating teams to formulate strategies for renting facilities to outsiders, building new facilities, hiring new staff, and many other endeavors. They itemize and categorize the necessary details into negotiable and nonnegotiable points. The negotiating team usually brings a report to a church board or congregation, who makes the final decision. A proposal full of glaring errors, oversights, or weaknesses can prove embarrassing. Conversely, the CES can earn respect through thoughtful preparation.

Unfortunately, some CESs fail to skillfully negotiate their salary/benefit package with church leaders. Somehow discussing money feels unspiritual. Yet, the New Testament only condemns the love of money. Too often church leaders initially offer a bare-bones minimum salary. They do not concede or volunteer anything in the process. That is how the business community operates.

Without being greedy, the CES needs to realistically assess the cost of living in the church's community. The salary may be too low to live in a responsible way. Many churches commonly ignore items such as book allowances, convention attendance, professional dues, and continuing education at seminars and schools in the salary package. A wise church will see the CES as an asset that increases in value with continuing education and exposure to other professionals.

In the past, churches have sometimes looked at a school-teacher's salary as a model for the CES. Though both work in education, the comparison ends there. The CES:

1. Receives much less vacation time
2. Must recruit, train, and supervise volunteers to accomplish the educational purpose of the church
3. Is on call twenty-four hours a day
4. Has virtually no job security

A better model might be a management-level job with commensurate numbers of people and programs supervised. Sticking with a school model, a school principal would compare more favorably with the responsibilities assigned to the CES. Soon the church must learn that the place to hunt bargains is not in the salaries of its leaders. The CES may need to lead the way through skillful negotiation.

Conflict Management

Anyone who works with people soon realizes how easily personalities clash. So many biblical illustrations exist that the church should expect conflict.[6] Similar to negotiating, conflict management does not put the CES on one side or the other but in the middle functioning more like a referee. Almost invariably, people who disagree assume the other has bad motives. Bad motives do occur, but they are certainly not the norm. Instead, different perspectives, objectives, or priorities usually create the trouble whether among teachers, or between teachers and congregation members. The CES begins on common ground, reminding each party of common beliefs. The new commandment from Jesus serves as a wonderful beginning place for resolution.

Each conflict must be faced and dealt with. Unresolved conflict causes waves of stress and strain throughout the ministry of the church. Sometimes the wisdom of Solomon is insufficient to happily resolve the tension. At other times the parties bow humbly before God when confronted. When restoration and healing occur, an even stronger ministry emerges. When the CES deals with the conflict swiftly yet fairly, the result is tremendous confidence among workers. Over time, the CES's reputation may even prevent problems as people begin going to one another. Everyone functions more comfortably knowing that a problem will be handled in a healthy spiritual atmosphere.

The following procedure may facilitate initiating a compromise. After an initial meeting to gather facts, another meeting should be set several days away. The time delay helps cool tempers and gives the CES time to consider a fair procedure for all parties involved. Careful thinking, seeking counsel, and sometimes even asking people what they feel would make things right can all lead to constructive answers. Gentle confrontation, firmness, following policy or procedure, fair mindedness, and patience must mix together in the CES to deal with these chronic problems.

Small Group Management

Small group skills are the bread and butter of the CES. The CES will face countless combinations of people in committees, task forces, agencies, boards, and staff meetings. Some of the tasks accomplished in groups are: (1) arranging/scheduling calendars, (2) writing policy manuals, (3) maximizing individual participation, (4) assigning subcommittees, and (5) synthesizing massive amounts of information. Performing these in concert with other people on the appropriate committee presents a formidable challenge. When many people consult before making decisions, programs change slowly. Although inefficient by business standards, people, not programs, are the focus of the CES and the church. In addition, people feel ownership of a ministry when they help make the decisions.

People learn to make good decisions by making decisions and living with consequences. Part of training leaders means coaching them through good and bad decisions. The time taken to make decisions may also mean fewer mistakes. In the church, mistakes are extremely difficult to overcome. Businesses simply cut their losses and move on. But the church can butcher the flock on the altar of efficiency. Churches deal with human lives. Ignoring, damaging, or railroading people through decisions spells trouble for them and for the church. Because God is patient, "Go Slowly" makes a helpful motto for the church.

OTHER DUTIES

Most denominations require attendance at national and district level meetings annually. These can provide essential networking for the CES. Because the CES gets the job done through people, he or she often needs the help of practitioners who are more proficient. These meetings, including travel time, can require a week or more out of an annual schedule. However, at such meetings the CES usually receives great encouragement by talking with others experiencing similar frustrations and exhilarations. Sometimes the most important work at a convention occurs over coffee and not at the meetings, as helpful (or boring) as they may be.

One last task that sneaks into a schedule almost unnoticed relates to the new staff member. Because every church differs, each new staff member requires orientation. No Bible college or seminary course prepares one for a specific church. The CES who assists in this orientation may discover the new staff person needs one year to finally feel at home. The CES may find that answering questions takes considerable time. New staff need guidance deciding such questions as:

- Which decisions can I make alone?
- Which decisions do I send to the staff for discussion?
- Which decisions do I refer to the official ruling body?
- Who really works? Who merely talks about work?
- Are there any unwritten rules and procedures?

Rarely can a new staff member make an immediate significant contribution. Experienced staff members normally will invest significant time and energy in coaching the newcomer.

ANCILLARY MINISTRIES

Unexpected ministries develop for the CES. These consume time from the regular schedule but probably never appear on anybody's job description. Here are four creeping time consumers.

Community Responsibilities

Common courtesy requires the CES to assist in community-wide projects such as Sunday school conventions, area-wide teacher training efforts, and evangelistic crusades. Although the events tend to be occasional in nature, they consume hours of time throughout the year for planning and coordinating. Sometimes conditions within the church simply will not permit additional responsibilities. However, the wise church board will plan some of these into the CES's schedule. Every church ought to be interested in the well-being of the larger kingdom of God. Provincialism normally proves to be short-sighted.

New CESs in the community often gravitate toward the CES with the longest tenure or largest church for help and support. Taking time to set up and conduct tours for other churches who are exploring facilities is an expected form of hospitality. Sharing information, procedures, and policies exhibits a Christian attitude instead of a competitive one. But all take time.

Coordination with Church School or Day Care

If the church operates either a church school or day-care center, or is considering doing so, the CES logically functions as the liaison staff member. Although the school and the day care should have paid directors, coordination is necessary between church programs on Sunday/Wednesday and the weekday programs. The CES will cushion and coordinate such issues as arrangement of chairs, and proper, acceptable clean-up of rooms. He or she will help to answer such questions as: Whose posters go on which walls? Who pays for equipment repair? Without involvement in this vital and time-consuming effort, the CES will find that seemingly trivial items that come up for discussion are deteriorating into complaint or even conflict.

Special Education

In the past, churches have unconsciously discriminated against people with special needs. As generous as the ministry of Jesus was to the disabled of His society, many church buildings actually hinder their entering or moving around. Church designers have been sensitized to these needs, but older buildings need renovation.

Another especially sensitive area of ministry has largely been ignored until recent years. Some children and adults require special education. Frequently, when churches begin to reach into these unique communities and provide helpful programs, parents respond with deep appreciation. For many, time at church may be their only relief all week. In wealthy homes, help is easily affordable. But in poorer homes, the family must bear all of the responsibilities. The time commitments in caring for these special individuals is enormous and emotionally exhausting.

The job of the CES includes making sure both groups—those with physical limitations and those with mental or emotional disabilities—participate in program provisions as soon as feasible. Keeping this important goal in front of the appropriate committees will not necessarily be a popular task. However, the CES may need to function as the conscience for the church in this matter.

Cultural Observer

Much too often developments and trends in our own culture surprise the church and its leadership. We spend more time reacting to and bemoaning current developments than anticipating and addressing them head-on. Someone needs to stay out in front of trends and developments. Alvin Toffler suggests that we need to position people for receiving change.[7] The church's educational program needs evaluating in light of the future and its impact on the congregation.

The key cultural issues today include the role of technology, the need for more human interaction and sharing, and the impact of relativistic thinking. These issues should affect programming planned to help adults function in a Christian way. If the CES's thinking or programming stagnates, the church will suffer significantly. Reading, discussing, and thinking through forward-looking periodicals and workshops may help. Continuing education helps only if it includes stretching and enriching kinds of experiences.

SUMMARY AND CONCLUSION

The career path for CESs remains clouded. Few survive twenty years in the field. Some move into a senior pastor slot, some into teaching or missions, while others leave the ministry altogether. This will probably remain the case until the problems of job stability and recognition of advancement are clearly addressed.

In this chapter we have pointed out the fluid nature of the CES's job in the church. The wide range of activities and skills required indicate the need for both advanced and continuing education. No program can ever rise above the competency of the leadership. Churches should be willing to pay for expert help. In turn, the church should expect both qualitative and quantitative results. Both of these measurements should be used to evaluate the ever-expanding role of the CES.

— NOTES —

1. PACE—The Professional Association of Christian Educators (formerly The National Association of Directors of Christian Education, NADCE), 8405 N. Rockwell, Suite 222, Oklahoma City, OK 73162; (405)841-1712.
2. NACBA—The National Association of Church Business Administrators, 7001 Grapevine Highway, Fort Worth, TX 76118-5103; (817)284-1732.

3. ACMC—The Association of Church Missions Committees, PO Box 800, Wheaton, IL 60189-8000, (708)260-1660. ACMC is an organization that collects and dispenses missions education information for churches. This tremendously useful service reflects what actually works.
4. Douglas L. Fagerstrom, ed., *Singles Ministry Handbook* (Wheaton, Ill.: Victor, 1988), p. 61.
5. Turnover rates vary from denomination to denomination, but a recent study reveals that in eighteen months 1,200 Southern Baptist pastors were fired or relocated.
6. James and John tried to outmaneuver the other apostles for favored position in the kingdom (Matt. 20:20-28). Barnabas and Paul could not agree about the future ministry of Mark (Acts 15:36-41). Peter and Paul did not agree about fellowship with Gentiles in Antioch (Galatians 2:11-14). Euodia and Syntyche's disagreement caused stress in Philippi. The list could go on. From the beginning, human relationships within the church have caused stress.
7. Alvin Toffler, *Learning for Tomorrow* (New York: Random House, 1972), pp. 3-18.

Principles in Practice

AT A SMALL CHURCH

Calvary Baptist Church
Eau Claire, Wisconsin
Sunday school size: 100

by John Vincent
Senior Pastor

In one of his Christian education classes, Dr. Howard Hendricks described a pastor who had spent much time planning for a teachers' training class that Hendricks was invited to teach. The meeting was to start at 7:30, but only five of the teachers had arrived by that time. The pastor told the five that he was discouraged about the poor attendance. After the session, the pastor asked Hendricks to evaluate his preparation and planning for the teachers' meeting. Dr. Hendricks responded, declaring that the pastor had totally shredded the motivation of those who had come out to the meeting.

Hendricks's words left a lasting impact on my life concerning one of the major purposes of a pastor in a small church. Perspective concerning numbers is vital for the pastor of a small church helping in Christian education. We should not focus on numbers as much as on our enthusiasm for those now involved in Christian education in a small church.

In my ministry I have learned that the number one emphasis for Christian education is leadership development. Motivating is not only essential but has been the focal point of my ministry. I am reminded of how the Lord taught Gideon concerning numbers: He reduced Gideon's band from 32,000 to 300 alert and eager volunteers (Judg. 7:3-6).

Leadership development is vital to provide the environment for growth, both spiritual and numerical. Leadership development includes instilling in volunteer leaders an understanding of both felt and perceived needs. A deacon in one of the churches I pastored taught me much about understanding the needs of those in the flock. Even though he was not personally interested in potlucks or Christian films, he would attend and be involved in both of these events when the need of the church demanded it. In training leaders, I constantly look for men like that deacon, who know how to be involved in the church to meet the needs.

In a small church, a pastor involved in Christian education is constantly confronted with developing underdeveloped areas of ministry. This probably is due to lack of or changes in leadership. For instance, I have tried to work closely with a young man and woman who lead our junior high ministry. Our children in Awana and Sunday school usually continue to grow and develop until they reach the junior high years, but at that point many of them drop out. My deacon board recommended that I be involved with this young couple to train them by example. The best results come when I not only tell the volunteer leaders what to do but show them by example how to do it.

Concerning missions education, I have found that most small churches do a good job on their annual or biannual missions conferences. However, it is crucial that the pastor lead in ongoing missions education. This past year we have tried to encourage our youth to be involved in missions activities and to seek God's will concerning their role in missions. Previously we had sent young people on overseas missions projects, which is very important. However, this past year we developed a goal of involving our young people in local missions before they move into cross-cultural missions. We believe that by observing them in their ministry locally, we can assist them throughout the year in developing their spiritual gifts, spiritual lives, and ongoing ministries. One such way we have done this is through the ministry of camping. We sent two young people this past year to work for a month in our own camp. They raised their own missions support, which equaled what they would have made in a summer job.

Another important task for a small church pastor is to plan recreational activities that promote relationships and fellowship. At Calvary Baptist, monthly swim and gym nights have been important in promoting deep and growing relationships. In addition, we have discovered that an evening of table games brings people of all ages together. Through an annual family retreat, we also involve younger families, including their children. One of the deacons and I plan and present this weekend retreat, which binds our younger families together for fellowship and outreach that continues throughout the year.

The pastor serves as a more intimate role model when he is directly involved in Christian education ministries. Some of the best relationships I have established to influence people's spiritual lives have developed through my personal involvement with other volunteer staff. Camping is one of the greatest ways of building relationships with those whom I have recruited and trained. This past summer at camp, as dean of junior age children grades four through six, I had to model the Christian life under the pressure of some difficult situations. Camps are great places to make decisions and handle major difficulties.

The small church pastor involved in Christian education can become so tied up in the diversity of programs, and in trying to meet the immediate needs, that prayer can be put on the back burner. The struggle that all pastors have is not spending enough time in prayer. This is not only real, but at times tragic. Without the preparation of personal prayer, we have lost our skill and our heart for negotiating, conflict management, and small group management.

Salary negotiations are important for an extended pastorate. This past year I presented a detailed breakdown of my past four years. This helped our leaders to evaluate and allowed me to state openly and honestly the needs of my family. I believe a pastor needs to show a great deal of sensitivity and willingness to compromise as well as being open and honest about his current financial situation.

In the area of conflict management, the small church pastor needs to be one who takes immediate, decisive action when he becomes aware of a problem between volunteer staff. One of the best ways of doing that is to encourage those who are involved to talk directly, as Christ tells us in Matthew 18:15-17. As they explain why something is not right or is different from the past, conflicts often can be resolved. When that doesn't occur, mediation may be necessary involving other mature believers.

The pastor himself needs conflict management skills. I have been to a number of conflict management seminars that have been extremely helpful. One conflict taught my wife and me a great lesson. The teacher of our junior-age boys lightly struck one of his students. Of course, the parents of the child were very upset and came to me. In dealing with the problem, I immediately went to the teacher and tried to get the boy's parents and him together. I also said that my wife would be willing to be involved in discussing this conflict situation. About two days later these two men, the teacher and the boy's father, came to our front door. Not knowing what to expect, I reluctantly opened the door, and to our delight found they had resolved the situation by themselves. The reason they had resolved it was our willingness to become involved with them. There is great joy in seeing believers unite together to serve the Lord.

Small group management concerning decision making is an important part of the stability and growth of a church. Communication must be emphasized in all areas of ministry. I need to draw out quieter board members for their ideas and suggestions. On every board are some who serve as active initiators and others who are the brakes. We need both to seek and find God's will. People must be open and honest before making a final decision; sometimes we must slow the pace to ensure that our decision is one of honesty rather than a result of peer pressure.

A small church pastor involved in Christian education needs to be the motivator and encourager of his people in the ministry for evangelism, edification, and the glory of God. One of my major goals is to hear from the lips of our Lord, "Well done, thou good and faithful servant."

AT A MEDIUM CHURCH

Mid Cities Bible Church
Bedford, Texas
Sunday school size: 400

by Dwight Walker
Pastor of Christian Education

The education specialist trains and assists people so that they can utilize their gifts and abilities in a lifetime of ministry to Jesus Christ. As a new education specialist, my job is to reach this goal by building a vision into the lives of my staff in a personal way. For programs to be successful, people must accept them as their own ideas. They should be made a part of the planning process. Also, people who volunteer for educational ministries need to feel accepted and appreciated for the things they are doing. As a result, I spend a lot of time getting to know and befriend all of my teachers and directors.

As I get to know them, I look for two characteristics. First I try to determine their kind of personality. This helps me to know the age groups with which they will work best. Second, I talk to them about their dreams and gifts. People will spend more time and effort in the educational ministry if they enjoy what they are doing. These people are more dedicated to the work of ministry than those who are asked to fill an empty slot on Sunday morning.

God has honored this approach by providing staff in unique ways. One day I took one of the businessmen in church out to lunch. He had helped my family move into our house and expressed an interest in education. During lunch we discussed various aspects of ministry, his personal goals, and his dreams about ministry. I had intended to ask him about being director for the intermediate children's department, but all of that changed as he laid out a plan he had for the adult ministry. Had I pushed him to work with the intermediate department he would have, but his talents for work-ing with adult ministry would have gone by the wayside. Later on, God did provide someone who was qualified and enjoyed working with children. Through this experience I learned that God owns the ministry; we are called to be His facilitators.

An effective educational program requires planning. My goal is to plan in such a way that the people of the church can participate in ministry most effectively. Ideas and strategies are approved and supported from the teachers up to the education specialist instead of being dictated by the education specialist down to the teachers. In this way the whole education program is owned by the whole faculty. This system produces a sense of teamwork.

With people's busy schedules, the education specialist must be flexible in planning activities and training sessions. With this in mind, I set aside special Sunday mornings for teacher training. I have found that weekly meetings are no longer effective, but the need for trained teachers is great. Two months before teacher training Sunday I begin to prepare a number of substitute teachers. Their job is to take the place of the regular teachers on the training Sunday. Since it would be impossible to replace all teachers, I pull out only one Sunday school division at a time.

On the training day the regular teachers are trained in the how-tos of the curriculum, hands-on development of learning activities, and basic counseling methods. The day begins at 9:15 A.M. and ends at 2:00 P.M. They attend the 11:00 A.M. service and receive a free luncheon afterward. Training includes a lot of role play, group work, and discussion. Teachers can devote time to organizing and brainstorming their own ideas for implementing strategies in the classroom. We conclude the session with exchanging thoughts, and prayer. This strategy is effective because it utilizes time already set aside by the teacher.

In a similar manner, substitutes for teacher training Sunday are trained in a special three-session class on Sunday morning. The format is similar to the teacher training format except that special emphasis is made on the specific lesson to be taught on that day. Training begins at least five weeks in advance. This allows the substitutes to feel comfortable with the material. Another positive aspect of this strategy is that a network of well-trained substitutes begins to form. These people can become a valuable resource for prospective full-time teachers.

To implement new programs from the teachers upward to the education specialist, I have put together a committee in our mid-size church. They evaluate curriculum, brainstorm for new approaches to ministry, and make long-range plans. This committee consists of teachers, directors, parents, and myself. The committee reviews the whole education ministry as it applies to the church's mission statement. Parents and teachers work together as coworkers in the raising of the children to be godly men and women. Through this group, special needs of the education program come before the church membership. This committee also functions as a safety cap that insures that the ministry is run by the laity and is true to the mission of the church. Parents who feel a part of their children's learning process can become more committed to reinforcing lessons learned in Sunday school.

Conflict management plays a significant role in setting the tone of the education ministry. At times teachers who are dedicated to their work misunderstand the actions of other coworkers. This may be due to differing objectives, approaches to ministry, or stress. Proper management will make the ministry stronger. As people confront me with various problems, they are looking to me for stability, focus, and trustworthiness. I try to spend time listening to each side of the problem. Later, I bring the two parties together, and we discuss each other's goals and dreams for the ministry. We then focus on the problem, seeking to understand the circumstances that caused it. Hopefully a mutual understanding of each person's perspective can be reached. Many times misunderstandings have occurred during a time of high stress.

In order to manage conflict successfully, the CES must spend time in building friendships. A strong sense of trust must develop between the education specialist and the staff. People also need a clear understanding of the program's goals, purpose, and how they help to fulfill them. I meet with each of my directors regularly. These informal meetings focus on building relationships. A meeting may include a family outing or lunch. In turn, I encourage my directors to meet with and build strong friendships with the teachers. As friendships are developed, a sense of teamwork emerges. People who know each other well are more able to forgive each other when misunderstandings occur.

Specific job descriptions for everyone in the education program also will limit conflict. People who know and understand what they should do are more productive and have less stress. At our church, every job description contains information on roles and responsibilities. The job description packet also includes material on learning styles, simple first-aid procedures, and discipline policies. The packet gives the big picture of how the education program works and what each person's responsibility is in it.

Finally, all people involved in ministry need to feel important and appreciated. Once a year we have a teacher appreciation banquet. Throughout the year teachers are recognized for their work. We have a teacher of the week, and the four teachers are profiled in our monthly newsletter. We also ask different teachers to present their testimonies, hopes, and goals before the church. An education fair, held twice a year, demonstrates what the children are learning. Each Sunday school class sets up a booth in the fellowship hall, and students sometimes use such creative methods as puppets and drama. The adults who walk through the fair have an open window into the educational program. Parents learn to appreciate the teachers' hard work, and become aware of the various needs in the program.

AT A LARGE CHURCH

Medinah Baptist Church
Medinah, Illinois
Sunday School Size: 450

by Richard Van Dyke
Minister of Education

One of the phrases in my job description reads ". . . and anything else the pastor deems necessary." During my four and one-half years a number of duties have been added to my job description.

Our church initiated a Labor Day Retreat five years ago and that retreat is my responsibility. We use a local Christian camp for four days. Most of our people bring pop-up campers or motor homes. We have four adult meetings as well as four corresponding children's sessions and planned activities during the weekend. It is an excellent time of fellowship for about one hundred people. A second special getaway comes each spring. About twenty couples attend the annual marriage retreat. The Friday night meeting takes place at the church, and then the couples spend Saturday and Sunday at a local motel and resort. I usually lead the Sunday morning sessions, and one year my wife and I led the entire five sessions at the retreat.

Our church does not have a Christian education committee, but we do have a group of coordinators. The preschool coordinator is responsible for coordinating Sunday school and children's church curriculum, recruiting, and assisting all staff in the two-to-five-year-old Sunday school and children's church. The elementary coordinator has the same responsibility for first through sixth grade; the youth pastor is responsible for junior and senior high; and an adult coordinator oversees the adult classes. The children's church coordinator, Sunday school superintendent, and occasionally the Awana commander also meet with this group. This group is my "eyes" and "ears" in these ministries.

Missions is a significant part of our church. We promote more involvement in missions by our children in two ways. First, each month we emphasize a different missionary through our children's church ministry. Ten to fifteen minutes each Sunday a teacher will describe a missionary's country and responsibilities. Second, most of the Sunday school offering in the elementary grades goes toward a child-oriented missions need as expressed by our missionaries. One quarter we bought puppets and tape tracks to send to our missionaries in Spain who are involved in a puppet ministry.

One important duty I have, though it is not related to Christian education, is coordinating the ministry of greeters. We have people who greet at our doors as well as people who serve at our information table. I coordinate the greeters, ushers, nursery workers, and Sunday school class secretaries so that we effectively register visitors and work to bring them back again and then assimilate them as quickly as possible. We believe we're doing a fair job of assimilating new people, as 60 percent of our adults are involved in some ministry (Sunday school, children's church, Awana, ladies' Bible study, choir, ushers/greeters, etc.).

Of course, training of current staff as well as new teachers is a key responsibility. I offer a teacher training class once or twice a year for six weeks for new staff. I also lead a bimonthly meeting of our Sunday school and children's church staff. In addition to teaching the group, I am able to express any concerns I have and the direction I'd like to go and then get their feedback. Each fall I direct a leadership training seminar for our staff and other local churches. We bring in special speakers for three one-hour sessions in preschool and elementary education.

In the areas of counseling, conflict management, staffing, and preparation of programs, dealing with people does consume much time. I am convinced that the CES must have clearly written across his forehead the word "approachable" and must have as one of his character traits "interruptible." These were Jesus' traits, and it is certainly not too much to ask of a CES.

Relationships with Church Staff

And Saul hurled the spear for he thought, 'I will pin David to the wall' " (1 Sam. 18:11). Few senior pastors tote spears to staff meetings, but many would admit the urge to skewer a popular young assistant. Problems in staff relationships are nothing new. Nehemiah had his problems with Sanballat and Tobiah, who saw the rebuilding of Jerusalem's walls as a threat to their own interests and tried to sabotage the work. "Do not forgive their iniquity . . . for they have demoralized the builders" (Neh. 4:5). The subtle undermining of someone else's ministry is still a popular method of forwarding one's own program. Even among Christ's companions there was a jockeying for position. Christ had to tell His disciples, "Whoever wishes to be first among you shall be your slave; just as the Son of Man did not come to be served, but to serve, . . ." (Matt. 20:27-28).

The key to productive staff relationships is the practice of mutual servanthood. This requires considerable commitment by everyone involved, but it's worth it. In our survey of more than one hundred CESs, unsuccessful staff relationships was the number two problem. Marvin Judy, church management expert, found similar results in a survey done more than twenty-five years ago.[1] More complaints centered on staff relationships than on the combined concerns of space limitations, budget deficits, and teacher training. The seriousness of the problem depends on whom one asks. Staff members in assistant positions will report unworkable situations in the same churches where the senior pastors will report that all is well.

If modeling is the most effective teaching tool, and congregations look to the church staff for shining examples, these reports of disharmony are not only significant but alarming. Where can growing Christians look for an example of community? How will they learn to serve if there are not servant models? Uncooperative, self-serving church staffs breed uncooperative, self-serving congregations. Is it any wonder that the number one problem reported in the survey was the reluctance of church members to be recruited for service?

How does it happen? How do men and women filled to overflowing with good intentions create such misery for each other?

ROLE EXPECTATIONS

As a church grows, pastor and board may decide to call an assistant to share the responsibilities of the ministry. The "second man" usually gets the job of overseeing the educational and/or youth program. If the applicant has planned and trained for this ministry, that's fine. Unfortunately the job often is given to a candidate who, like the senior pastor, is a "generalist" rather than a "specialist." Because number two's abilities and ambitions mirror those of number one, number two may be seen as a threat and limited to "flunky" work that will keep him in the background. "I have no written job description," commented one CES, "so I do whatever the senior pastor decides he doesn't want to do!" Sometimes the educational program is entrusted to a pulpit-hungry applicant who accepts it as a necessary evil in the job package. Some senior pastors make short work of assistants with ambitions to the throne, using the short-term "Henry the 8th" school of management.

The expanding staff is similar to a growing family. The first-born suffers insecurity and jealousy upon the advent of a second child. Further suffering is inflicted should the younger child prove brighter, stronger, or more attractive than the elder. A wise parent will nurture their individuality and strive to bring out the best in each child.

A candidate should be selected whose skills complement, rather than duplicate, those of existing staff. Some senior pastors will value the same abilities in candidates that they see in themselves, but this attitude will lead to duplication of effort in some areas of ministry and the complete neglect of others. Consider, for instance, a people-oriented senior pastor with little administrative ability who hires only those in whom he discerns the same relationship skills. The church winds up with a warm, friendly staff that couldn't administrate a child's birthday party.

There are usually fewer problems with jealousy and insecurity when there is little overlap of roles. Clear role expectations are a vital part of healthy staff relationships. Concise, written job descriptions are crucial not only to the candidating process but to the continuing work of the team. Is the new position on staff intended only to lift menial burdens from the shoulders of the senior pastor? Is the position one of special responsibility, distinct from the senior pastor's area of ministry? Search committees should work out the details before a candidate is called. Problems can arise when special interests influence the interpretation of a role. The board and senior pastor need to concur on the role expectations and educate the congregation in the matter.

The congregation's clear understanding of the role of each staff member is vital to the staffer's relationship with church members and the view he holds of his own contribution to the ministry. "What exactly does Pastor Steve do?" can be answered by educating the congregation before he arrives. Items in the bulletin, appearances in the pulpit, and the endorsement by the senior pastor can all aid in the acceptance and understanding of a new staff member.

The roles of existing staff members change with each new addition. Tasks must be redefined and sometimes redistributed. As the staff grows, it becomes crucial to clarify roles and establish clear lines of responsibility and authority. Organizational charts are helpful tools. The charting of an organization is a good test of its coherence. Some church staff retreats include an exercise in which members are asked to visualize the church in chart format, showing the importance and relationship of individuals and groups within the congregation. A similar exercise involves making Venn diagrams in which circles representing staff members overlap to show the extent of interrelationships (see chart below). The variety of interpretations of the same church body can be illuminating and a little frightening. Charts and job descriptions are important tools, but they cannot create good relationships.

Some role expectation problems start with the CES himself. It is important that anyone training for this position understand that

RESPONSIBILITIES OF CHURCH STAFF

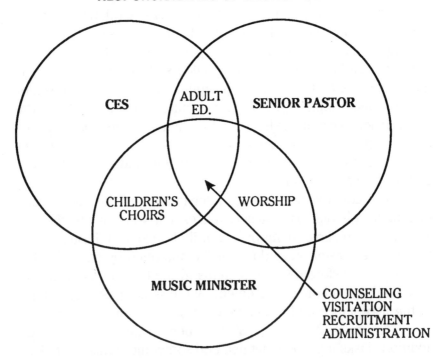

his responsibilities will lie mainly in the area of adminstration. This may come as a blow to those who expect to spend most of their time expounding the Bible knowledge they worked so hard to accumulate during their seminary years. To do the job right, a CES must have the business and management skills to complete the tasks defined by a biblical philosophy of Christian education.

Two-thirds of the CESs in our survey reported that their major role was coordinator/administrator. Their descriptions listed: recruiter, trainer, planner, director, encourager, and enabler. When asked what skills they would look for in a candidate for the position, CESs reported that they would search out a people-oriented organizer. Bible knowledge, although vital to any Christian, was ranked low on the list. Near the top were: a servant's heart, experience, perseverance, a sense of humor, and a love of children. The candidate should be an equipper, a motivator, a communicator, and a problem-solver. He should be well-trained and have a sound philosophy of C.E. He should be flexible and teachable. He should be a team worker. Responses stressed the importance of the acceptance of the "assistant" position. The educational ministry, while equal in importance to all the other programs of the church, is simply not a "limelight" job. A healthy staff team perceives all ministries as of equal value.

THE CES AS CHANGE AGENT

A church's traditions are usually firmly entrenched by the time it hires its first CES. The five year olds meet in the dark, damp basement. Junior class opening exercises use up most of the lesson hour. The primaries always have and always will sit in miniaturized pews. Fresh from seminary, the CES arrives and wants to change everything by next Sunday morning. He moves the five year olds, thereby displacing the senior adult class. He alters the format of the junior class to provide quality teaching time. He sets up learning centers and floor-sitting space in the primary classroom. He is fired within the year.

What happened? One of the roles of the CES is that of change agent. A church that wants to provide a quality program for its educational ministry should be open to whatever change is necessary to achieve that goal, but the church is people and people resist change.

When beginning a new ministry, the CES should take time to evaluate the current program. Programs must be designed based on the unique characteristics and needs of each church. A program that enjoyed success at a CES's last church should not be arbitrarily imposed on his new situation.

The first few months is the time to build relationships with workers and establish trust. Once the CES has the trust of his volunteer workers, he can begin to initiate change. The development and communication of goals and rationale for change must be a team effort. Without a share in the planning, workers will never feel ownership of the program. Without understanding the reason for a change, workers can interpret a critical evaluation as a personal attack and resign. Although a resignation from an inflexible, uncooperative teacher can appear to be a blessing, the CES's duties as a shepherd include helping his staff as well as his students. Change, after all, is not an end in itself. Sometimes the old way of doing something is still the best way. A new CES should find out the history of a program, including previous changes. It may be that the suggested "improvement" has been tried already and failed for reasons he will be doomed to discover.

By carefully evaluating existing programming, seeking the advice and support of volunteer workers, and developing a coherent proposal for change, a CES can avoid most of the pitfalls of a new regime. When a newly implemented program succeeds, it is to the honor of God and the credit of all involved. If a program fails, the CES is less likely to go down with the ship because the other people on board are bailing with him.

The CES should take the same approach when acting as proposal-maker among other staff members. He must clearly communicate the reason for change and let the staff consider the implications for each program. Because each staff member wishes to shield his own ministry from the winds of change, each will stand in the way when those winds shift in his direction. The CES's proposal must become the staff's proposal, or it may not even be on the agenda at the next meeting. The change agent must be a team player.

PART OF A TEAM

"There is a lack of fellowship with the other ministers at our church."

"I have broader duties than any other staff member, but very little support," wrote one CES. "I have a lot of responsibility and very little authority," echoed another.

"The people that make the decisions that affect my work don't understand the situation."

"Our senior pastor has no leadership skills."

These are some of the responses we received from CESs nationwide. More than one-quarter of them indicated they had a better relationship with the congregation than they did with fellow staff members.

"Senior pastors need to know more about teamwork!" advised one of the CESs we surveyed. This is probably true, but since good teamwork demands empathy with teammates, we need to look at the position of the much maligned senior minister. Many senior pastors currently heading multiple-staff churches were trained to be a one-man show. They probably never expected to be placed in the position of leadership over other pastors. A gifted preacher in a small church may suddenly find that, by virtue of his preaching skills, his church has grown to the point where specialists are needed to share in the responsibilities of the ministry. Now he must be a leader and discipler of peers and the administrator of a large institution.

In his book *The Multiple Staff and the Larger Church*, Lyle Schaller describes the role of senior minister in anthropological terms. "In most larger congregations," says Schaller, "the senior minister is, and should be, the tribal chief, the number one medicine man, and the chief administrative officer. . . . Many ordained ministers are convinced by both their call to preach the gospel and their training that their role is to be a preacher, not a medicine man or tribal chief."[2]

This stressful situation creates insecurities and sets the stage for mistrust of the bright young specialists whose strengths shine a brighter light on the senior pastors' weaknesses. Some church members may even refer to some other minister on staff as "their pastor."

Those in training for the Christian education ministry today must be aware of the likelihood that they will be placed in a multiple-staff situation. Often the first additional staff person is the CES; he creates the multiple staff. An understanding of the mechanics of teamwork will be crucial to the future success of the CES ministry.

Management maven Peter Drucker lists four requirements for productive work: (1) understanding of specific operations; (2) understanding of how those operations work in cooperation; (3) direction and quality control; and (4) the right tools.[3] We can translate these four requirements from the secular to the sacred. The effective CES manager will have (1) understanding of each team member's program; (2) an understanding of how all programs cooperate in ministry; (3) acceptance of responsibilities and authority in the pursuit of the common goal; and (4) the right skills.

Every CES spends several hours a week in meetings. Some are well worth the effort, some are not. What characterizes a worthwhile session? A well-planned agenda and an atmosphere of acceptance. Both will contribute to a productive staff and fulfill those four requirements.

A good agenda includes topics that staff members want to discuss. Topics are listed in a logical sequence, and time is allotted for discussion and feedback. The list keeps vital issues in sight and minimizes chances that discussion will be derailed by staff members with agendas of their own. A leader skilled in group dynamics will keep the discussion "on track" and productive.

An atmosphere of acceptance is built on shared vision and each individual's sense of security. Each member's program is recognized as important and distinct. Maslow's hierarchy of needs stresses the importance of "belonging," along with the need for achievement and recognition. When the individual staff member's programs are understood and respected, some basic needs are met. As a result, he will show concern for the needs of the group.

Weekly meetings are an opportunity to share information about individual ministries and work out ways in which programs can support each other in common purpose. "Iron sharpens iron, so one man sharpens another" (Prov. 27:17). Sharpening programs by evaluation and honest disagreement is impossible in an atmosphere of criticism and defensiveness. One way to improve the atmosphere is to begin the meeting with a devotional time. "Commit your works to the Lord, and your plans will be established" (Prov. 16:3). Studies on the nature of leadership and servanthood can be led on a rotating basis among staff members. Some churches also include a time of informal fellowship. Others find it helpful to end the meeting with a shared meal.

The setting of the meeting is also important. To meet in the senior pastor's office automatically reinforces his position as leader and puts everyone else in a defensive stance. Meeting at a round table on neutral ground provides more equanimity.

Each staff member must be given the opportunity to update the rest of the staff on the progress of his own programs and be made current on the status of other ministries. "A fool does not delight in understanding, but only in revealing his own mind" (Prov. 18:2). Each member should have the freedom to make evaluations as well as receive feedback. Each member should share in making the plans and decisions that affect the team, and expect to be held accountable for their administration. Among staff people who have learned to trust each other, criticism of an idea will not be interpreted as a personal attack.

Many staff teams find it helpful to get away on a retreat once or twice a year. It is important that a retreat of this kind be held in a setting that is unlikely to be disturbed for anything but the direst of emergencies. Some take "get away from it all" a step further and head for the hills in a stress-free camping experience. A retreat can be used as a time for challenges that can be made only after a team has learned to trust. Creative exercises can build such trust. Author

Kenneth Mitchel recommends that staff members predict how the ministry of the church could be sabotaged in forty-eight hours.[4] Such an exercise will show weak spots in the organization. Another exercise requires staff members to visualize the church as one individual and then to describe the individual to the group.

The retreat should be a time for "clearing the air" and sharing relational experiences as well as talking shop. It should be a unifying factor. For some staffs, the common purpose of feeding the Lord's sheep is not a loud-enough rally cry. For others, the feeling "it's them against us" will unite a staff against a congregation, hardly a worthy goal.

TAKE ME TO YOUR LEADER

The team's need for leadership varies from church to church, but all workers need someone to whom they can look for guidance and to whom they are accountable. The tasks of the manager, according to Drucker, are: (1) The purpose and mission of the institution, (2) making the work productive and the worker achieving, and (3) managing social impacts and responsibilities.[5]

How these tasks are completed depends largely on the integrity and leadership style of the CES as a manager. "The integrity of the manager," says Drucker, "is his subordination to the requirements of the common task."[6] Some CESs may chafe under the burden of "enabler" of volunteer workers. It takes a sense of selflessness to work hard to make other workers look good. This is the high calling and heavy burden of the team leader. Marvin Judy has described authority as "that ability lying within a person which enables his peers to be released for greatest potential productivity."[7] Authority can be granted by an institution, but the most effective authority is earned.

Whether or not a manager has the respect of his peers/subordinates may depend largely on his leadership style. The leadership style may be direct (autocratic), cooperative (democratic), or laissez-faire. In laymen's terms, these styles may be described as: "You'll do as I say," "Let's decide what we're going to do," and "I don't care what you do." Obviously, the favored model is the cooperative leader. Nonetheless, cooperatively led teams have a built-in danger of endless discussion with little decision making. Decisions based on consensus usually take longer than decisions based on majority vote, but they are easier to implement because of their popularity. Rather than wait for consensus on every decision, however, a cooperative leader will make a decision based on shared goals and insights gleaned from each team member.

"Where there is no guidance, the people fall, but in abundance of counselors there is victory" (Prov. 11:14). The smart manager trusts in the abilities of his team but not to the point of the laissez-faire leader who leaves them without guidance or coordination. Occasionally, an ambitious young pastor will lead as an autocrat. The autocratic, or direct, leader often resents any offers of guidance from a senior pastor and tries to run his own show. Usually, staff members look to their leader for a measure of direction and at least the pastoral care to which they and their families are entitled as members of the congregation.

Much has been said about the obligations of the senior pastor as leader of the team. Although his ministry is no more important than that of any other staff person, his job description gives him the authority and responsibilities of team leader. In an atmosphere of mutual respect, what are the obligations of the team members, including the CES, to the senior pastor?

Loyalty. The staff must avoid cliques, which create power struggles. Often a third staff member is lobbied to choose sides by one of the original pair. Unless the leader has displayed a lack of integrity and betrayed the group's common purpose, however, team members should submit to his authority. "Keeping away from strife is an honor for a man" (Prov. 20:3). When a staff member has a problem with one in authority over him, he must go to that authority to voice the dissatisfaction, not to the congregational gossip-mongers. "He who conceals hatred has lying lips, and he who spreads slander is a fool," Solomon warned (Prov. 10:18).

Support. The role of the servant is to make the master look good. In the ministry, we are all servants. The senior pastor is sometimes praised for the results of the work of assistants. Conversely, a problem created by the senior pastor often lands on the doorstep of an innocent coworker. The ideal to work toward is mutual helpfulness. Words of praise and encouragement can reduce the painful insecurities that may plague a senior pastor surrounded by young hotshots. "Pleasant words are a honeycomb, sweet to the soul and healing to the bones" (Prov. 16:24).

Submission. No one should submit to authority beyond the bounds of what he knows to be the higher laws of God. Short of that, Christians are advised to submit to those in authority. The ideal staff situation would be one in which team members submitted willingly to a respected leader who had earned his authority. In a less-than-ideal situation, workers may find it necessary to pack up and leave. Before getting that suitcase out of the closet, however, a disgruntled staff member should examine his relationship with the senior pastor and other church leaders, identify the problem, and explore possible solutions. Make sure the problem is not one of pride. Remember, "whoever loves discipline loves knowledge, but he who hates reproof is stupid" (Prov. 12:1). If there is no relief in sight, the CES must depart before congregational loyalties can become polarized.

Sometimes a recent seminary graduate may find fault with what he considers outmoded methods and be impatient to make improvements. He must balance the obligation to share the knowledge for which he was hired with respect for tradition. Changes should be made slowly and in concert with other staff. "It is not good for a person to be without knowledge, and he who makes haste with his feet errs" (Prov. 19:2). One CES recommended that a newly hired team member be given one month with no work obligations other than to build relationships and get the "lay of the land."

Christian love. The added dimension of a church staff's relationships is the Christian love that must pervade the usual concerns of human relationships, leadership, group structure, personal goals, and all the other factors of management. To some, the obligation to treat fellow-workers as brothers in Christ may come as an inconvenience. To others, it is cast aside in the interest of running the church as smoothly as any business. To all of us, *koinonia,* a fellowship banded with love, must be the glue that holds the whole thing together.

BODY PARTS

Paul, in his first letter to the Corinthians, used the example of the human body to illustrate how the various members of the Body of Christ work together. "That there should be no division in the body," he wrote, "but that the members should have the same care for one another" (1 Cor. 12:25). No part of the Body was to deprecate itself because it was not some other, more highly honored member. No part of the Body was to consider any other part dispensable. "And if one member suffers, all the members suffer with it; if one member is honored, all the members rejoice with it" (v. 26).

The Helping Hand

If the CES is an "enabler," as many said in the survey, we can liken his job to the "hand" of the body. The brain uses the hand to perform tasks, but anyone who has broken an arm knows how frustrating it can be to have to sit and think about the things you could be accomplishing if you only had the use of your hand.

What about the feet, the ears, and the other parts of the body that represent our brothers and sisters in Christ? What is the CES's relationship to them?

The Brain: The Church Board

The church board is, hopefully, the brains of the outfit. These are men, and perhaps women, who have been chosen by the congregation to use the resources of the church for the enlightenment of the people and the glory of God. The idea that godly men and women cannot be shrewd businessmen should be given the same credence as the myth that pretty girls are brainless. The authority and responsibility accorded to people in this position require a Christian lifestyle and administrative skills (1 Tim. 3; 2 Tim. 2; Titus 1).

The size, makeup, and authority of the board may vary from church to church, but the basic requirements remain the same. Usually, a subcommittee that includes some board members oversees the educational program. Lay leaders must be perceived as partners in ministry and valuable living resources, not as necessary evils. The CES must be careful to respect the contributions of church members willing to dedicate time and effort to administrating their church. He should support and encourage them as he would the volunteer teaching staff. (We discuss the relationship with board members in the next chapter.)

The Eyes and Ears: The Secretarial Staff

The church secretary is the eyes and ears of the body. Anyone who wants to know what it would be like to have no secretary should go to the office wearing a blindfold and earplugs. Any competent secretary has mastered all the necessary office skills. A church secretary must add to those skills superior relational abilities, diplomacy, dedication, and more than the usual degree of patience. Church staff should respect the secretary's position by carefully defining and limiting the job's responsibilities. Often a church secretary will be called on to work unreasonable hours. A staff member should schedule his own day so that the report that needs typing before tomorrow will not be dropped on a secretary's desk at a quarter to five. The inclination to abuse a secretary's good nature can run rampant if she attends the church where she is employed. She must not be asked to serve the lunch at the board meeting or fix the coffee for the adult class.

A secretary can be the barometer of a congregation. A staff member can solicit the opinion of a trusted secretary regarding the feeling in the congregation toward a particular program or individual. As a part of the ministry team, a secretary should be included in decision making that affects her job or about which she may be better informed than the ordained staff. Peter Drucker cites the example of the IBM worker who sat idle beside a machine waiting for it to be reset for the next task. When questioned by a supervisor, the worker answered that she could easily have reset the machine herself but was not allowed to. The supervisor redesigned the worker's job to include greater responsibility and variety. Productivity rates soared.[8] "To enable the worker to achieve," said Drucker, "he must therefore first be able to take responsibility for his job. This requires: (1) productive work; (2) feedback information; and (3) continuous learning."[9]

The Feet: The Staff Team

These fellow-workers are the feet that will enable the people of God to get the work done and really go places. Whenever a staff member daydreams about an obnoxious coworker being "called" to the Arctic, he should think about what it would be like to hop around on one foot all day. Concentrate on the contributions he or she makes to the overall ministry. Support and encourage whenever possible. Many workers who begin as an irritating grain of sand eventually turn into pearls. The oyster lets the sand grain remain, and coats it with layers of a lustrous substance instead of rejecting it. The oyster's response to the grain is what makes it a thing of beauty.

If criticism is necessary, voice it privately. Other team members must not be forced to take sides. If all else fails, the problem should be taken to the senior pastor. Most interpersonal problems on church staffs could be avoided by clear role expectations and policies to be followed when areas of ministry overlap. Members must respect each other's rights to the floor, the pulpit, and the calendar.

To develop a sense of oneness and concern, staff members should meet socially as a group on a regular basis. It would be natural for the directors of the children's and youth programs to spend more time with the CES than they might with the music director, just as the music director might spend more time with the senior pastor in planning the worship service. By actively seeking interactions with all staff members, the CES can prevent power blocks from developing.

Self-evaluation is a healthy habit. Each staff member should examine his relationship to the team and his contributions to the team's goals. Any gear in a machine will disrupt production if it fails to synchronize with the others. Congregations sacrifice to provide salaries for staff members, and any staff member who fails to function is a poor steward of the funds dedicated to God's work.

The Heart: The Congregation

The congregation is the heart of the church. The CES will be involved with many of the congregation through their volunteer work in the educational ministry and their participation in classes. However, to others who are active in the music or evangelism programs, he may be "the invisible man." The visibility of the CES position should be raised by having him appear on the platform occasionally and give updates on the educational program. The CES should attend social functions, such as church dinners and class parties, whenever possible. He must not build relationships solely for the purpose of having a file of names for teacher substitutes. Every staff member should enjoy the fellowship and community of his church.

The CES's Family

Where does the family fit in? Every vocational and volunteer Christian worker must answer that one for himself. Our survey solicited a wide scope of comments on problems and frustrations in the ministry, but only a small percentage of responses mentioned the welfare of the CES's own home. A few commented that the ministry left little time for family, and one or two confided that their spouses were unhappy about either financial limitations or their role as "his wife" or "her husband." Is it any wonder that the divorce rate among clergy is skyrocketing?

Church meetings are hard enough on families whose mom or dad must attend one or two a month. What about the family that must sacrifice a member to several meetings each week? New Testament standards for church leaders stipulate that they must have one spouse and be able to keep their households in order (1 Tim. 3:2, 4-5). They won't be able to maintain order if they're never home. Church leaders, whether volunteer or vocational, must balance their schedules to provide time with the families God has committed to their care. Spouses who want to be involved in the work should be welcomed but not abused. Those who have decided not to participate should be encouraged but not pushed. Just as the senior pastor is expected to care for his staff as members of his flock, each pastor must show his family the concern and respect he would show to members of the congregation.

Judy describes the church staff as "organismic." "By organismic I mean each person on the staff is not an entity unto himself, but a part of a total organism . . . united and dependent upon other members of the staff."[10] The helping hand, with active, cooperative eyes, feet, heart, and brain, will contribute to a church body that is healthy and attractive.

UNITED WE STAND

Lyle Schaller has written many books on church management. His "Seven C's" summarize the characteristics of a good team.[11]

1. *Compatibility.* The team is compatible.
2. *Continuity.* Long-term relationships and pastorates exist.
3. *Competence.* The team has the ability to lead.
4. *Confidence.* The congregation trusts the staff.
5. *Coherence.* The program is consistent.
6. *Complementarity.* The team is well-rounded.
7. *Conceptualization.* All agree on the church's role and purpose.

Schaller's formula for teamwork and all the other advice on the subject can easily be summed up in the words of the apostle Paul:

Love is patient, love is kind, and is not jealous; love does not brag and is not arrogant, does not act unbecomingly; it does not seek its own, is not provoked, does not take into account a wrong suffered, does not rejoice in unrighteousness, but rejoices with the truth; bears all things, believes all things, hopes all things, endures all things. Love never fails. . . . (1 Cor. 13:4-8)

Christ has given a warning that applies to all church leaders: "Any kingdom divided against itself is laid waste; and a house divided against itself falls" (Luke 11:17). If we create division, the house that falls is His house.

— NOTES —

1. Marvin T. Judy, *Multiple Staff Ministry* (Nashville: Abingdon, 1969).
2. Lyle E. Schaller, *The Multiple Staff and the Larger Church* (Nashville: Abingdon, 1980), p. 106-7.
3. Peter F. Drucker, *Management Tasks, Responsibility Practices* (New York: Harper & Row, 1974), p. 199.
4. Kenneth R. Mitchell, *Multiple Staff Ministries* (Philadelphia: Westminster, 1988), p. 74.
5. Drucker, *Management Tasks,* p. 40.
6. Ibid., p. 245.
7. Judy, *Multiple Staff Ministry,* p. 47.
8. Drucker, *Management Tasks,* p. 260.
9. Ibid., p. 267.
10. Judy, *Multiple Staff Ministry,* p. 30.
11. Schaller, *The Multiple Staff,* p. 103.

Principles in Practice

AT A SMALL CHURCH

Park Springs Bible Church
Arlington, Texas
Sunday school size: 300

by Bob Cave
Pastor of Christian Education

To mark my fourth anniversary of service as pastor of Christian education at our church, the congregation and leadership surprised me with a dinner and a roast "tooting" my ministry. The event included a sentimental slide show of some of our years of ministry with them, and an all-expenses-paid weekend getaway trip for my wife and me.

This represents a high point in my relationship with the congregation and, in particular, our church leadership. It has taken years of effort to build those relationships and establish rapport and credibility with the shepherds and sheep. During those four years, God saw fit to call each member of the pastoral staff to other churches for ministry. With this staff turnover came a corresponding change in the membership of the board of elders that governs our church. Only one elder who was on the board when I was hired remains in that position. This kind of turnover has given me lots of opportunities to practice building and rebuilding relationships!

Fortunately, the men that serve in leadership positions share a strong commitment to build relationships. Building meaningful bonds with others is not a one-way street. It requires time and attention on the part of all.

I dislike change more than most people. Therefore, if it had been up to me, I would not have chosen the turnover in leadership that has occurred, particularly in the last three years. However, those staff changes caused me to place a higher priority on relationships. Just over one year ago, we restated our philosophy of ministry in terms of relationships. Our ministry statement is:

The ministry of our church is to make disciples. Disciples are made by building three vital relationships; our relationship with Jesus Christ (believers growing more like Jesus Christ), our relationship with one another (believers building up one another in Christlikeness), and our relationship to the world (believers influencing others towards faith in Jesus Christ).

Various versions of this statement grace our publications and are communicated regularly to congregation and leadership. At least annually, our senior pastor presents a series of messages reminding the congregation to concentrate on these important vertical and horizontal ties. With such a public stress on relationships, there is extra pressure to establish and maintain model relationships among the staff and board. To facilitate this process, we have set aside time for this purpose.

Regular weekly staff meetings emphasize communication and prayer. Humor plays a major role in preventing any of us from taking ourselves too seriously, whereas prayer for both corporate and individual needs helps us to build relationships with each other. We also develop staff friendships with a monthly staff lunch that replaces the weekly meeting. The luncheon takes place either potluck style at church or we eat at a favorite local restaurant. Business is minimal as we invest time in each other. We invite our secretaries as well, arranging for volunteers to handle visitors and phones in their absence.

Relationships with board members are built in a similar manner. All the pastors make an effort to take leaders to lunch. Although some business is addressed, I work at understanding and encouraging these men. When I seek to serve, assist, pray with, and encourage other leaders in their ministry, they often develop similar attitudes and actions not only toward me but to others in the church family.

Recently we began monthly meetings in the homes of pastors and board members designed to train our leaders and develop relationships. After a breakfast meal, we study a ministry issue or skill to better prepare ourselves for ministry. We include much time for prayer, primarily for individual needs and some pressing corporate needs. Occasionally, we bring our wives and meet together especially for fellowship. These "board socials" normally are fun times, but one such gathering turned into a disaster. That month, the regular board business meeting lasted well past midnight. We decided to adjourn and discuss the last issue or two at the beginning of the board social. Our wives took a tour of the house and sat out by the pool as the issue became controversial and we discussed and debated. At the conclusion of the business the men were drained, and the ladies had fought a losing battle with mosquitoes. Most couples opted to make their exit shortly thereafter. We no longer attempt to combine business with pleasure in that fashion.

One of the most significant contributions to ministry team-work is the hiring process. Care is taken to select individuals who fit the team. We look for individuals who have complementary gifts and skills (not clones of existing staff members), share a similar philosophy of ministry, and understand ministry teamwork. When I was hired, I don't think I was significantly better trained or possessed more impressive credentials than other applicants. A decision was based heavily on my compatibility with the existing team. Using such instruments as the SOI (Style of Influence),[1] we are able to evaluate qualities of potential as well as present staff members.

Leonard Bernstein, the famous orchestra conductor, once told an interviewer that the most difficult instrument to play was second fiddle. "I can get plenty of first violinists," Bernstein said, "but to find one who plays *second* violin with as much enthusiasm, or second French horn, or second flute, now that's a problem. And yet if no one plays second, we have no harmony." My experience as a Christian education pastor has been one of playing second fiddle. With some effort, the playing has resulted in some beautiful and satisfying harmonies with other pastors and leaders.

My father taught me (and showed me) that the main job of an employee is to make his boss look good. In ministry, there is never any lack of "bosses." I am responsible in various ways not only to the senior pastor and board but also to the congregation and ultimately to the Lord. If I concentrate on making those groups and individuals look good, rewarding relationships should result.

AT A MEDIUM CHURCH

Melonie Park Baptist Church
Lubbock, Texas
Sunday school size: 400

by David Jacquess
Pastor of Christian Education

We have a team concept approach to our pastoral group. The staff consists of pastor/teacher, a pastor of youth, pastor of counseling, pastor of music and worship, and pastor of Christian education and administration. Each person is considered a specialist in his field and has a clear job description with no overlapping of duties. There is no "jockeying for position," because each pastor considers his position a lifelong calling. No one is stair-stepping to a higher position.

Each pastor has specific gifts in his area and has true respect for the others on staff. Our pastor/teacher is by far the best speaker from the pulpit. Our pastor of counseling is by far the best trained and gifted counselor, and so on. We each accept our calling as part of the team and truly consider the others on the team as gifted specialists, trained and capable in their specific areas. As a result, we feel secure in our own roles and with the roles of others on the team.

During weekly staff meetings, we discuss insights from our personal devotions the past week, our schedules for the coming week, and any difficulties we are having. We have also studied through different books together. We rotate leadership for our weekly meetings. Several exercises mentioned in chapter 3 seem worthwhile, and we plan to try them to help improve our accountability and relationships.

We submit goals to the elders twice a year and hold each other accountable for fulfilling these goals. Two events contribute to team unity. We meet every other week in the pastor of counseling's office for a half day of prayer. In addition, we have a yearly retreat and invite our wives to join us. The retreat always includes some kind of enrichment or evaluation of each other's performance over the past year.

The team concept is also evident in the pastoral salary structure of the church. Each pastor is paid from the same scale despite his position. This helps to eliminate the hierarchical approach to the pastoral team. For instance, the pastor/teacher is paid on the same basis as the pastor of youth. This strongly communicates the importance of the pastor of youth to the entire body as well as to the pastor of youth himself.

I believe our successful team approach comes from four attitudes among the staff. First, the pastor/teacher's willingness to share authority, responsibility, and recognition with the other staff. Second, the pastor/teacher's willingness to be paid on a scale that is probably less than others in similar positions. Third, each team member must be a self-starter with the training, experience, and motivation to do his job with excellence. Fourth, each team member must be willing to be a servant and consider others above himself.

Three books by Kenneth Blanchard have helped us in our staff relationships and in working with others in ministry: *The One Minute Manager, Putting the One Minute Manager to Work,* and *Leadership and the One Minute Manager.* I highly recommend these books. Although written for the secular business market, they include many suggestions to help people reach their full potential. Blanchard recently became a Christian, and many of his ideas are easily supported by Scripture.

The new CES should consider himself a servant, ready to help and encourage those with whom he works. During the first six months in my new job at Melonie Park, I met with the current workers. I asked teachers, "What do you like best about your ministry?" "What is frustrating about your ministry?" No one had asked them these questions before, and they got excited about someone's caring about their opinions. Most of the frustrations were simple things that were easily corrected. Over time, I could slowly make suggestions and influence the direction of the Christian education ministry at the church.

A key element to the CES's position is that he or she consider himself a spiritual job consultant. He should help people find the ministry that God has for them. This ministry will be the one that matches the individual's spiritual gifts, personality, and passion. The CES must approach this process considering what is best for the potential servant and God's kingdom rather than simply to fill a need in his program. After prayer and discussions the CES may discover that a person who has shown interest in an opening in the nursery department has the passion, personality, and gifts to work with youth. He should gladly refer him to the youth pastor, no matter how badly he needs a nursery worker. God has given each church a complete body; we must work to help people plug into God's program and not our own.

AT A LARGE CHURCH

Faith Bible Church
De Soto, Texas
Sunday school size: 800

by Jerry Hull
Pastor of Children's Ministries

Once in an African tribe a little child wandered off into the tall jungle grass and could not be found, although the tribe searched all day. The next day they all held hands and walked through the grass together. This enabled them to find the child, but sadly the boy had died during the cold night. In her anguish and through tears the mother cried, "If only we would have held hands sooner." I serve in a church that has five full-time staff positions, and we find that "holding hands" is essential to our ministry. Effective teamwork is the product of good, open, and honest relationships in which we see the need to "serve one another," "love one another," and "esteem one another as more important than ourselves."

Maintaining those good relationships on any multi-staff church team takes time, effort, and flexibility. I believe that each staff person must cultivate a concern for every area of ministry, developing an appreciation for the difference of personalities and perspectives each staff member brings to the pastoral team and church. We must be willing to be as excited about what other ministries are doing as we are about our own area of ministry. It is easy to focus on what I am doing and forget the big picture of what God is doing in the total church program.

We strive during our staff times to build a team concept. Our friendships and good working relationships remain a priority for us. We take time for staff lunches, meetings, and fellowship that help us in planning the year's calendar activities and tackling the tough issues together. For instance, once we discussed what we should do about teens walking the halls during the evening service. Developing our team relationships requires practical effort on the part of each staff member.

As children's pastor I am accountable to our senior pastor, who really does care that all areas of ministry are done well. He keeps our churchwide vision focused in the right direction. Each year through prayer, discussion, and planning the staff develops a vision statement of our specific goals and objectives for Faith Bible Church in six areas: worship, evangelism, outreach, education, fellowship, and missions. In addition, our senior pastor uses the pulpit to communicate the importance of members serving the Lord, exercising our gifts, and making ministry a priority in our lives. He makes announcements of children's worker needs and the particular opportunities for service. In his teaching ministry our pastor presents several sermons each year on spiritual serving and gifts to tie in with our emphasis for a quarter or for the year. He is also an encourager: visiting classes, affirming teachers, calling spontaneously to say "thanks," and sending personal letters and cards of appreciation.

The support of our worship pastor matches that of the senior pastor. The worship pastor and I plan special services together that highlight areas of our Christian education ministries. Each year we present an Awana closing program and several age group appreciation services and banquets. We coordinate what goes into our weekly announcement bulletin. In addition, at times we use drama and skits in the services to highlight the need for people with gifts in music and teaching. The worship pastor helps me to identify people who can serve in junior camp music programs, direct children's choirs and musicals, and lead songs in Sunday school and children's church. He also helps me in developing age-group music and instrumental training classes.

My task is easier thanks to the coordination of the youth ministry with the children's work. Our youth pastor and I began training teens for ministry through a service plan called "SWAT" (teens "Serving With A Testimony"). Our goal is to raise another generation trained to serve the Lord effectively. We give teens practical instruction to serve in VBS, children's church, puppet ministry, and as Awana leaders and camp counselors for younger children. The objective is to bring teens alongside experienced teachers in a discipleship role, giving them both hands-on training and godly role models who will impact their lives. Many kids who have grown up in our children's ministry are now serving in it.

Working with the youth pastor has resulted in several large family events. We have planned such churchwide family activities together as family fun nights, ski retreats, and missions projects. A yearly highlight where youth and children come together is our Fall Festival. We also combine adults and teens for some Sunday morning teaching classes. These special classes help parents prepare their kids for adolescence and work on family communication and relationships.

This cooperative attitude among the pastoral staff extends to my relationship with our adult pastor. With his help, I am able to discover gifted people through our discipleship program. We want them to make service a natural part of their Christian growth. The adult pastor directs the adult Sunday school electives on teacher training and evangelism, and a newcomer Sunday school class introduces people to the church and also challenges them to become involved in a ministry. Each church member fills out a "ministry and gift survey" when he joins the church. We are careful to communicate the results of such surveys and interviews with all the pastoral staff for follow through.

The pastoral staff wants to keep growing together. It takes time and planning, but it's important. We alternate staff meetings with staff lunches and take time to spend together as we can. It may be racquetball or helping together with a church youth garage sale. We also have gatherings with our wives, either for dinner or a night of fellowship. Some days a special concern brings us together for a time of prayer to hold another up through a personal struggle or help each other in his area of ministry. As members of a team that is "holding hands together," we are more able to find and lead that lost child, youth, or adult to Jesus.

— NOTE —

1. Available from the Center for Christian Renewal, 200 Chisholm Place, Suite 228, Plano, TX 75075.

Relationships with Volunteer Leaders:

The Church Board and the Christian Education Committee

The C.E. specialist must function as both leader and servant in his relationships with volunteer church workers. He must lead by providing vision and guidance. He must serve by meeting the needs of the workers. The CES's uniform includes both a crown and an apron. These two skills are especially important in the CES's relationship to the church board and the C.E. committee. Paid church staff tend to develop a condescending attitude about volunteer workers. Few volunteers will have the biblical and theological background of a seminary graduate, but many will have had valuable experience in the front lines. The CES, especially one who is newly hired or inexperienced, should solicit their support. Referring to Nehemiah's rebuilding of the walls of Jerusalem, Frank Tillapaugh says, "Many lay people out there in our churches today are burdened for the work that needs to be done. And these people are not necessarily among the trained clergy. They haven't been to bricklayers' school, but they can help rebuild the wall."[1]

The volunteer leaders of church boards and Christian education committees bring special aptitudes and abilities to the leadership roles. Board members often have spiritual maturity and business
savvy. Education committee members may add to these qualities
a personal interest or career background in teaching. In our survey
of those serving in a CES capacity, only two-thirds reported a master's
degree level, but close to half of those specified education. Confidence
in the priesthood of all believers, along with good management skills,
are tools for the CES in his work with the church board and C.E.
committee. What Paul told the Christians at Ephesus was meant
for all Christians: "We are His workmanship, created in Christ Jesus
for good works" (Eph. 2:10).

DUTIES OF THE CHURCH BOARD

Organizational differences exist among denominations, but
essentially the church board is the group that handles goal setting,
policy making, personnel management, evaluation, budget setting,
and long-range planning. In addition, the board oversees facilities
and coordinates the church's various programs. It has legal responsibility for church activities and administrative responsibilities, and
is charged with the spiritual oversight of the church.

The board usually delegates many of these tasks to committees that report to the board on a quarterly or yearly basis. Each
committee generally includes one or more board members or church
staff. Whether they are called elders or deacons, church board
members are usually elected from the congregation for a specific
term of office. The board also includes all church staff, but not all
churches designate them voting members. An ad hoc committee
or task force is appointed to handle a short-term concern, whereas
a standing committee exists on a continuing basis with a regular
change of members. A steering committee organizes a new project
prior to the formation of a standard committee. Most boards and
committees will use Robert's Rules of Order to conduct business.

The CES beginning a new ministry has probably already met

the board members while in candidate status; now, as a new team member, he must complete some research before his first board meeting. He needs to learn the history of the group and review the minutes of the last six months. Briefed on the current projects and board protocol, and armed with an organizational chart and a planning calendar, the CES is ready for his debut at the board meeting.

Ted Engstrom, president emeritus of World Vision, offers ten key roles and responsibilities for board members of Christian organizations:

1. Appreciating, recognizing, and encouraging everyone who makes a contribution to the group
2. Decision making
3. Reviewing, refining, approving, and tracking the master plan
4. Networking—bringing appropriate resources to bear on the need at hand
5. Keeping an overview of the entire organization
6. Problem solving
7. Record keeping
8. The senior executive—hiring, evaluating, and releasing
9. Providing spiritual leadership
10. Maintaining a standard of exellence[2]

How do these duties apply to the Christian education specialist? Responsibilities of the CES could include:

1. Providing a brief report on current major projects in Christian education
2. Sticking to the agenda by referring minor projects to the Christian education committee
3. Being aware of the total church program
4. Keeping records of attendance, budget, and personnel of all educational ministries
5. Helping board members understand and implement a proper biblical philosophy of education and ministry
6. Sharing goal setting for the educational ministry
7. Providing encouragement and feedback for other staff

8. Showing concern for other areas of ministry
9. Accepting authority and responsibility
10. Providing candid evaluations

Some church boards become too concerned with organization and neglect the spiritual dimension. The spiritual element brings balance and guidance. Meetings begun with prayer provide a spiritual springboard for communication and acceptance. Whenever a question arises about policy or ethics, the board should consult God's Word for answers. Members should lift up in prayer the needs and concerns of their colleagues. When the nameless face at the end of the table is recognized as a fellow Christian striving for a common goal, the atmosphere has been prepared for progress. "Let us consider how to stimulate one another to love and good deeds, not forsaking our own assembling together, as is the habit of some, but encouraging one another" (Heb. 10:24-25).

MEETING THE CHRISTIAN EDUCATION COMMITTEE

As a committee of the board, the C.E. committee will include at least one board member. Other committee members will represent various ministries of the educational program. When the number of members exceeds ten, the committee will find discussion and decision making an unwieldy process. At this point many large churches appoint members to represent age-group areas that span different ministries. The representative for children, for example, would represent the children's Sunday school, churchtime, and club programs.

As a church staff member, the CES is usually an ex-officio member of both the board and the committee. Of those in our CES survey who reported a C.E. committee as part of their church structure, 41 percent of the respondents indicated that they served as chairpersons, 36 percent as members, and 23 percent as advisers only. Whatever the status of the CES, his attitude toward volunteer church workers will affect his performance.

As a member of the church board, the CES is basically a resource person to the C.E. committee. He provides information, advice, and encouragement. His participation ensures that the educational area coordinates with the other ministries of the church, but he rarely assumes a leadership role. Leadership and management skills are vital, however, to the CES's role as a chairman, member, or adviser of the C.E. committee. Whoever has the best group management skills should preside as chairman, but the discipleship and development of each committee member will be the job of the CES. Leadership means developing the potential of every subordinate. Author John Naisbitt cites the recognition of the individual a key element of a leader. "Any well-trained person can be a manager," Naisbitt writes. "A leader is an individual who builds followership by ethical conduct and by creating an environment where the unique potential of one individual can be actualized."[3]

The CES can best serve the individuals by first getting to know them. A survey of interests and abilities is a helpful tool, especially if the CES must assemble his church's first C.E. committee. The list of questions could include:

1. *Church membership and attendance.* Are you active?
2. *Spiritual life.* Are you growing spiritually?
3. *Family.* Does your family support your participation?
4. *Skills.* Do you devote special gifts to the task?
5. *Goals.* What are your personal goals? Ministry goals?
6. *Availability.* Are you able to attend meetings regularly?
7. *Motivation.* What prompts your participation?
8. *Teachability.* Are you willing to grow?
9. *Employment.* What kind of work do you do?
10. *Interests.* Do you have particular hobbies or talents?

Manipulation and exploitation occur when managers use people to achieve goals. These problems are less likely to develop when the growth of the individual is one of the goals. The words *administrate* and *minister* both stem from the old Latin word for service. The CES must remember that his role as leader is that of servant. Kenneth Gangel lists several ways to serve committee members:

The needs and wants of people have been classified and codified in many different ways, but basically they boil down to a desire for development, opportunity for fullest use of gifts and abilities, appreciation and credit for work done well, recognition of achievement, attention as an individual, interest and challenge in the work task, firm but kind supervision, and fair understanding of what can be expected from the organization in return for their efforts.[4]

DUTIES OF THE C.E. COMMITTEE

In order to properly delegate tasks, the CES will need not only an understanding of his workers but a clear vision of the work to be done. What are the tasks of the C.E. committee? The following represent ten common tasks:

1. Communicate and promote the educational ministry
2. Evaluate programs and personnel
3. Recruit qualified teachers
4. Select curriculum
5. Set budget for educational programs
6. Coordinate a calendar of events
7. Provide supplies, equipment, and facilities
8. Provide continuing training and support for teachers
9. Engage in long-range planning and goal setting
10. Keep records of attendance, personnel, and finances

The CES's Role on the Committee

Everyone can help with some tasks, such as teacher recruitment. Other responsibilities can be delegated to workers under the guidance of the CES. The delegation of a responsibility must include a degree of authority, so the CES must be certain that the skills and motivation of the worker are equal to the job. The person in charge of vacation Bible school, for example, needs to be a skilled organizer. The secretary should be a detail-oriented person. Those involved in curriculum evaluation ought to be experienced teachers well versed in the teaching/learning process. Workers deserve a clear description of their responsibility and an understanding of how they will be held accountable.

Another responsibility of the CES to the committee will be the training of its members to complete tasks and achieve the goals of the ministry. Training should include a biblical philosophy of education, the basics of the teaching/learning process, and skills in decision making, problem solving, and evaluation.

Much of the CES's success with the C.E. committee will depend on the amount of time he devotes to planning. Most of those surveyed reported that they had fewer hours to devote to planning than they spent in meetings. If more time was spent planning, fewer hours would need to be spent in meetings. An administrator who values not only his own time, but the time of his workers, will carefully plan the agenda for the hours they spend together in meetings. If the CES is not the chairperson, this is a task they should work on together. If everyone has done his homework and the chairman can manage the group dynamics, no meeting should last longer than two hours. By sticking to an agenda and a time schedule, the chairman ensures that major projects will be discussed and only minor items risk postponement to the next meeting.

A Productive Committee

In the New Testament, the gift of administration is described using the Greek term for the helmsman of a ship. The helmsman was captain and navigator. He directed the progress of the ship by knowing the landmarks, the strength of the rowers, the use of the sails, the currents, and the signs of changing weather. He stood in the stern of the ship with his eyes on the horizon ahead. When the rowers were at work, they faced the stern and trusted the helmsman to direct them. In his role as administrator, the CES needs to figure out a way for his workers to keep on rowing and yet be able to see where they are headed. The ancient sailors might have rowed with more enthusiasm if they had seen the lights of home ahead.

As an administrator, the C.E. specialist will perform four functions, as recognized by most management experts. The CES will act as the planner, leader/director, organizer, and controller. In each of these roles, he will perform various duties, as shown on the chart "The Role of the CES As Administrator."

A skilled leader and a motivated group of workers are fundamental to the success of a C.E. committee. What else is needed for a productive and growing committee? Here are six elements that keep a C.E. committee productive. First, the committee needs *clarity of purpose*. The purpose of the committee must be understood and supported by the group. Goalsetting must be a group activity. Goals must be based on biblical standards.

THE ROLE OF THE CES AS ADMINISTRATOR

These four functions are recognized by most management experts as the role of the administrator. The CES, in ministering throughout the year, will perform these functions:

PLANNER
□ Forecasting (estimating)
□ Establishing Objectives
□ Developing Policies
□ Establishing Procedures
□ Programming
□ Scheduling
□ Budgeting

LEADER/DIRECTOR
□ Decision Making
□ Communicating
□ Motivating
□ Selecting People
□ Developing People

ORGANIZER
□ Developing Organizational Structure
□ Recruiter/Trainer/Delegator
□ Establishing Relationships

CONTROLLER
□ Establishing Performance Standards
□ Performance Measuring
□ Performance Evaluating
□ Performance Correcting

Second, the committee must have the right *organization*. The structure of the committee must be designed to achieve the purpose. Lines of authority and responsibility should be clear. Areas of responsibility cannot be allowed to overlap. An organization that cannot be charted is not well organized.

Third, the committee needs adequate *information*. The committee must have the information it needs to make intelligent decisions. Decisions based on "feelings" and "assumptions" are poor decisions.

Two key elements are *participation* and *motivation*. Every committee member must be permitted input and provided with feedback. Active participation also requires that each member know that he will be held accountable for the task to which he is assigned. Motivation can be nurtured but not imposed. Manipulation and motivation seem to produce the same results, but they do not. Consider the example of two children in the middle of the lake. One has been given swimming lessons and lots of encouragement. The other child is "being taught to swim" by being thrown into the lake. Both make it to shore. The first child pursues an athletic career and wins Olympic gold. The second child will never go near the lake again.

Finally, the productive committee has *unity*. Decisions should be based on a general consensus, with few dissenters. Agreement adds cohesion to a committee. Guard against assembling a group of "yes men," but work for agreement based on objective evaluation of the facts.

COORDINATION AND BALANCE

The smooth operation of the C.E. ministry must be based on coordination. Cionca writes, "Four ingredients are essential for good coordination: a positve team spirit; a functional Christian education committee; a responsible decision-making process; and an annual assessment."[5]

Anyone who has enjoyed a day at the circus has been dazzled by the kaleidoscope of action and color. Trained tigers leap through flaming hoops. Dozens of clowns tumble from a tiny car. Elephants parade, and acrobats fly overhead. So many acts perform that it's hard to decide what ring to watch. The seeming lack of coordination is what made the term "three-ring circus" apply to any out-of-control situation. In reality, the ringmaster has the big top under complete control. Everything has been carefully orchestrated to give the impression of constant action and an endless assortment of attractions. Several acts can perform simultaneously because the ringmaster knows he can trust his people to do the work they were trained to do.

The performers can do their best because they trust the ringmaster to maintain order and direct the show. There is a tradition of "family" among circus people and a dedication to their art that motivates even the riggers and roustabouts who set up the tents and the trapeze but never share in the applause.

The CES who administrates a church's C.E. program must sometimes deal with "three-ring" situations. Let him trust his workers and lead in a way that warrants their trust in him. He should build a team spirit among them and develop their strengths as a group and as individuals. He should serve them in a way that prepares them to serve the church.

— NOTES —

1. Frank R. Tillapaugh, *Unleashing Your Potential* (Ventura, Calif.: Regal, 1988), p. 71.
2. Bobb Biehl and Ted W. Engstrom, *Increasing Your Boardroom Confidence* (Phoenix: Questar, 1988), p. 28.
3. John Naisbitt and Patricia Aburdene, *Megatrends 2000* (New York: Morrow, 1990), p. 308.
4. Kenneth O. Gangel, *The Church Education Handbook* (Wheaton, Ill.: Victor, 1985), p. 16.
5. John R. Cionca, *Solving Church Education's Ten Toughest Problems* (Wheaton, Ill.: Victor, 1990), p. 113.

Principles in Practice

AT A SMALL CHURCH

Plano Bible Chapel
Plano, Texas
Sunday school size: 300

by Lin McLaughlin
Pastor of Christian Education

The opening paragraph of chapter 4 captures the essence of working with volunteers. We must wear the crown and the apron. Leading and serving church volunteers are ongoing functions for the CES. These functions sometimes require sacrifices, but they also bring great rewards.

Leadership is necessary because direction and vision do not just happen. As a "helmsman" of the C.E. "ship," the CES navigates, or administrates, according to a direction. Navigation presupposes direction, because unless there is a course and a destination, navigating is worthless. As the old saying goes, "If you aim at nothing, you are bound to hit it."

When I first came to Plano Bible Chapel, I began to formulate a purpose, some goals, and some objectives based on ongoing discussions with the senior pastor and the elder/deacon board. Although I had some ideas about what a C.E. program should look like, it was not my purpose to impose my agenda on the church. As much as possible, I wanted the direction from the Christian education program to reflect the collective thinking of the senior pastor and the elder/deacon board. With this in mind, I knew that the planning process would be fluid, that there would be give and take, and that the task would be continually evolving. A good helmsman is always able to make midcourse corrections. A good leader and administrator is able to provide new direction as ongoing evaluation mandates it.

Serving is vital because people, especially volunteers, are important. They are not a means to an end. They are the end. Their growth, their maturation, their role, and their contribution are paramount. Sometimes I like to think that a program simply gives me an excuse to watch a person blossom in ministry. Of course, this is an exaggeration, because programs are important, too. Moreover, people and programs are not mutually exclusive. Rather, they serve each other. The CES, however, needs to maintain a priority on people, because it is easy for programs to overshadow them. I sometimes fall into the trap of thinking that people can wait but deadlines cannot. Many times it should be the other way around.

Furthermore, people are not perfect and neither am I. Knowing that is one thing, but being patient with imperfect people and an imperfect me while implementing a program is another thing. Paul's admonition remains valid. "Warn those who are idle, encourage the timid, help the weak, be patient with everyone. Make sure that nobody pays back wrong for wrong, but always try to be kind to each other and to everyone else" (2 Thess. 5:14-15). The CES will sometimes work with idle (unruly) people, with timid (fainthearted) people, and with weak (spiritually and morally) people. Admonishing, encouraging, and supporting these people are appropriate ministries for him. This is where leadership and servanthood blend together into the role of the shepherd.

For an effective, productive relationship with the church board, the CES must keep good records. Actually, good record keeping helps the CES in several ways. He can maintain the big picture of what is happening in the C.E. program of his church. The records will help him use equipment, facilities, and other resources wisely. It helps him accurately project personnel and equipment needs for the future. Most important, it helps the CES effectively communicate this information to the board.

For instance, I track the attendance for each grade of Sunday school and compute the square footage available to each child based on the attendance and the size of each classroom. By reporting the attendance, along with the proper ratios of square feet to children in comparison with the actual ratios, I helped the board to see the need for making plans for a new education building. This process of communication is a lot different from casually entering a board meeting and saying, "I think we need a new building." It would be easy for any one of the board members to argue with my opinion. It would be much harder for them to argue with objective facts. One of my seminary professors used to frequently say, "Always do your homework before making a proposal to the board." That piece of advice has been very helpful over the years.

I have an unorthodox approach to working with what is in effect my C.E. committee. I rarely meet with them as a whole committee; instead, I usually meet with them as individuals, and sometimes with two or three members at once. I do this for several reasons.

First, I find it difficult to get everyone together at the same time. Scheduling meetings is much easier, if less efficient, with one to three individuals. Second, this approach allows me to give personal attention to the leaders who serve our educational programs. A large committee meeting limits changes from the formal business atmosphere to an informal relational one. Easier, more open relationships can occur in a setting with one person or even a few people.

Finally, I have observed that the tendency for upward delegation frequently takes place in a large committee meeting. In other words, the committee ends up delegating most of the work to the CES when it should work the other way. By meeting with one to three individuals I am able to effectively delegate and supervise the various leaders of our educational program. I find that planning and coordination rarely require the whole group to meet.

This arrangement is not for every church. Leadership is situational, and I have found this specific application results in the most effective leadership in my church setting. Fortunately, the principles hold for relationships with most church committees.

AT A MEDIUM CHURCH

Northview Bible Church
Spokane, Washington
Sunday school size: 470

by Gary Prehn
Minister of Christian Education

When starting a new ministry, the CES must prove himself or herself to the church board and earn their respect regardless of how much training or years of ministry the CES brings to his new church. In most cases the CES is hired by and under the authority of the church board. The board gives the directives, and the CES's task is to implement the Christian education goals that the board sets for the upcoming year. The CES, the pastoral staff, and the C.E. committee will have some input regarding those goals, but the CES must recognize that the board initially hired the CES to implement the goals and tasks assigned. To earn the board's respect, the CES should faithfully fulfill the tasks given him. As board members observe the CES's track record and the quality of his work, they will gradually ask him for ideas and recommendations.

In both of my ministries it has taken almost four years to earn the full respect of church boards. During the first year with a new church, the CES often attends the monthly church board meetings and just listens. He offers his comments only when board members ask for them. Later, when he is confident that he has earned the right to be heard, he may independently make suggestions.

One way I communicate my zeal for Christian education is by distributing a one-page ministry report to the board each month. I list the number and types of meetings and visits I had, and the number of times I taught or spoke. I summarize projects over the past month and indicate recruitment and training activities. This is a fine approach for letting the staff see one's duties in action. Record the tasks accomplished that the pastor or the board had assigned.

In addition, the CES should distribute a set of minutes from each C.E. committee meeting to the church board. These minutes keep them informed of the activities and status of all the C.E. programs in the church. The C.E. specialist demonstrates to the board his awareness of situations by the monthly reports, and they avoid being caught ignorant of a situation because the CES failed to inform them. For instance, for years our church participated in a nearby Bible camp program. One year the leadership of the camp changed, and the quality of the counselors and the quality of the program deteriorated significantly. As a result the C.E. committee decided not to promote that particular camp until conditions changed. A number of us wrote letters and met with the camp leaders to help improve the camp even when we were not promoting it.

We kept the church board informed of these efforts. Meanwhile, two vocal families in the church complained to various members of the church board that the C.E. committee was not doing its job promoting camp. Armed with current information the board members supported the C.E. committee's actions instead of reacting and telling us to do a better job of promoting the camp.

The authors are right; learn some history about the church board. To work effectively with the board it is vital to learn about past decisions and the reason for those decisions. Do your homework and find out what has occurred in the past. Talk with individual board members about ideas you are thinking about suggesting before you submit formal plans. I learned this lesson the hard way when I recommended a tandem approach to Sunday school. In my previous church we ran a successful tandem Sunday school program in order to accommodate the nearly 650 poeople who attended classes each week. We had two services and two Sunday school/children's church programs back to back. There was a fifteen-minute break between the two hours. Sunday school for preschool through junior high and eight adult classes met during the early service. The senior high and three or four other adult Sunday school classes met at the later service. We also offered a children's church program for the preschool through junior high grades at the second service.

At my second church the leadership wondered what to do with anticipated growth in the Sunday school program. My first thought, of course, was to recommend a tandem Sunday school approach. In one staff meeting I suggested the tandem Sunday school to the senior pastor, but he was not at all in favor of it. I learned from him that it had been tried about three years before I came and did not work. Families did not like being pulled apart and made to go at different hours for church and Sunday school. I talked in private with my current C.E. elder and met with the same response. I talked with a former C.E. elder and again encountered a brick wall. I soon realized that the church's negative experience strongly influenced the board and made them unwilling to attempt a tandem Sunday school again. As a result the C.E. committee and I dropped the idea of a tandem Sunday school and offered instead an alternate proposal.

Though discussed in chapter 3, the CES's relationships with the senior pastor and other pastoral members deserve mention here, as they influence board decisions. The wise CES will discuss significant Christian education recommendations with the senior pastor before bringing them to the board. There are three reasons for this. First, you avoid catching the pastor off guard, that is, unprepared. Senior pastors don't like surprises, especially when they come from one of the staff under them. Second, the senior pastor will probably have a good idea of the reaction of the board to any recommendation you set forth. He is a good sounding board and can probably make suggestions that will help the recommendation to pass. He can also go before you and sell the idea to a few key board members so that your proposal will be accepted at the board meeting.

Finally, you do not want to be in the position where you make a recommendation to the board only to discover the senior pastor is strongly opposed to it. Better to discuss, modify, or even scuttle a plan with your senior pastor in private, such as a tandem Sunday school, than to bring the plan to the board and put the pastor in the awkward position of finding fault with it. The chances are that if the senior pastor is not in favor of a recommendation it will not pass anyway, so the CES might as well get his input and gain his support before the board meeting begins.

For a strong relationship with members of the C.E. committee, the CES should stay in touch with each member at least monthly. The CES should do this in addition to the monthly meeting to show his interest and concern for them and their ministry. Some programs, such as Sunday school or Awana, constantly have the specialist's attention and direct involvement, but it is very easy to overlook other ministries, such as the nursery or the college-age group. The CES can set up a reminder system to call the nursery supervisor on the third Thursday of every month and call the college coordinator every fourth Thursday. As well as finding out how they are doing and how their ministry is going, the CES can inquire about the progress they made on an assignment given at the last C.E. meeting. Many people need to be reminded or encouraged to complete tasks assigned to them. Such calls help them to follow through so that they don't show up at the next meeting apologizing because they didn't get their task completed on time. In addition, a monthly call helps the members feel remembered and want to succeed.

The CES always should support the policy decisions of the C.E. committee. If he does not, they will become discouraged and drop out of service. For example, church members have a tendency to pull rank and go to the CES when they don't like the policy for serving in the nursery. Our policy manual states that every family in the church needs to serve one hour a month in the nursery for every child they have in the nursery or find a substitute to fulfill that hour. A situation arose where a couple had two children in the nursery. The husband sang in the choir and the wife taught in the elementary Sunday school department. The parents did not feel obligated to serve in the nursery because they served elsewhere in the church. Dissatisfied with the nursery supervisor's insistence, they appealed to me to make an allowance for them.

The parents were upset with me, yet I sided with the supervisor and upheld the policy that had been established. If I had not done this I would have demoralized the supervisor and created additional problems. Dozens of other parents would have then come and asked for the same exemption. The staffing of the entire nursery program would have been undermined. The CES must stand by his C.E. committee members. He must be wary of people who try to get him to overrule a C.E. decision. Before making a decision, the CES should talk with the C.E. member responsible and obtain the member's perspective.

For the C.E. members to succeed, the C.E. specialist should give them ongoing guidance and training. Once goals are set for the coming year the CES should ask members to submit at least quarterly progress reports. Nudge them along by reminding them about the goals they set for their department and help them to reach milestones along the way. Offer them an article to read; loan them a cassette tape that will give them ideas or practical helps to improve themselves or assist them in running their program.

AT A LARGE CHURCH

Central Church
Memphis, Tennessee
Sunday school size: 2,500

by Bill Barber
Minister of Education

It is important that the CES find a good match combining his/her philosophy of education and ministry with the church's goals. I first came to Central Church for a weekend of training and consultation. I returned seven weeks later after accepting the position of minister of education. I returned because church leaders said, "We agree with your ideas for programs and want you to lead us in carrying them out." At the same time, I faced pressure in my new position: The Sunday I arrived they began using a new schedule that I had suggested earlier.

Often the CES and the church board both want to put on their best face when courting for a new position. Neither is completely honest with the other. The CES will sublimate desires thinking that they can be discussed later. The board does not lay out the full reasons they want to hire a CES. It is only during the next couple of years that these two begin to bump together, creating the rocky marriage that too often leads to heartache on both sides. For instance, recently I talked with a church board member from another church. The church is having a problem with a lay couple working with teens. The teens do not respond to their direction. Parents are upset because the teens are refusing to participate. The pastor refuses to acknowledge that there is a problem because the couple represent a powerful force in the church.

Now the church has decided to hire a CES. They will then let the CES resolve this problem. They are in the process of writing a job description. "Will you include this responsibility in the job description?" I asked the board member. The board member laughed at me for asking such a foolish question. The main reason for hiring a CES won't even be discussed until he/she is on the job. This is a great set-up for failure.

I remember visiting a church as a candidate for a CES position. I had made an assumption that this church used brand X curriculum. After all, their previous CES went to work for brand X publisher. As I met with the church board the question of curriculum came up. I told them that I would only work in churches using brand X because it best matched my philosophy of education and ministry. The chairman of the board was a surgeon. He told me he could understand a preference of one brand over another. He preferred a certain brand of surgical glove, but he would use another brand. I asked him if he insisted on a certain scalpel for a particular kind of incision. He said he did. I soon agreed that their curriculum, brand Z, was well suited to their objective. However, I was not comfortable with their objective. Eventually we reached mutual agreement that I could not meet their needs.

Curriculum is a tool. The one the CES chooses depends upon the objective he or she has. As a CES, you must first decide what you want to accomplish. Then you select the best tool. The goal this church wanted to accomplish would be best achieved by using brand Z. If that were my goal, I too would use brand Z. My philosophy and goals led me to brand X curriculum. That does not mean that a church that has a different philosophy and goals is wrong. However, a problem develops when the brand X person and a brand Z church each secretly thinks that the other will change. That is an unrealistic assumption and an unfair expectation.

When I came to Central Church to discuss with the board the possibility of accepting the CES position, I was already committed to spending a certain number of Fridays per year conducting seminars in other churches. They agreed that this was fine. One man asked how I would feel if they cut that number back in future years due to growing responsibilities at Central. I told them that my commitment to the other organization had already been made. That decision needed to be made now. It was quickly affirmed that it would not be a problem. Even after sixteen years it is still not a problem.

Open, honest discussions between the CES and the board during the hiring process are essential. In addition, the CES must be aware of expectations the church has of the spouse of the CES. Usually church boards have much higher expectations of wives of a CES than husbands of a CES. I am very proud of Elsa's involvement in our church. However, her prime responsibility has always been to the family. That has always been clear to the boards with whom we have interviewed.

In developing programs at Central Church, I have tried to follow the model of Nehemiah. Nehemiah had a passion to rebuild the city. He then was given authority from the king. Next, he spent time checking out the exact conditon of the walls. Finally he enlisted the workers. The CES must have a passion for the ministry of Christian education. It is not just something to do to get some experience so that "better" positions might become available. He/she must also have objectives. Those who come to a position of leadership with no idea of what needs to be done are sure to fail. The reason the church has hired a CES is to have someone to lead them. At Central Church I needed to be willing both to lead and to be comfortable as a full-time CES, not as one ready to move forward to another position.

Nehemiah checked out the city in one night. It took me one month to do that at Central. The first month at the church I met individually with each of the seventy-six Christian education lay staff members. I listened to their dreams and heartaches. I was then able to select the early childhood department and one children's department to develop as models. Within eighteen months the staff exceeded two hundred and the model was working in all the departments.

One exercise that has been most productive for our Christian education committee has been the establishment of standards. These have enabled us to measure where we are and what our next steps should be. The committee members have grown in their understanding of what is Christian education.

All our committee members are deeply involved in Christian education ministry, either as Sunday school teachers or department leaders. In addition, some also assist in our one-week children's camp each summer; a few help in our midweek small group meetings. This enables our C.E. board to be a practical group who knows from experience what is best. I also value their commitment to the Word of God.

The first board meeting I attended as a staff member was spent dealing with a major problem. I was delighted to see each member search his Bible for principles that might apply to this problem. I remember praying that the Lord would never let me forget that scene. I knew there would be times that I would disagree with a decision. I wanted to remember that they were people guided by the Word.

Recruiting the Teaching Staff

When more than one hundred ministers of education were asked to name their greatest frustrations, the problem mentioned most often was recruitment of workers. "I hate it! I feel like I'm forcing people to serve!" declared one associate pastor from California. Some of the C.E. specialists, responding to our survey, complained bitterly that the workers delegated to the task of recruitment were reluctant to do the job. Others admitted to procrastinating because the task was so time consuming and discouraging. Although hired as the administrator of the educational program of a church, one CES was somehow expected to do the entire job alone. "That's why we hired YOU!" another staff member explained.

In some cases church members rebuff recruitment efforts by keeping a list of excuses by the phone. Gifted individuals skip church during recruitment drives. Potential workers sidestep into offices and supply rooms to avoid the CES in the church hallway. Why such an aversion to joining the education team?

Most leaders recognize that each Christian has been gifted with abilities intended to be used for the good of his brothers and sisters and the glory of the Father. "As each one has received a special gift, employ it in serving one another, as good stewards of the manifold grace of God" (1 Pet. 4:10). Christians are to seek opportunities to serve and then do it "with gladness" (Ps. 100:2). However, many members fail to respond because of ignorance. Others avoid involvement due to improper strategies or management by the CES. Consider these three barriers to recruiting the volunteer teacher.

BARRIERS TO SUCCESSFUL RECRUITMENT

Ignorance and Apathy

Many Christians view service as an option, not a mandate. Some are unaware of their own abilities or how to use those gifts in the church. Others decline involvement because of the low status of educational ministry.

Is this reluctance to volunteer one's services a national plague, or is it unique to the church's educational ministry? Interestingly, although the total number of Americans volunteering their services has decreased, the percentage of those volunteers who work in religious organizations has increased, according to the 1988 Statistical Abstract of the United States. Service to religious organizations placed first among types of volunteer activity.[1] And *Newsweek* magazine reported, "The new Yuppie rallying cry is volunteerism."[2] President George Bush's "thousand points of light" speech referred to the "vast galaxy" of volunteers.[3] Where are all these people? The churchworker recruitment system may have scared them off. Two barriers to recruiting revolve around the strategies of the CES.

Inadequate Recruitment Strategies

"Press gangs" were an overly aggressive form of naval recruitment in nineteenth-century England. Armed patrols snatched men off the street and presed them into service as sailors. In many churches, the press gang technique is used to fill teaching positions.

A CES prowls the hallway for the last-minute recruit. "You're my last hope!" "Just babysit them for an hour!" "It's just for today!" he declares. With these desperate words and false promises of additional helpers, he launches a worker into ministry. This kind of recruitment is unfair to workers and an affront to the high calling of servant.

Teachers must be recruited before they are needed. Given time and motivation, an individual can identify his gifts, choose an appropriate ministry, and receive the necessary training. The worker who is plugged, unprepared, into a hole in the teaching staff will experience failure, frustration, and rapid burnout. Like most of the press gang victims, he will jump ship at the first port.

Mismanagement

Workers burn out quickly when they are placed in a situation mismatched to their abilities and interests. Without training or support, they go up in smoke. Sometimes the CES places them in a position too soon. When they leave their teaching position, they probably will not return. That means another post to fill and perhaps bad publicity for would-be replacements.

Just before Easter, the pet store window is filled with bunnies. Droopy-eared and wiggle-nosed, they are snapped up by parents as pets for their children. For a while Thumper is the adored carrot king, but by Mother's Day he will be hasenpfeffer. An eager recruit can soon become a weary worker, and eventually another casualty. Recruitment includes the care and feeding of workers. The CES must offer a continuous strategy of education, evaluation, and preparation to maintain current teachers and attract new ones.

A TEAM EFFORT

The individual who says, "Let George do it," needs to learn that everyone is George. The entire church staff should promote recruitment. Twenty percent of the CESs polled reported that the laity had a lack of vision and little appreciation for the importance of the C.E. ministry. This may be reflective of the view held by the rest of the staff.

The CES may have low visibility, since much of the educational ministry is "behind the scenes." Staff members in higher profile areas should use their influence and share the burden. The pulpit ministry, for example, should emphasize service. "If the senior pastor stresses the importance of something," reports a C.E. pastor in Kansas, "the people are more apt to listen."

The success of this plan may rest on the relationship between the CES and the senior pastor. Cooperation among pastors in a multistaff situation is crucial to successful worker recruitment. If the heads of various programs within the church are willing to join forces and pool resources to develop God's people for His glory, the tree bears fruit. If leaders cannot see beyond the needs of their own particular program, gifts will be misused, workers abused, and the tree will bear nothing but resentment.

The vocational and lay leaders can develop a strategy several ways. They can assemble a clearinghouse of names and skills, compiling lists of eligible recruits from Sunday school rosters, church attendance records, and references from other workers. From such lists the leaders can match the individuals to the roles that can develop their God-given talents. By combining forces to develop workers, the leadership can better serve the entire congregation.

SPIRITUAL GIFTS IN THE CHURCH

And how about that congregation? "Too many receivers, not enough givers," complained one minister of education. The "receivers" need to understand that service is not the dark side of God-given abilities but the natural progression of the recognition and development of those spiritual gifts. Some churches promote that truth with each new member. Membership classes include sessions on gifts and opportunities for their usefulness.

A sermon series or adult elective class on spiritual gifts also can encourage church members to assess their talents and apply them to service. Questionnaires can be distributed that survey the congregation's interests and skills and provide a resource file for later follow-up and worker recruitment. A Texas pastor calls his church's survey "S.O.S.—Service Opportunity Survey." Several churches have Ministry Fairs, where members can visit booths representing various ministries. One special advantage to this approach is the personal contact and exchange of information in an unpressured setting. The potential worker can pursue his interest in one program without being drawn and quartered by representatives from every worker-hungry ministry in the church. This method, however, is only a warm-up for the more formal recruitment procedure, not a substitute for it. Cooperation among program leaders will prevent workers who have rejected or resigned from one type of service from slipping through the system. Such a worker can be directed to a more appropriate ministry.

A VISION FOR CHILDREN'S MINISTRIES

One Arizona minister reported a problem in "getting people to understand that the children's ministry is not second rate . . . it is equal to the other ministries in the church!" The higher prestige associated with teaching adults makes it easier to recruit their leaders. Since there are usually more children's classes than adult classes to supply with teachers, the CES must recruit the most workers to fill the least popular positions. Comments from the survey reveal the low status of children's education in the church. Among the more popular excuses Christian education specialists report are:

"Get the kids' parents to teach" (from a single adult).
"It's my one chance to be with adults" (from a parent).
"I've done my share" (from a burned-out worker).
"I wouldn't know how" (from an inexperienced worker).
"I don't have the time" (from a young adult, a middle-aged adult, and a senior adult).

How can the status of the children's department be raised so that workers will view teaching there as a high calling instead of menial work? Once again, the solution may lie in staff cooperation. An area specialist who has a holistic view of the ministry will rejoice to see workers in service that utilize their gifts, even if that service is in some other staff member's program. When children choose up sides for a ball game, the captain whose hand wraps around the top of the upended bat chooses first and picks the best athlete. The last to choose gets stuck with the kid doomed to spend his life up to his knees in the left field weeds. Each captain looks to the welfare of his own interests. In the ministry, however, we're all on the same team. If a church leader equips his own program by stripping other programs of their workers, his area prospers at the expense of the holistic ministry.

A director of children's ministries in Arizona wrote that one of his greatest frustrations was "people who don't work in the children's area and don't understand the enormity of staff responsibilities." One Sunday school superintendent threatened to send all the children marching militantly into the adult worship service to demonstrate the need for children's church workers. Some churches do just that, perhaps in a less intimidating manner, on one special Sunday during the year. Some worshipers are amazed at the number of children who need leaders, while parents get to finish that roll of film that's been in the camera since Christmas. Whether the children march or the CES simply speaks, the educational ministry and its needs must be kept before the congregation.

The C.E. specialists responding to the survey offered dozens of suggestions to promote the children's educational ministry. Here are several that we received.

1. *A Children's Sunday.* Students and teachers present the children's ministry to the congregation through music, drama, slides, and testimonies.
2. *An entire month of emphasis on the educational program.* Using special speakers and resources, leaders can present the church's educational philosophy in depth.
3. *Frequent teacher recognition and appreciation.* This is done in front of the entire congregation.
4. *Inserts and items in the bulletin and newsletter.* This will

keep before the church the projects and needs of the ministry.

5. *"Volunteer of the Month"* success stories.

6. *Prayer groups* to support the educational ministry and the work of recruitment. "Therefore beseech the Lord of the harvest to send out workers into His harvest" (Matt. 9:38).

7. *Higher status for the minister in charge of the educational program.* Too often the educational ministry simply falls to the low man on the totem pole, regardless of gifts and interests. This is a specialized profession requiring training and a variety of abilities, and deserving of more respect than it usually receives. The senior pastor and other staff must model the respect due the director and the ministry.

8. *A display area in the foyer* for student art, photos, and posters of classroom activities. To be effective, displays should be changed often.

9. *A well prepared slide-tape presentation of the ministry.* The leadership can show the presentation to new members and to the congregation at a church dinner or during the service.

10. *Good promotional pieces.* People may judge the status of a program by the professionalism of the publicity. Someone in the church with graphic arts skills can design attention-getting brochures, flyers, and posters.

FINDING AND DEVELOPING THE STAFF

In the educational ministry the right man is usually a woman, since women do most of the work in the children's department. Nonetheless, church leaders have tried for years to recruit men to team teach in the children's classes, and for good reason. With the high rate of single-parent families, Christian male adult teachers in children's classrooms become important role models. Whether man or woman, however, the right teacher has abilities and interests that complement the job description. In this way the CES can develop workers instead of simply plugging holes in the teacher ranks. Like the Dutch boy who stuck his finger into the hole in the dike, we have only temporarily solved the problem. CESs who use untrained and improperly recruited workers may feel like the Dutch boy, plugging a leak here or there while standing in the cold mud.

An associate pastor in California sets as his goal to "make it my job to make my people successful!" Keep in mind that workers remain part of the congregation for whose welfare each minister is responsible. Workers are not unlimited resources to be used (and used up) in pursuit of a successful program. Ministers are sometimes surprised to find that they have been using willing workers with as little concern as they would checkers on a gameboard. The female CES may be more sympathetic to the needs of volunteers than many male CESs. Like her largely female teaching staff, she faces the pressures of home and family. "When the church office closes," one female CES says, "I rush to get the housework done, drive my youngsters to baseball practice, and feed my husband his dinner so he can attend an evening meeting."

What if the available recruit's gifts put him in line for a position that is already filled? The answer should not be to reroute the recruit to an unsuitable opening. Instead, the CES should provide training and let the trainee benefit from observing the model and experience of a master teacher. A trained and willing worker will not be kept waiting on the bench for long. Recruitment is a pre-need process. With turnover rates in teaching staff of up to one-third yearly, anticipation is part of the solution. A pastor in Pasadena, California, described recruitment as "constant, continuous, never-ending," and that's the way it is.

What if the CES is unfamiliar with the spiritual gifts of the people? As one minister of education reports, "The church is large and I haven't been here very long. I don't know the people well enough to know their maturity and gifts." A Texas CES had the problem of prying workers out of ministries to which they were unsuited. One answer is to form a screening committee to review talent/interest surveys and decide what program in the church would provide mutual benefits for worker and ministry. Such a committee familiar with church policy and churchgoers can help a CES avoid the embarrassment of recruiting a worker who is unacceptable due to lack of membership or some other reason. The committee's recommendations can also protect potential workers from being "pounced on" by representatives from every program in the church.

Surveys and questionnaires can provide some basic information, but there is no substitute for personal contact in the recruitment process. Person-to-person contact is a prerequisite to effective recruitment, according to 39 percent of the ministers in our survey.

Five tried-and-true steps for recruitment mentioned by survey respondents all emphasize personal contact and interest in the potential teacher's welfare. First, meet with the prospective recruit. "Make an appointment, don't do it on the fly," advises one California pastor. "Let them know that a lot of prayerful consideration went into their selection as a candidate for the position." A CES in Connecticut says simply: "Personal affirmation."

Second, provide the prospect with a detailed *written* job description. Many of those who responded to our poll recommended this highly. Discuss the job description with the outgoing worker whenever a replacement is made to insure its accuracy and completeness. Include information on length of service, available resources, and training required. Those who are unwilling to make a time commitment of at least a year may be better suited to a special program of limited commitment, such as vacation Bible school, than the job of teaching a Sunday school class. "A commitment of convenience," an Illinois pastor calls it. Regular attendance of leaders is especially vital in children's classes to maintain continuity and build trusting relationships.

Third, make arrangements for the recruit to meet with a person experienced in the position. Provide time to observe the ministry. Anyone who has taken on a position without an accurate idea of its responsibilities knows the foolishness of diving into untested waters.

Fourth, answer all the recruit's questions and give him about a week to pray about it. "Allow the Spirit to work," advises a New Jersey youth worker. Often the recruit needs time to sit down and assess the family schedule, especially if the prospect is a single parent, part of a two-income household, or has a job requiring occasional weekend travel.

Finally, ask for his decision. If it's "yes," it's on to the training stage. At this point, some churches ask a new teacher to sign a covenant promising faithful service. The church, in turn, promises to provide training, resources, and encouragement. If "no," accept the answer. "Give them the freedom to say no," says an assistant pastor in New Orleans. After all, Webster's definition of a volunteer describes someone "willing to offer himself for any service of his own free will." Nothing there about arm-twisting or manipulation through guilt feelings.

At this stage, a negative response is better than a half-hearted commitment, sporadic attendance, and a grudging ministry. The answer may even be "later." Follow-up notes should be kept on willing recruits prevented from serving by circumstances that may change later on.

Something worth remembering throughout the entire process—smile. Children "catch" the attitude of their teacher. If the teacher expresses a positive attitude, so will the children. The same cause/response happens between the recruiter and the prospect. "You're my last hope. Nobody else will touch this job with a ten-foot pole!" is not the honey with which happy flies are caught. If a teacher finds no joy in helping children experience the love of their heavenly Father and the wonder of the world He made for them, that teacher should resign. If the CES has no enthusiasm for introducing talented and godly people to the high honor and limitless opportunities of the educational ministry, then *he* should quit.

HELPING TEACHERS TO MATURE

The word *recruit* comes from the Latin *recrescere,* meaning "to grow again." In order to develop workers for God's service, the church must help them grow. Even if they are "old hands" who have been teaching since the invention of chalk, they can benefit from training. Master teachers can grow by being trainers of new workers. Without the right training and support, a bright, shiny recruit will soon collapse in a heap of good intentions and scribbled student activity pages.

The parable of the talents (Matt. 25:14-30) illustrates the role of the CES as enabler. In this parable, Jesus presented three servants who were left in charge of varying amounts of money while their master went on a journey. Upon his return, the servants were called to account. Two had invested wisely and could return a profit to their master. One had buried the money and could return only the original amount. The master praised the prudent servants; "Well done, good and faithful slave," he said to each (21, 23). But he rebuked the third servant. The point of the story was the proper development and use of God-given gifts. The role of the CES is that of the banker who made it possible for the faithful servants to invest the amounts with which they had been entrusted. Though the banker is not mentioned directly in the parable, without his help the two servants would have had no profit.

Through careful and prayerful discernment of gifts and recruitment of workers, the church can enable people to serve the Lord and receive the commendation "Well done!"

— NOTES —

1. U.S. Department of Commerce, Bureau of the Census, National Data Book and Guide to Sources, *Statistical Abstract of the United States, 1988*, 108th ed., no. 599, "Percent of Adult Population Doing Volunteer Work: 1981 and 1985."
2. Annetta Miller, Carolyn Friday, and Sue Hutchison, "The New Volunteerism," *Newsweek* February 8, 1988, pp. 42-43.
3. Barbara Kantrowitz, "The New Volunteers," *Newsweek*, July 10, 1989, pp. 36-38.

Principles in Practice

AT A SMALL CHURCH

Stone Mountain Community Church
Stone Mountain, Georgia
Sunday school size: 300

by Andy Chappell
Pastor of Christian Education

There will forever remain a constant quest for the CES, the "magic formula" for successful recruiting. Such a quest is a pipe dream, however; there is no common strategy for all CESs. Successful recruiting for the C.E. team requires learning what works effectively in a particular ministry situation. Not all CESs have the personal recruiting magnetism of a salesperson, or a church leadership or congregation committed to sound Christian education. In some churches adults may even be negative to discipling God's people.

But the future can be bright. Having a sound philosophy of recruiting, a good idea bank of successful solutions, a Spirit-controlled patience, and the grace of God makes effective recruiting possible. The CES should pray and develop ideas and the creativity necessary for his or her own situation. Ideas come from many sources: reading articles in books, attending seminars, discussions with colleagues, and remaining teachable.

The authors have identified major problems in ministry recruitment and offer a good idea bank. One barrier to recruitment I would add: "Overextended family commitments." In our ministry setting in suburban Atlanta, overworked fathers, chronically fatigued mothers, and extracurricular children's programs tend to be our largest obstacles. Add to that an ever-increasing enrollment of home-schooling moms, and you have parents whose free time seems occupied and who typically consider children's ministry a drudgery.

I believe recruitment must be shared not only by the church staff but also by the church leadership and Christian education team members. No successful recruiting can be carried out by just one person. People will volunteer for a number of reasons. They may truly desire a ministry position. They may desire the personal gratification that comes in serving and being cared for. However, some will volunteer because someone on the team who has a personal relationship with them has asked them, and they will do it as a favor to their friend. I know for certain that some of our staff members are with us for this latter reason. Some volunteer simply because they like the CES and want to help him or her.

The authors' suggestions for solutions are currently working very well in our church. We use the "team strategy" to compile lists of members' skills and gifts. In addition, we emphasize "Every Believer Ministry" and recognition of one's spiritual gifts. We currently incorporate this education and testing in our new members' class each quarter. Moreover, each year the congregation completes a basic information survey on two consecutive Sundays during our morning worship services.

The Arizona minister who fears that adults perceive children's ministry as being "second rate" is sadly correct. At my church we must constantly battle this attitude. The younger the age of the learner, the more difficult it is to secure heartfelt service from adults, both from prospects and those in actual ministry. When I read the second suggestion for raising the status of children's ministry, I shouted, "Amen!"

The CES can create unnecessary problems by offering too many programs that require too many C.E. staff members. Our Bible church has five pastoral staff members and naturally generates many programs. Someone must fill all those slots with people. In a multiple-staff church we can create many openings for too few prospects and actually over-program a church's total ministry schedule. In order not to over-program and thus not overextend our congregations, the church leaders should offer only programs that are vital to the congregation's needs. In some cases, staffing ministry positions is a problem because the church cannot realistically support a program.

The authors are correct: "the educational ministry and its needs must be kept before the congregation." The congregation can easily forget or not even understand what occurs behind closed classroom doors. The authors' ideas for promotion are excellent. They may not apply to every ministry setting, however. We have had good success with a couple of the ideas. For effective teacher recognition we publish the names and positions of the entire Sunday school staff in the bulletin, listed together as a staff team. Once a year we honor our staff on "Teacher Appreciation Sunday." The teachers are called to the front, awarded an appreciation certificate, and publicly thanked by me as well as by applause from the congregation. Each fall we also list the teachers and their positions in a bulletin board display. Some years I have even had photographs of the teachers posted so the congregation knew who they were and the parents knew who their children's teachers were.

Suggestion number seven is helpful and practical. A higher status for the CES means both professional contentment and a stronger church program. If a CES is only an administrator behind a closed office door, the congregation will probably see him as a professional "headhunter." But if he is seen as valuable in the "visible areas" of the church, the C.E. ministry can actually increase in success. In my ministry I oversee not only children's ministry but adult ministry as well. I serve as "back-up preacher" for the senior pastor, teach a weekly adult Sunday school class, lead a men's ministry, and periodically teach in some of our women's ministries. I am *very* visible! The only other thing that I would like to do one day is to become a regular part of the platform team during the worship services for even greater visibility.

The California associate pastor's goal "Make it my job to make my people successful!" has the makings of a great desk plaque. If an adult will provide the commitment to teach, the CES must provide the tools and support to complete the job. I would add two suggestions for "follow through" in this area. First, the CES should provide a written "ministry" description ("job" sounds too labor intensive and negative) outlining what is expected, what the church will provide, and a ministry termination date. Leaving an out for the worker may sound disastrous for the recruiter, yet with this approach I have an approximate return rate of 90 percent following the summer off for teachers that serve during the school year.

Our school year staff serve only a nine-month term unless they tell me they decide to continue. The assumption is that their term is over at the end of the spring quarter. Summer staff will also serve more willingly if they know it is only for three months. That is why it is easier to recruit for VBS than for Sunday school. The workers know that their service ends after five days, and they serve willingly. A pre-agreed ministry termination date helps greatly.

The "five tried-and-true steps for recruitment" are fine, though I find it difficult to carry out face-to-face meetings with prospects for various reasons. Telephone interviews and mailed information material to the prospect have worked best for our situation. Another distinction of our program is that we do not use a teacher commitment form. So far my staff members have all been faithful without it. If a volunteer really needed to leave the staff for an important reason, he would leave with or without a signed commitment form.

To maintain a proper perspective the CES should constantly ask himself two questions. "Am I creating a staff team of Christian educators who see their ongoing contribution to this local body of Christ as 'teaching'?" That question concerns the C.E. ministry. The second concerns the C.E. minister: "Do my staff members feel 'glad' that they are part of Christian education at this church?" Answering "yes" to these two questions should mean effective recruitment and retention of the volunteer teaching staff.

AT A MEDIUM CHURCH

Pantego Bible Church
Arlington, Texas
Sunday school size: 350

by Jane Tune
Director of Children's Ministries

As the authors note, church members who recognize their spiritual gifts often are more willing to serve. At Pantego Bible Church we offer Discovery, a four-week seminar designed to help each person understand his or her temperament, spiritual gifts, and passion (what fires the person with enthusiasm). On the fifth week, each person has a personal interview. This is to help people find the area of service in our local church where they can best express their unique giftedness.

The Discovery networking book links our members' gifts to ministry needs. The book describes all the opportunities in the many ministries at our church. This is a valuable tool for old members as well as new. If their schedule changes or they discover a new interest, members usually can find a job that fits their enthusiasm, circumstances, and time.

Once the names are generated for certain positions in the children's ministry, I follow five steps in the recruiting process: prayer, empathy, education, counsel, and follow-up with encouragement.

Prayer comes first, asking God to prepare the hearts of those people He wants involved. Equally important is asking God to help me guide each person in the right decision.

Empathy is a characteristic gleaned easiest by having been in the position for which I am recruiting. Having been a teacher in school and church, I can talk honestly with people about the joys and frustrations involved. There will be both.

Next, I try to educate the person in all areas of the job. People need to see what is to be taught. All duties and expectations of time, talent, and dependability need to be clear up front. Then I counsel the person to take the time to pray for God's direction and get the support of spouse and family if applicable. This is my responsibility to the Lord, to point the individual to sources of wisdom and comfort. In addition, I need to be available to answer all questions during the decision-making process.

Finally, I usually give the person one week before I ask for a decision. During that week I need to be praying for God's decision. When I follow up by phone or in person a week later, my response to their yes or no is crucial. Encouragement is the key here. The potential volunteer needs to know that I respect his or her decision. I need to be prepared to accept the "yes" with enthusiasm and begin the training and "confidence building." I need to accept the "no," and with God's words and sensitivity be able to guide him into another area more suited to his gifts. This is where the Discovery program helps the individual get direction. I may need to refer him lovingly to another ministry with a contact person's name. Depending on what the reasons were for the "no," I may need to continue to pray and contact him at a later time.

The second week I was working as director of children's ministries, I used the above-mentioned steps. One woman wanted to fill a vacancy with her husband and herself the next Sunday. However, I used all of the steps including waiting one week. I asked them also to observe the class on Sunday together. We talked on the telephone three times. One time, I told them to pray about it as they have three small daughters. This class has twelve boys and four girls. They considered this, watched the class, prayed, and planned together. It was clear they were hesitant.

The day before the week was up they called. They are now teaching and love it. Their comment a week later was that teaching wasn't as scary as they had thought it would be when they first wanted to do it.

If I surround every aspect of recruiting in prayer, I am not allowed to pull in "warm bodies" or to "strong arm" people. I can have the God-given confidence that He will bring in and strengthen His people.

AT A LARGE CHURCH

Wheaton Bible Church
Wheaton, Illinois
Sunday school size: 2,200

by Gary Dausey
Associate Pastor of Education

With as many as 2,400 students each Sunday (though as low as 1,700 in the summer), we need a sizable teaching staff to facilitate this ministry. As a result, recruitment of volunteers is essential to our program's effectiveness. The most important component of our recruitment program is ensuring that our present teaching staff are well placed, are utilizing their spiritual gifts, and are personally fulfilled in their teaching roles. This is important to us, not only because it's right, but because we recognize that each teacher who continues to serve is one less that we need to recruit.

Wheaton Bible Church uses a spiritual gifts assessment tool in our new members' classes to identify the spiritual gifts of our people. One of our pastors later interviews the new member candidates and discusses how the particular gifts could be used in the church. The interviewing pastor then forwards the information to the appropriate ministry leaders within the church. In addition, we emphasize the role of spiritual gifts in several of our adult classes and from the pulpit.

Building a satisfied staff requires much planning and action; it doesn't happen automatically. In our setting it begins with a clear and concise philosophy of Christian education and detailed written job descriptions. As this chapter suggests, letting the person know what is expected of him or her, up front, is essential. This not only includes actual teaching responsibilities but also expectations regarding training and length of service as well. In addition, our church maintains a strong volunteer staff by:

• providing personalized direction, support, and encouragement to the teaching staff

- maintaining a good physical teaching environment, good teaching materials, and good equipment
- building a spirit of team unity and camaraderie through informal social gatherings
- offering multiple options for time commitments (most of our workers are recruited for one-year periods, but we do provide options for shorter commitment)
- promoting regular formal training opportunities both in-house and through outside seminars

Recognition of our volunteers is important and can occur in many ways. At Wheaton Bible, we honor our teachers through our Sunday School Newsletter, in our worship services twice a year, and at an appreciation dinner in the spring. We have found visual displays to be effective, including bulletin boards and photo badges of the teacher with his or her class. Much of this is consistent with the suggestions listed in this chapter.

We have chosen to decentralize our recruitment, giving that activity, insofar as possible, to the ministry that would most benefit from it. This means that our college pastor is responsible to recruit his own staff, as is true of our high school and junior high pastors, and the director of our children's ministries. The children's director has the largest responsibility for recruitment for two reasons; her area involves more students, and we insist on a much smaller student-to-teacher ratio, depending on the age. She maintains a teaching staff of more than 200 volunteers.

To make her recruitment task more manageable, the children's director assigns each of her six departmental coordinators the task of recruitment for his or her own department. Each coordinator has a recruitment team of five others, who assist with phone calls and who form a prayer team. Names of potential candidates are coordinated and shared with the departmental coordinators. We wholeheartedly agree with chapter 5 on the role of prayer in the recruitment process. It must be the Holy Spirit who moves a person to take on a ministry, not a high pressure recruiter.

We recognize that decentralization of recruitment is not a

national trend. In fact, many churches have chosen to make recruitment a highly centralized task and have made it a function of a pastor or director of volunteer services. When recruitment is decentralized, however, the coordination of information between the various ministries of the church about the potential volunteers is critical.

The advantages gained by moving recruitment to the departmental level include a better knowledge of the needs within each classroom, a better idea of the type of person best suited for a specific assignment, and a more personal relationship between the departmental coordinator and the new teacher. This is all consistent with the person-to-person contact described in this chapter.

A diverse, church-wide recruitment plan uses a variety of resources: video presentations of our classes shown on monitors in our church atrium, tours and open houses of our children's ministry for adults, bulletin inserts (each highlighting the testimony of one of our teachers), articles, and announcements in church-wide publications. We also have a booth and sign-ups at our annual Ministry Opportunities Fair, similar to the program described in chapter 5.

Training Christian Leaders and Teachers

Sooner or later some church leader will ask the CES, "What are we doing to train our people?" Training workers to accomplish the educational objectives of the church should be the main reason for hiring a CES. Two professors from Denver Seminary recently asked CESs to list the ten most frequently performed tasks. In the summarized results of their survey, training appears three different times on the list (see below).

Task Analysis

The ten most frequently performed tasks in educational ministry were:

Percent	Task
97	Demonstrate an ability to get along with people
95	Train workers
94	Recruit workers

94	Demonstrate an ability to work with a church staff
93	Demonstrate the art of listening
93	Plan and lead a teacher training session
92	Counsel volunteer workers
91	Lead groups
89	Use the laws and principles of learning
87	Promote teacher training

Training occupies second under the heading "Train workers," sixth under the heading "Plan and lead a teacher training session," and tenth under the heading "Promote teacher training."[1]

The survey by Brown and Williams places training consistently among the major tasks performed by CESs. In another part of the survey the professors put training among the most difficult issues anticipated in educational ministries in the 1990s. "The fourth major concern is how to train workers effectively,"[2] they write. Among practitioners, training remains both a major focus and a major obstacle for Christian education in the church.

Church programs routinely use volunteers with no professional training. These well meaning and spiritually gifted people need help in developing their teaching and ministering skills. However, church leaders must remember that volunteer teachers exercise the final option to attend or implement training. A few workers believe they have "arrived" and boycott all training efforts. Most have matured enough to realize their ongoing needs. They attend meetings publicized well in advance, occurring at convenient times, and utilizing excellent resources. Public recognition of those who continue their education contributes enormously to creating a wholesome attitude toward training over time.

The CES must recognize certain limitations in any church training program. No church has even had a standardized set of trained teachers. Only in our dreams will all teachers arrive at some predetermined level of expertise at the same time. Even planning different levels of training each year will not move the entire staff up the skill ladder at the same pace. Each year new teachers replace veterans who for various reasons cannot serve. These new teachers will not have the benefit of the specific training offered two or three years ago. In spite of the best efforts, teachers remember and implement only parts of the training.

A difference exists between instituting a training program and sustaining a training program over time. A few precisely defined changes can be implemented each year, but only carefully designed practices will continue as standard operating procedure for future teachers.

Not all training needs to be done in a group setting. Motivated teachers read books or articles, listen to cassettes, view videos, and receive personal consultation. However, in formal training sessions, the trainer must be ready for a variety of topics from department to department.

Each church program utilizes different skills or learning processes. The four areas shown below represent some of the skills and processes teachers need to know.

1. Leading a small group discussion versus delivering a lecture to a large group
2. Designing or implementing an affective versus a cognitive lesson
3. Teaching children versus teaching youth or adults
4. Working in a classroom versus an informal setting

Each of these and others like them require unique attention in the training effort.

In addition to these practical considerations, training should include spiritual encouragement. All the training in the world will not replace the work of God in the lives of trainers, teachers, and students. Occasionally, God chooses to work in spite of poor training. However, this should not become an excuse for laziness or irresponsibility.

No single approach to training can account for all these variables. An ongoing training program needs a multifaceted strategy. The following six procedures have proved extremely effective over time: (1) plan annual in-service training events; (2) utilize published curriculum with built-in training; (3) develop a well furnished media center; (4) attend periodic conventions and seminars; (5) organize a routine for new teacher orientation; and (6) record the training profile of each teacher. These strategies receive extensive discussion in the following section.

TEACHER TRAINING STRATEGIES

Annual In-service Training

Training workers in their own church to serve in specific programs forms the backbone for Christian education training. One major question nags at this whole training effort: "How do we get people to come?" All other questions pale in comparison. The finest training in the world cannot happen without people to train. Only after devising a successful way to get people to the training effort do curriculum and schedule issues become relevant.

Nothing can guarantee perfect attendance; however, attendance will improve dramatically when the C.E. staff makes the training sessions attractive and easy to attend. Three simple elements can help attendance at a training meeting. We call those elements "prime rate," "prime rib," and "prime time," and each can increase teacher attendance.

In banking, the term *prime rate* refers to the best (lowest) interest rate that lending institutions charge their best business customer. For training of volunteer teachers, the prime rate is the lowest rate charged for child care. Child care may be free or at very low cost, thanks to a C.E. subsidy. Parents must decide what to do with their children. Whenever parents want to attend a meeting outside the normal church hours, they must find someone to watch their children. Their first concern relates to children, not training. "What will parents do with their children?" holds the key to parental attendance.

Perhaps this problem hindered teacher training less when homes normally had one working mate and two functioning parents. Now, the growing number of single-parent families and two-income homes requires creative solutions for child care. Busier schedules for everyone limit the number of evenings or Saturdays people can reasonably take away from their children, even for the best of teacher training. With the prime rate, the C.E. staff will either hire group caregivers or offer a child care fund to defray expenses; this will improve attendance almost immediately.

The Bible acknowledges a wholesome place for food beginning in the Garden of Eden and continuing through the feasts of Israel to the Communion supper. People have to eat, and they still enjoy doing it together. *Prime rib* consists of planning refreshments and meals to coincide with training. Prime rib will attract workers. The refreshments need not be fattening. Workers will appreciate salad luncheons, vegetable and fruit trays, and juices or diet drinks. In most cases, the more exotic the meal, decoration, and program the better the attendance. Prime rib is an important piece of the teacher training attendance puzzle.

The media designate the early night hours (8:00 to 11:00 P.M.) the *prime time* period when most people watch, or are available to watch, television. During this time, ratings go up and so does the cost of advertising. It's the ideal time, the convenient time, for viewing. Similarly, church leaders must find the prime time for training people in our occupied culture. The most popular time for church attendance is Sunday morning. It is the "prime time" to offer training.

If rooms are available, people who lead evening or weekday programs can easily receive training on Sunday mornings. If not, they may be able to meet Sunday mornings in a home near the church. Attendance should reach nearly 100 percent when scheduled at this time on Sunday.

The strategy of group training is most effective for early childhood, children, and youth teachers. Group training is less effective for adult teachers, who tend to resist this type of training. The most successful strategy for training adult teachers links the CES with each teacher two or three times a year in a team-taught setting. Planning the lesson months in advance, and reviewing the principles and methods together as friends, will help adult teachers become less apprehensive about new techniques. Since the teacher observes them working successfully in his own class, the usual excuse that "these simply won't work with my people" evaporates.

The following model of group teaching does not apply to, nor has it been field tested with, adult teachers. However, it has consistently worked with teachers from all the other age groups.[3] The model consists of two phases, but it also includes the three incentives to attendance—prime rate, prime rib, and prime time. It addresses mainly the training of Sunday school workers, as other programs can utilize the Sunday school hour without interrupting their own program.

Phase I involves setting aside two Sundays each year for training. The best times come in the fall and spring quarters. Planning a training event for Sunday school workers during the Sunday school hour means making a curriculum adjustment and providing alternate programs for the children or youth. Published materials come in quarterly form with twelve content lessons plus a final review lesson. Deleting the review lesson often satisfies the regular teachers who prefer to maintain continuity through the quarterly publications. This procedure leaves one Sunday free for something special.

The CES can combine a whole department or division, assembling the children in large groups supervised by parents. Large group activities can include films, special music, clowns, illusionists, or evangelists to serve children during the hour. Simultaneously, their teachers can meet in a vacated room to have refreshments, pray, and receive training. This arrangement provides a refreshing relief from normal responsibilities, does not add to people's schedules, and occurs while children receive excellent care. Maximize those precious minutes with the teachers and workers with a carefully planned schedule.

Phase II involves scheduling one or two special three-week training series a year. Conduct these during the Sunday school hour by department or division. The CES can train a specially prepared SWAT team to replace the regular teachers for three Sundays. In law enforcement, SWAT stands for Special Weapons and Tactics. The designation fits their job. They will demonstrate new, rarely used, or unusual teaching methods and approaches that the regular staff can observe.

This special team of people should be selected and trained

months in advance. They should not come from the regular core of teachers, but they should be the most gifted teachers available. Former teachers and local experts make excellent candidates. Since the assignment is short-term, people who would not otherwise be available can often be enlisted. The SWAT team should use the standard curriculum but emphasize specific features that may normally be ignored.

The first year or two, regular teachers can simply observe the SWAT team in action. On those Sundays, the regular teachers should not have any responsibilities. Instead, they should evaluate the specific features being emphasized. They will certainly feel more secure evaluating than being evaluated. Watching creative approaches while resting from regular responsibilities makes a powerful learning opportunity. Sometimes just seeing others struggle with a problem child brings enormous comfort to a volunteer teacher. They definitely feel less alone or incompetent. Later, new teachers can stay with the SWAT team while veterans receive advanced training elsewhere.

This approach adapts easily to other configurations such as observing one week and training two weeks. Or, the C.E. leader can provide a lunch (a prime rib benefit) after church on the final Sunday for the SWAT team, the regular teachers, and their families. Following lunch, employ teenagers (prime rate) to watch children as teachers spend one hour reviewing the helpful things they learned during the previous weeks. The CES can make a summary of the helpful things they recalled and publish it periodically during the year to remind everyone of the procedures that sparkled during the SWAT team classes. SWAT team members make an excellent substitute corps as well.

Combining Phases I and II requires five to ten hours annually. Considering the fact that workers teach about fifty hours a year (assuming two weeks for vacation), they can devote ten to twenty percent of their time to improving their skills.

This schedule can be sustained over a long period of time without fatigue or exhaustion threatening the teaching staff. In fact, the opposite tends to occur—the staff receives periodic relief from responsibility while gaining enriching skills and information.

Whenever possible, these special sessions should be recorded on videotape. New teachers can quickly upgrade their skills whenever they come on staff by viewing the videotaped sessions. Other teachers can review and analyze the event.

Published Curriculum

No reason exists for a modern American church to use home-grown materials. In recent years, the major publishing houses have vastly improved materials in content, methodology, and overall educational strategy. True, no national publisher can emphasize each church's doctrinal distinctives; however, teachers can add those where desirable, or they can create short-term classes on church distinctives. Where materials have a perceived weakness, teachers can enrich and supplement rather than originate. A good curriculum furnishes an important part of teacher training. Here are nine benefits of using a published curriculum in the classroom:

1. All the lessons link together sequentially.
2. Individual lesson plans are fully developed (a distinct advantage when using substitutes).
3. Creative methodologies occur regularly and are explained clearly for the developing teacher.
4. The lesson hour is laid out in minutes so that the teacher senses movement.
5. Resource packets contain visuals, activities, and other helpful teaching aids.
6. The lessons are developmentally sound for each age group and reviewed by education specialists.
7. The color and layout of material have eye appeal for the students.
8. The routine of using provided formats and methods almost self-trains the teacher.
9. Some information about student characteristics and teacher tips exists in the best materials.

Editors, curriculum specialists, writers, and artists periodically evaluate and upgrade the material. Publishing houses often provide consultants to assist in running training programs for individual churches. A phone call or letter usually brings a prompt response and normally no charge for the use of their experts. Knowledgeable churches regularly take advantage of this feature to enrich their overall training strategy. Usually, a specific person supervises the doctrinal content. Publishers are sensitive to concerns voiced in this area and respond immediately.

Individual churches cannot duplicate the millions of dollars and expertise to develop a church-wide curriculum. A simpler approach trains teachers in how to use published curriculum like any Bible study tool. Teachers can easily adapt a quality curriculum to the distinctives of an individual church.

Media Center

Churches can now collect an amazing array of quality training materials. Books, courses, journal articles, cassettes, and videos should be available free of charge to teachers. The CES should work closely with the media center director to develop a diverse yet relevant list of holdings.

The director of the media center can encourage reading and viewing by promoting specific titles each month. In addition, the CES may circulate copies of the tables of contents of important books and encourage teachers to read only relevant chapters. Large books sometimes intimidate below-average readers. Recommending one specific chapter reduces that initial fear immensely. Tapes or books that explain the Bible or theology should find their way onto reading lists for teachers. Teachers need to grow in their understanding of the Scriptures as well as in their abilities to communicate.

Media center volunteers should study book display strategies that encourage people to pick up the materials and take them home. Talking to a large bookstore owner may unearth valuable ideas. Streamlined check-out procedures make it easy for teachers to utilize training materials. Never underestimate the learning capacity of the motivated adult.

Conventions and Seminars

Within driving distance of almost every area is a Sunday school convention. The address of each convention appears in the Resource List at the end of this book or can be secured by writing the National Association of Evangelicals.[4] The great variety of workshop titles and amassed expertise make these training conventions highly beneficial. Normally conventions are used more by people from smaller churches than from large churches, who often can hire professionals to do their specialized training.

Conventions provide much more stimulus than just training. The displays often generate a natural interaction and energy. New materials appear so frequently that publishers sometimes have difficulty keeping their field staff informed. Teachers can both lead and learn in these discussions of curriculum. This feature alone justifies the effort and expense of attending conventions. People return with renewed energies for their classes. The effect of meeting other teachers who struggle with similar frustrations brings great encouragement.

Of course, getting people to attend is *the* problem. Someone should make all the prearrangements so that teachers experience no red tape at registration. The church should cover all the costs. Teachers merely pick up their name tags and information packets at the door. The creative CES may sponsor a breakfast and have the participants travel together for fellowship and mutual encouragement. The local CES should recommend recognized workshop leaders or titles to each teacher. By highlighting the teachers' schedules, the CES can help people sort through the dazzling array of workshop titles.

New Staff Orientation

Although some training can be accomplished as the new teacher acts as an intern, many routine items should be discussed prior to his assuming any duties. The prepared CES will provide a checklist of items for handy reference. What should be on the list? Here are some suggested items:

1. Discipline procedures
2. Location of supplies
3. A sample of the curriculum being used
4. Substitute procurement procedure
5. Attendance-taking procedure
6. Absentee follow-up procedure
7. Teacher resources available in media center
8. AV check-out procedures
9. Arrival time
10. Church doctrinal statement
11. Dates and times of next training events

Of course this list will need to be adapted to the individual church. Anything routine should be included.

Teacher Profiles

The CES can construct a fairly accurate annual assessment of the progress of the church's teachers by tracking them in these five major training areas. Such an assessment can also provide subtle motivation for those who, for whatever reason, choose not to take advantage of the published curriculum, media center, and conventions. The C.E. committee can mail quarterly reviews and progress reports to the teachers. Most people enjoy seeing their progress. With this system, levels of achievement might receive special recognition. The CES could recognize training for excellence in teaching in addition to years of service.

In the past, such record keeping would consume inordinate amounts of time. Today, however, a personal computer enables the CES to know at a glance what each teacher has done in a given year. In addition to monitoring the teachers' reading, listening, and viewing patterns, the CES can track attendance at workshops, conventions, seminars, and consultations. These reports help teachers spot their own weaknesses in training and set goals for the following year.

MAJOR TRAINING TOPICS

As the CES develops a workable attendance strategy, he or she must also devote time to developing the content of training. Two great content needs exist in teacher training. First, teachers need to know the Bible and its theology. Second, they need to learn the best ways to communicate those truths so that others learn to obey them (2 Tim. 2:2). Almost any Bible college or seminary catalog will suggest topics for biblical and theological study. Innumerable books provide outlines of such topics. Each C.E. committee or CES must evaluate the local church's needs and decide which areas to study in groups and which areas individuals will develop independently.

Assessing Bible knowledge is fairly easy. Evaluating teaching expertise is harder. After all, what standards measure a good teacher? The following belong among those standards. They need regular attention and deserve a place on training event agendas.

Classroom Time Management

Limited teaching/learning time exists each week, so it must be carefully used. Rarely do volunteer teachers think specifically about each minute's use. They become preoccupied with filling time, not maximizing it. Though they may not scrutinize each minute, teachers can maximize sixty to ninety minutes for the benefit of students. To do so, teachers should ask three questions: (1) Which moments and activities seem wasted? (2) Does each activity efficiently move the student toward the learning objective? (3) Which activities are absolutely essential? Only relentless scrutiny will uncover those wasted moments and transform them into productive opportunities.

Using Activities to Promote Learning

The lecture method has dominated the teaching profession for a long time. Many teachers and especially volunteers believe they are not teaching unless they are talking. Talking does not equal teaching, and listening does not equal learning.

Activities that challenge and involve the mind and body of the learner consistently produce excellent results. Lecturing is most effective when done in ten- to twelve-minute blocks interspersed with activities. Teachers need to feel confident about using a variety of activities that promote learning. Many activities may be described in the curriculum. Until the teacher sees these activities run successfully in the classroom, however, he may be afraid to experiment. Even more important, the teacher must believe that these activities provide the best kind of learning.

Discipline Procedures

Even professionally trained, experienced teachers struggle with discipline at times. The rest of us struggle with it all the time. Church teacher morale gets damaged more by this problem than almost anything else. Since corporal punishment is not an option, churches need to agree on consistent procedures for teachers to follow.

The CES needs to provide a safe buffer between the volunteer teachers, the problem child, and the parents. Each department should have regular strategy sessions to encourage teachers and develop creative discipline techniques. At these meetings the leader should be sure everyone understands the procedure. He or she must remind everyone to handle even ornery children with love and care. The goal is to have teachers who are firm but gentle in asserting themselves.

Creative Use of Space

Rarely do churches have enough space. Educators have long known that the setting for learning contributes to or detracts from learning. Volunteer teachers frequently focus so intently on the lesson that they do not notice the setting nor do they understand what part it plays. Annual evaluations and records of improvements help the teaching staff see progress and recognize the importance of environment.

The following questions and others like them can lead to excellent discussions at teachers meetings. How does the color and lighting of the room contribute to the learning atmosphere? Do wall decorations stimulate and reinforce Bible truths? Who is responsible for neatness and clean-up? Is there occasional variety in the decor?

Dealing with Competition

Competition that pits one student's accomplishments against another can prove destructive for the underachiever. Each department and each teacher must be aware of competitive tendencies among themselves and in their classrooms. Competition should be used only where opportunities can be equalized. For example, memory achievements by children may be positive, but often such achievements reflect the support of parents more than the children's interests. In addition, children can easily equate these achievements with spirituality.

In contrast, group competition can be very useful when children help one another to achieve a common goal. In group competition, care should be taken to mix high and low achievers throughout the groups.

America's competitive society makes competition an attractive motivator and its use an ongoing issue. Teachers need to discuss how and when to use competition to promote learning among all their students.

Support and Encouragement

Training involves more than acquiring knowledge and skills. In his book *The Care and Feeding of Volunteers,* Douglas Johnson emphasizes that content and skills must be balanced with affirmation. Volunteers need gratitude, recognition, and courtesy, according to Johnson.[5] Teacher training is certainly a key part in the discipling process but disciples become discouraged. The CES and department leader should encourage them. Numerous times the New Testament reminds us to encourage one another.

Large doses of nurture and support should find their way

into each training session. Weary teachers need to celebrate the victories God has graciously given. Workers need constant reminding about how significant they are to God's work in their church. Personal notes from the CES, the pastor, the C.E. committee, or other church leaders reinforce the church's positive attitude toward its corps of volunteers.

Bob Herrington, a veteran CES and a personal friend, suggests this encouragement should manifest itself during every department meeting. He offers six suggestions for effective encouragement:

1. *Support.* "Does anybody care what I do?"
2. *Sharing.* "Has anything good happened?"
3. *Scripture.* "What does God say?"
4. *Prayer.* "Where do we need God's help?"
5. *Planning.* "What do we need to be doing?"
6. *Purpose.* "Why are we here and doing what we are doing?"

By shifting these six elements, a variety of agendas can easily develop. Any one of these could provide the focus for a particular session with the other elements given smaller amounts of time. Variety in the training keeps the meeting stimulating and fresh.

Training workers requires constant attention and creative planning. It rightfully belongs as a major focus and challenge for Christian education. The CES must solve the attendance puzzle, as he offers pertinent help in a time-efficient format. Individual development and progress should be tracked to evaluate the overall status of teachers.

Although teacher training never ends, the CES will receive tremendous satisfaction as he watches work multiplied through many hands. Those hands need training to work with excellence in the service of the King.

— NOTES —

1. Beth E. Brown and Dennis E. Williams, Summary Report: Christian Education Field Survey (Denver: Denver Seminary, 1988), p. 1.
2. Ibid., p. 4.
3. Metropolitan Baptist Church in Oklahoma City utilized this procedure for several years to solidify its training efforts.
4. The National Association of Evangelicals, 450 E. Gundersen Dr., P.O. Box 28, Wheaton, IL 60189; (708) 665-0500.
5. Douglas W. Johnson, *The Care and Feeding of Volunteers* (Nashville: Abingdon, 1978), pp. 24-25.

Principles in Practice

AT A SMALL CHURCH

Grace Community Church
Columbia, Maryland
Sunday school size: 250

by Tim Siemens
Pastor of Family Care

The authors wisely avoid quick and easy solutions, reminding us that each church will have a different focus. Two of their ideas for improving teaching skills seem very practical: track the annual progress of each teacher, and make teachers feel special. The CES should be able to give teachers a review and to tell them (1) how their teaching has improved, (2) examples of their effect on the children, and (3) how their ministry has furthered the cause of Christ. At our church, we send notes of encouragement that include these ideas. I do not track attendance at training sessions and conventions, however. Nor do I monitor who checks out books/videos for individual teacher development. I am not convinced there is much of a payoff in this work.

Recognition has great value in motivating teachers for additional training. Our curriculum design committee interviewed teachers and found several ingredients seemed necessary for the teachers who continue: the need to feel significant, the need to be a part of a team, the need for ongoing training, and the need to be protected from isolation from other adults. As we pursued significance we found that teachers needed to be thanked, needed to feel that the church values the teacher's ministry, and that the teachers have the opportunity to tell the congregation what was happening in class (via church report, newsletter, or slide show). We have had sermons on the impact and importance of teaching/training and try to gather the teachers together by departments for an appreciation dinner as well.

We have used "prime rate" to encourage attendance at teacher training. The high school teens have helped with babysitting and child care. Some of our teens who wanted practice in babysitting have offered free babysitting for our training sessions. Having a special meal together (prime rib) and providing child care are great ideas.

At one time all our teachers attended one large training session. However, some teachers had no previous training. This frustrated the trained teachers, who didn't want to hear the basics again. Therefore we divided into two groups: trained and untrained. This helped, but the most effective design is for the age-group coordinators to develop their own team of teachers. For the first session the trained teachers help with the "new staff orientation." After that the team meets monthly to go over the lessons for the next month. Each person comes prepared to contribute some part of a lesson so that all the lessons are covered. That way the team knows the flow for the month and team members can step in to substitute if necessary.

However, we have lacked a plan for ongoing training beyond the mechanics of a specific lesson plan. The proposed format for Sunday morning training seems excellent, and we hope to assemble our own SWAT team, composed of our best teachers as a model for others.

We have open training to interested parents, including many who are helpers in their own child's class. During this time they are able to observe the learning process, learn how to communicate truth to their child, and become pre-trained as a potential teacher. We encourage parents to assist in their child's classroom. At the training session, we try to have the parents learn to teach the age group that their own child will soon enter. That way parents can experience what is "normal" for their child's next stage and be trained to handle it.

I believe personal relationships can resolve many attendance problems at training sessions. Recently we have had teachers form their own small groups. This allows time for personal interactions, which are important for a team, and spiritual input (they can study the theological ideas in upcoming lessons), and provides time to pray for children in their classes.

A published curriculum and a media center are great training aids, and Grace Community Church uses both. We have found the published curriculum to be age-appropriate and teacher-sensitive. My only disappointment is that our staff has become bored after teaching the same materials; the publishers do not change the curriculum significantly. Our media center has had limited use, but this probably is due to our location. The center is at the church office, but our Sunday services (and Sunday school) are held at a public school. We are in the process of compiling a table of contents for our teachers, too.

The authors provide a fine checklist of eleven items for orienting new teachers. Our church has assembled an information packet for new teachers that also includes: a summary of the whats and whys for the morning's schedule, philosophy of ministry statement, and listing of supplies available. The packet also summarizes age-group characteristics and a statement of what the teacher can expect from the church, including training, resources, encouragement, and prayer.

Choun and Lawson mention knowledge of the Bible and theology, and teaching methods as major topics in training teachers. In addition, a basic training session should discuss a definition of a good teacher. Otherwise our teachers have nothing to aspire to nor do the leaders know what we are training our teachers to do. *The 7 Laws of the Teacher* are excellent to give teachers a vision and understanding of what teaching involves. A second major topic to cover would be the process of learning.

I agree with the authors that activities promote learning. Good teaching will motivate by curiosity and encourage participation and interest. Many parents have said that their children want to return because church is fun at Grace. It's fun because it's active learning and participation. Some children have even awakened oversleeping parents so that they could come to our learning center.

AT A MEDIUM CHURCH

First Christian Church
Phoenix, Arizona
Sunday school size: 300

by Roy Reiswig
Associate Minister of Adult Education and Discipleship

Our greatest (and continual) challenge is to bring teachers to the point where *they* recognize their need for training so much that they are willing to participate in a training session. We may provide the best in trainers, location, child care, snacks, and schedule, but the training is effective only if the teachers recognize their need to learn more about how to communicate the truths of Scripture to their students.

Prime rate could refer to the overall cost of a seminar, not just child care. Whenever possible, the church should provide any seminar at no cost to the teachers. The C.E. committee should allocate the expense in their annual budget. Relative to child care, the CES could approach teens to care for the children as a service project, their contribution to the ministry of a congregation.

Although we don't serve prime rib at our training seminars, I agree with the *prime rib* approach. We make sure that meals and/or snacks are attractively served. We ask someone with the gift of hospitality to set this up; this allows the individual to be a part of the ministry team. In today's health-conscious society, I've found our workers enjoy sliced fresh fruit, vegetables, or cheese and crackers. In addition we offer light beverages for our non-coffee drinkers. When people have a snack and drink in their hand they are more likely to relax and visit with others in the room.

Selecting a convenient (prime) time is critical to the success of any training session. Sunday morning is the most popular time for most volunteers to attend. I've tried every other possible time of the week and have learned that those who need the training the most simply will not come if it is not prime time.

Refreshments are a good idea, as previously discussed, but

I'd suggest they be available *before* the sixty minutes begin, rather than during the training hour. Having the entire Sunday school staff together provides an excellent time for encouragement, appreciation, challenge, and an education-oriented stretching experience from the minister(s) of Christian education. In fact, you might include club program and/or Wednesday program staff in this meeting. A specific theme or focus would be good, such as outreach, fellowship, personal and spiritual growth, and commitments. A supplemental article to send home with each teacher to read would also be good.

The two-phase teaching model seems practical; there is great merit in conducting training on Sunday mornings. Under Phase II, the authors propose scheduling one or two three-week training series per year. I believe it's a good idea to continue to use Sunday morning for training if possible and to conduct this training one department or age group at a time. However, in most churches it may not be feasible to train an expert team of teachers to model for the existent teachers. I suggest the minister of education and/or department leaders provide age-graded training while substitutes or perhaps parents teach the classes for three weeks. The children could be used one Sunday for an actual demonstration teaching session. This plan provides a break for the teacher as well as a prime-time training schedule. Using substitutes five Sundays a year for training is enough, so I wouldn't recommend a second three-week series.

Concerning published curriculum, criticism against publishing companies has been a constant during my twenty years of ministry. Many teachers and even Christian education ministers are highly critical of whatever publisher they are using at the time. Two or three years later, after a complete shift to another publisher, the criticism begins again.

This criticism is unfair. Publishers are not perfect; the apostle Paul does not write for any of them. Nor can the writers prepare the lessons with one specific church as their only market. Nonetheless, few congregations can invest the money, time, and creativity to produce quality materials such as the curriculum publishers can. Published curriculum can be an effective springboard, a guide for strong Bible teaching. The teacher can use much, change some, and delete what he cannot use. However, we should not discard all pub-lished curriculum just because some church leaders seem to be writing their own curriculum.

One major training topic to include in a training session is how to prepare a simple lesson plan. I can remember preparing my first sermon and worrying more about its length than its content. Many teachers fall into that trap. The CES can assist them in manag-ing their time by providing a lesson plan form (including places to put in a time schedule) and modeling good time budgeting in dem-onstration lessons.

"Talking does not equal teaching, and listening does not equal learning," the authors declare. They are right. Activity-oriented learn-ing is learning. Published curricula have many good ideas for ac-tivities that promote learning. During one training session the CES could lead the teachers in a study of Jesus' teaching methods.

Finally, healthy doses of support and encouragement will go a long way toward staff retention. Teacher appreciation day and/or dinner, personal notes, a word of encouragement on Sunday are all important to maintain a good staff. The past year we combined an afternoon of training with a Saturday evening appreciation din-ner. Another church I know recognized their teachers in the morn-ing worship and then had an appreciation luncheon at noon.

AT A LARGE CHURCH

Christ Community Church
Tucson, Arizona
Sunday school size: 1,800

by Gordon West
Children's Pastor

I strongly agree that the proper recruitment and subsequent training of our volunteers is crucial for the CES who wants to main-tain a healthy education ministry within the local church. In our church, lay leaders who predate my arrival have taught me as much as I have brought to the program. At Christ Community Church we prepare our leaders with solid in-service training and the use of a published curriculum series. Teachers also develop their skills by visiting our media center and attending an on-site annual teachers' convention.

For effective in-service training, we conduct an ongoing on-the-job training of our Sunday school teachers. The program strengthens our experienced teachers while upgrading the skill of our newer staff members. We ask our lead teachers (those overseeing three to six teachers, all in one room at one session) to train their staff members by modeling good teaching techniques on a weekly basis.

Each month the lead teacher chooses one portion of the lesson as the training "target" (the Bible story, the application page, the learning activities, etc.) and establishes a schedule of demonstrations for his teachers. The regular teacher will co-teach with the lead teacher one time during the month. While the regular teacher is prepared to do the whole lesson, the lead teacher demonstrates one portion (for instance, telling the Bible story), thus providing the teacher with numerous subtle lessons on both this specific target and on how to deal with his own students.

Lead teachers are normally former teachers who have been recognized for their excellence and promoted into leadership. However, these leaders are often dissatisfied with only relating to the adults they supervise. We have found that teaching one portion of the lesson each month allows these excellent teachers to become better acquainted with both their staff members and their students; to keep their own teaching skills and knowledge of the curriculum on the cutting edge; and to upgrade the other teachers' skills without having to "correct" them (an awkward position for any lay leader). Perhaps most important, this partial teaching allows the lead teacher to keep in touch with what drew them into the ministry in the first place, the children.

Prime time is a new concept for us. As a result of reading this chapter, the children's Sunday school leaders have developed a new plan. The majority of our children do not regularly attend the worship service. Exploring the prime time concept for training, we have decided to develop a new staff that can focus on children's worship and oversee a worship time during Sunday school once every two months. Thus six times a year, this replacement staff can enrich the students' understanding and participation in worship. Meanwhile, the regular teachers receive adult teaching covering the Bible content of the upcoming two units of lessons. We rotate one Sunday for each of the kindergarten through sixth grade departments. This allows us one Sunday each two months to do similar training for our children's worship staff. All of our fifth Sundays are devoted to making the normal worship service more approachable for children as we enjoy "Family Worship Sunday." Thanks for the idea!

For our large church, it is imperative to use a published curriculum and to stick with that curriculum throughout all our programs. Many former teachers return to their classes after short sabbaticals to find the same curriculum waiting. If we continually changed curriculum, we would always be in need of retraining teachers. We achieve continuity in our special programs by maintaining the same curriculum publisher. Summer programs (such as vacation Bible school) are major entry points for new staff members at our church. People are willing to "try it" for two weeks. Therefore, we use summer curriculum from the same publisher as our Sunday school materials. This allows our new people to have some basic knowledge of the larger program immediately.

As a larger church, we have stockpiles of resources for our media center. We invite teachers and students to look at our books, convention tapes, professional videos, and even our own classes put on video or available in print. We have begun to distribute self-study guides to our teachers. These brief brochures list materials for specific problem areas and helps for furthering skills. The self-study lists should allow motivated teachers to track their own progress in improving skills. The brochures also provide our educational leaders with a concise listing of the numerous available resources for themselves and their staffs.

Our Christian education staff believes large conventions have limited benefits. The cafeteria-style convention does not provide the specific, quality, focused training we desire our staff to receive. Furthermore, when a large church subsidizes the admission fees of its volunteers (in our case more than 400 people) the cost is actually greater than that to hire one or several professional trainers to do in-house training. As a result, we have developed a ministry to small neighboring churches and what we believe is the "best of both worlds" for our own volunteer teaching staff; a semi-annual mini-convention that includes teachers from other churches.

"Super Saturday" is a half-day conference held in the fall and spring on our church campus. Participants from as many as ten other churches join us for worship, refreshments, and twenty seminars, from which participants can choose three. There are several advantages to this approach. We can control what is offered our own staff in the way of educational philosophy while meeting teachers with creative ideas from other churches. We are able to design the conference to have tracks for beginning and advanced teachers and to train the staffs of smaller ministries, such as our special education program. Specific classes can be added as our leadership discerns weaknesses or new direction for our program.

Charging a nominal fee of the other churches who participate provides smaller churches with a less expensive, yet quality, training program and helps defray the cost we incur in reimbursing one or two professional educators who join us for each conference. We have found that the "expert" from out of town helps create enthusiasm for our participants, as does providing an inexpensive, casual luncheon after the classes and an inspirational film regarding the ministry of teaching. We include among our seminar leaders recognized leaders in our own congregation who have a specialty area (for instance, our school district superintendent and members of our own pastoral staff). Thus, valued congregation members who cannot make a long-term teaching commitment can provide valuable resources in a one-time training class. We also call on teachers from within our program who are excelling in a particular skill, thus adding a new face to the training staff and honoring an excellent worker. One public school teacher who serves in our summer programs attended a college course on assertive discipline. After this subject was presented as a Super Saturday seminar, the concept evolved into our first unified discipline policy for the education ministries. The teacher has been requested to repeat the course four times at our church and for another church across town.

We regard new staff orientation as crucial to the success of a new volunteer. At Christ Community, we spend a month to fully orient the new worker. I divide the orientation of teachers among several layers of leadership. Our professional staff members normally make the first contact after a person has been recruited. This personal interview is designed to provide an overview of our vision for the education ministry and an introduction to our published curriculum, to review key elements of the printed job description, and, most important, to listen to the person's personal testimony. Lay leaders then meet the person on a Sunday morning and start him through a month-long plan that takes him from the first week of observing someone else do everything to the fifth week where he is observed leading his own class group. Trained teachers are asked to allow new teachers to observe them "at work" and to help the teacher through the four weeks as they take on one more part of the lesson each week.

As an administrator for a large program, I have found the checklist idea to be invaluable; it assures that the elements of training that I believe are important for the new worker are uniformly imparted by the numerous leaders involved in the process.

To the authors' short list of major training topics I would add one more: How to lead a child to Christ. Our leaders find this subject to be very important to all our teachers, but equally frightening to most of them. We include it in the core curriculum. Covering simple techniques of how to effectively communicate the gospel to our students, especially if we are teaching children, is essential to the training process.

Relationships with the Church and the Community

In his work with church leaders, the CES will encounter many highly motivated, spiritually mature Christians. Many of those colleagues and contacts will reflect the CES's own ideas and level of commitment. An outward-looking ministry, however, needs windows more than it needs mirrors in the church. A truly visionary congregation will step outside the walls, into a world of attitudes, needs, and conditions that present both opportunities and obstacles.

EVALUATING THE CONGREGATION'S NEEDS

Why are some churches shrinking while others plan two worship services because the parking lot can't accommodate the crowd? People attend a church that meets needs. Years ago, individuals retained membership in the congregation, or at least the denomination, of their parents. The graveyards of country churches contained generations of the same families. Today's churchgoers are less concerned with tradition than selection. Greater mobility and greater distance from extended family have created options. A family with teenagers is likely to abandon the little brown church in the vale to drive thirty minutes to a large city church with a dynamic children's and youth program.

This does not mean that the small church is doomed to extinction. Most American churches, after all, have memberships of less than one hundred.[1] Members of megachurches whose rosters list thousands often mourn the lost intimacy of a small fellowship. Research does, however, indicate that any local church that wants to grow will have to recognize and supply the special needs of its congregation.[2] This is where the evaluation and planning skills of the CES are brought into play.

The CES who spends all his time "putting out fires" will find his ministry up in smoke. There must be time set aside for evaluation of the needs of the congregation and community. To some, a period of evaluation may seem to be marking time. In reality, it is a time for regrouping and planning a strategy. Six questions can help in the evaluation of the program.

1. What are the needs of the group?
2. Considering those needs, what are the aims of the program?
3. Which needs are already being met by current programs?
4. Do the results of the current programs justify the cost in time, resources, facilities, and staff?
5. Should existing programs be modified or scrapped?
6. What models exist of programs that would suit the situation?

Evaluation should be done in a group. No individual can possibly provide a well-rounded evaluation or perspective. Everyone, including the Christian education specialist, possesses some degree of prejudice. The goals of a program can be perceived as worthy or narrow-minded according to the perspective of the observer. Some discussions elicit emotional responses as well as objective evaluation. For some leaders, a discussion of mission outreach, expansion of facilities, or new trends in worship may activate hot buttons. For others, the church dinner menus or even the youth director's hair-cut can become key "program" issues.

A TIME FOR CHANGE

Preparing for Change

If evaluation indicates a need for change, the time has come for inaction—at least for a while. The epitaph on many a fledgling ministry reads, "He tried to bring change." Communication and consensus must precede changes in the local church, and for changes to be effective, they require committee action. Committees will take time, but they also provide the congregation with ownership and voice in the church. An experienced church leader understands that "his idea" must become "our idea" if it is to work. What the CES recognizes as a glaring mistake in a curriculum choice, club program, or schedule may be an honored tradition to the congregation.

The CES must take the time to communicate the reason for change and win the support of key people in the congregation before changing an existing program or initiating a new one. A good rule for the change agent to remember is that few people who need change know they need it.

A committee representing different age or interest groups should evaluate existing and would-be programs through a grid of felt and perceived needs. Certain biblical criteria must also be considered: "And they were continually devoting themselves to the apostles' teaching and to fellowship, to the breaking of bread and to prayer" (Acts 2:42). Clearly, most programs should provide for instruction, fellowship, and worship. Evangelism is also on the list, for Scripture adds that "the Lord was adding to their number day by day those who were being saved" (Acts 2:47). Applying Scripture, a committee that notices little time allocated for fellowship during Bible study classes might advise the scheduling of a time of sharing insights on Sunday mornings.

Planning for Change

Once a change has the congregational stamp of approval, planning can begin. Planning, like evaluation, must be a group action. Flexibility, creativity, and responsiveness to needs are all characteristics of a good planning session. The committee should deal with six planning issues.

1. How is this program designed to meet needs?
2. What resources of time, facilities, and personnel are required? How are training and financing to be done?
3. How does this program coordinate or compete with the other ministries of the church?
4. How will promotion be handled?
5. How and when will evaluation take place?
6. How will this program achieve shared goals?

I watched this process at work while visiting a church whose attendance at a weekday Bible study for women had declined. A task force was formed to investigate the situation. Members asked ex-attenders about their reasons for quitting the group and examined attendance figures over a five-year period, along with a record of teachers, topics, class times, and locations. When the task force submitted its findings to the committee in charge of the project, it was obvious that attendance figures had dropped with the local economy. Most of the women who used to be free to attend the weekday morning session had found employment.

As a result, the CES made plans to reschedule the study for an evening hour and provide child care. The church calendar was checked to avoid conflicts of facility use. The CES consulted directors of other areas of ministry to ensure coordination. He saw the group's interest in biblical answers to stress and family problems based on feedback; a survey of available curricula turned up several courses that met the group's needs. Pulpit, newsletter announcements, and an advertisement in the local paper promoted the first meeting. Flyers were sent home with the church's day care clientele.

The class reopened and prospered. Careful record-keeping and insightful forecasting helped the church eventually to plan for the study group's future expansion. Periodic evaluation of the program indicated a need for a quarterly fellowship event that involved the members' families. In time, the class exceeded its original number and became an important element in the church's program of evangelism and discipleship.

HELPING THE COMMUNITY IN CRISIS

An ancient Asian curse reads, "May you be born in important times." These are important times in American and international society. Unfortunately, these are also threatening times. The traditional family unit is moving toward extinction. Biochemical advances provoke new questions of ethics. Cults are on the rise. Nature is threatened by human life, and human life is threatened by a microscopic virus known as HIV. We seem to be drowning, gasping for understanding in a vast sea of information. For the Christian, "Jesus Christ is the same yesterday and today, yes and forever" (Heb. 13:8), but for the non-believer that truth is disputed and gives no consolation. The only thing the non-Christian can count on is the constant of change itself.

Although we need not be disoriented by change, we need to be aware of it. The CES who believes that his congregation has not been affected by changes in society lives with his head in the sand. Whoever ignores the world outside the local church lives in a fantasy. In *The Wind in the Willows,* a classic of children's literature by Kenneth Grahame, the Mole expresses curiosity about the world beyond his home. " 'Beyond the Wild Wood comes the Wide World,' said the Rat. 'And that's something that doesn't matter, either to you or me. I've never been there, and I'm never going, nor you either, if you've got any sense at all.' "

Church leaders who claim that their congregations are exempt from problems such as drug abuse, suicide, or homosexuality are innocents out of touch with their congregation. Some day these naive shepherds will wake to discover their sheepfold empty except for a well-fed wolf. However, the suggestion that programs be established in the church to help sufferers of these unsavory social ills may be met with reluctance. The sufferers may be unwilling to be identified or may be living in a denial stage; many church members will insist that such ministries will attract "the wrong element" to the church. It may take a tragedy of abuse or even death in one of the fine old families of the congregation to open eyes.

The variety of problems and the numbers of people involved have spawned a long list of special need ministries both within and outside the church. Thirty such ministries are listed below.

The list could be extended beyond the thirty. Certainly it could include the impact of AIDS, and the wise CES will make sure his church develops an AIDS policy that protects teachers and students alike, while welcoming those with communicable diseases. (See Appendix E for sample policies and procedures regarding members and guests with communicable diseases.)

The social needs represented by this list include not only the needs we think of as outside the church but also the daily concerns of many church families. For instance, many premature and handicapped children who years ago would have died as infants now survive thanks to medical advances. The local church must be ready to express God's love to these children and their families by adapting facilities and training personnel to answer their needs.

Biomedical advances have made it possible to extend active lives into advanced years and at the same time have provided birth

---

Ministries to Social Needs

alcoholism	child abuse	drug addiction
suicide	sudden infant death	divorce
incest	the childless	the widowed
working parents	runaway teens	homelessness
imprisonment	terminal illness	chronic illness
handicaps	learning disorders	mental retardation
single parents	parent/teen conflict	infidelity
unemployment	unwanted pregnancy	care of the elderly
mental illness	homosexuality	hunger
illiteracy	sexual abuse	prostitution

---

control that has reduced the number of births in recent years. As a result, senior adults will soon constitute the largest age group in the country. The church must make plans to activate these gifted and experienced folks for church ministry. Working couples who care for older parents in their homes will require senior day care centers where hot meals, recreation, and occasional nursing care are provided.

Working parents will need help with child care, and those dissatisfied with public schools will require more Christian day schools. However, a church should not begin a day school or child care center without qualified personnel, a well-rounded program, and an educationally sound, biblically based curriculum. In our survey, 9 percent of the CESs reported responsibility for a weekday program, and this percentage is likely to grow in the near future. Every CES should be aware that this ministry will require special knowledge and skills.

With the current emphasis on fitness, many churches have attracted new members by building family life centers with gyms, racquetball courts, and weight rooms. Courses in recreation and camping would benefit a CES who must manage a family center, plan year-round retreats, or direct a summer camp program. More and more working parents will be searching for school-break programs for children too old for day care and too young for employment of their own. The church that provides quality care and an appealing program will have both hands full of evangelistic opportunities.

Sadly, half the marriages in America dissolve in divorce. Many churches that years ago would have branded a divorced person and sent him out from their midst now provide special support groups for the divorced, the remarried, and parents of blended families. Marriages in trouble are offered help instead of cold shoulders. The traditional church has favored families over singles or childless couples. Now educational programs must include classes and special programs for the divorced and nontraditional families. Demographics show the decline of the "married, with children" unit; the church must open its arms and its programs to the new American family.

All this will sound overwhelming to church leaders who see the needs and feel burdened to help. The bright side of the situation is that they don't have to do it alone. Parachurch organizations exist to help the church in service to special needs.

THE PLACE OF THE PARACHURCH GROUP

"Two are better than one because they have a good return for their labor. For if either of them falls, the one will lift up his companion. But woe to the one who falls when there is not another to lift him up" (Eccles. 4:9-10). Parachurch organizations exist not to compete with the local church but to complement it. Churchgoers who fear that these groups will leech donations from the church coffers or recruit workers from the church's volunteer ranks have a narrow perspective of ministry. No local church, no matter how large, can expect to meet all the needs of every individual in the congregation. Parachurch organizations extend the teaching of the church by providing tailor-made programs and trained personnel.

Consider the resources, experience, and perspective a Pioneer Ministries program can add to a children's club program. Similarly The Navigators, with decades of experience in ministry to college students and adults, has strong programs in evangelism and discipleship that not only bring new Christians into the local church but also help the church in nurturing believers. Other examples of parachurch organizations whose goal is to assist local churches are Christian Camping International, which offers camp programs and campsites, the Association of Christian Schools International, with a program to develop weekday education, and SIM International, which emphasizes missions education and Africa missions.

"One of the major developments in Christian education this century has been the growth of organizations and movements having origin and continuing life outside the official church," Warren Benson writes.[3] Parachurch groups must not be perceived as "additions" to the church nor "usurpers" of the church. They are partners, working alongside the church. According to Benson, there are six major divisions of parachurch groups: children/youth organizations not sponsored by the local church; children/youth organizations under local church sponsorship; Christian day schools; mission boards; Christian publishers; and camping organizations.[4]

Examples of organizations not under local church sponsorship would include such groups as The Navigators, Child Evangelism Fellowship, Campus Crusade, Young Life, Youth For Christ, and Intervarsity Christian Fellowship. Though it is true that these organizations must solicit contributions from local churches and individuals, any church that tries to do the same ministry without these organizations would wind up wasting time and money. Why reinvent the wheel?

Awana, Pioneer Ministries, and Christian Service Brigade all are examples of parachurch groups that operate under the sponsorship of the local church. The organization provides resources, programming, and training for specific children's programs, but the leadership must come from within the congregation. Programs take place in the local church, and contributions from participants, once materials and registration fees have been paid, are used at the discretion of the local leadership.

Mission boards have long been accepted by local churches as arms of ministry. Few churches would be able to train, support, and supervise missionaries of their own, even in America. Not only do these organizations provide training and placement for missionaries who have the usual Bible college or seminary background, they also recruit volunteers whose technical skills make them valuable staff members. Many individuals have both greater interest and opportunity to serve as missionaries because of their church's association with a mission agency.

Church leaders often use Christian publications without realizing that publishers are parachurch organizations. Curriculum for Sunday school, children's church, and Bible study groups are professionally prepared and easy to use, thanks to those who serve through Christian publishers. Bibles, study guides, magazines, and devotional material can sometimes go where teachers cannot. Textbooks and other materials for students are valuable resources for those preparing for a vocational ministry, and valuable aids for the teachers desiring more background on Bible passages and events. If we include under this category the distributors of Christian music, films, and other audio-visual media, the teaching aids become more diverse and creative.

Camping organizations, like publishers, are less suspect in the eyes of local churches. A church may look askance at a para-church group that performs a ministry the church thinks it can do for itself. Few churches, however, would want the job of building and maintaining a campsite and providing camp programs for a wide variety of ages. For those groups and individuals in the vocational camping ministry, organizations such as Christian Camping International provide help in training personnel and providing guidelines and standards to follow. Churches that need camps to expand their educational, recreational, and fellowship ministries will find a variety of offerings. Some camps provide only the site and facilities. Others provide ready-made programs complete with trained personnel. Programs have diversified to include wilderness camping experiences, training in sports or technical skills, and sessions for seniors as well as children.

Parachurch organizations serving the needs of the inner city are a more recent partner with local churches. Those churches in suburban or rural areas that want to deal with urban issues usually are well-intentioned but poorly equipped to do the job alone. Missionaries to the inner city need training just as if they were headed into overseas service. The city has its own distinct culture. For the unprepared, crime, unemployment, health problems, and poverty can create immobilizing culture shock. Parachurch groups equipped to deal with urban social problems can readily locate available resources and community service to minister to those in urgent need. Such groups can provide specific ministry opportunities for volunteers from suburban congregations and help suburbanites to understand the ministry of a storefront church or rescue mission. Although Bible colleges and seminaries are helping to prepare church leaders by offering cross-cultural studies, even the most knowledgeable graduate will be suspect in the inner city until he has shown his desire to help and empathize with those to whom he ministers.

Only 16 percent of our survey respondents considered themselves "very involved" with parachurch groups. Another 36 percent reported limited involvement, and the remainder had little or no involvement. Some mentioned specific organizations that have already been discussed. Other CES specialists said they helped in the local community through hospitals, schools, athletic groups, and community service organizations. Reasons for nonparticipation included "no time or energy left over after local church duties" and "local church deserves all my time and energy." The local church leadership that does not encourage its staff and congregation to become involved with parachurch organizations has a narrow view of its own ministry. The job description of the C.E. specialist should include time for cooperation with a parachurch group who shares the church's goals.

In ministry, church leaders, and especially the CES, will benefit from the outside help of qualified parachurch groups. The preacher describes the predicament of the one who would be all alone when he fell: "Woe to the one who falls when there is not another to lift him up" (4:10). And woe to the church that falls down on the job because it was too proud, too suspicious, or too ignorant to make the trip with a fellow-traveler. Likewise, woe awaits committees and boards that think a church's goals can be reached without the support and participation of the congregation. Whether the ministry is to the congregation or the community, the CES will not succeed by doing the ministry alone. The CES should always seek strong ties with the church and the community.

— NOTES —

1. Lyle E. Schaller, *The Small Church Is Different* (Nashville: Abingdon, 1982), p. 9.
2. John Naisbitt and Patricia Aburdene, *Megatrends 2000* (New York: Morrow, 1990), pp. 290-91.
3. Warren S. Benson, "Parachurch Vocations in Christian Education," in Werner C. Graendorf, *Introduction to Biblical Christian Education* (Chicago: Moody, 1981), p. 348.
4. Ibid., p. 349.

Principles in Practice

AT A SMALL CHURCH

Kearney Evangelical Free Church
Kearney, Nebraska
Sunday school size: 250*

by Greg Gangwish
Associate Pastor of Christian Education

A couple of years ago our Christian education committee members had a great burden to reach more people and bring them to Christ, even though more than five hundred attended our morning worship service. Other concerns we wanted to address were the increasing administrative and pastoral care responsibilities for our adults. These concerns led the committee to evaluate the effectiveness of our current ministries and ask some tough questions about our goals and strategy for implementation. Prior to this time we did not have a well-defined purpose statement. After investigation and discussion we developed a purpose statement that echoed Paul's call to service in Ephesians 4:12-13.

We began to evaluate the needs of our congregation, specifically our adults. We conducted a survey and reviewed attendance records. The committee concluded that Sunday morning was our best opportunity to draw people into the life of the church. We discovered that almost 80 percent of those attending worship were not involved in ministry any other time of the week. Adult Sunday school was in place and, we believed, was potentially a key to significantly impacting our adults in their spiritual growth and evangelism.

Next, we visited larger churches within two hundred miles and discussed with their leaders the effectiveness of the Sunday

---

* Original attendance before the church's Operation Jethro. As a result of the program and continued interest, Sunday school attendance now averages 400.

school and related ministries. As a result of our investigations, the chairman and chairman-elect of our C.E. committee and I identified a model of our Sunday school structure that we believed would address the church's needs. The model was an age-graded program for adult classes. We knew for the model to succeed we would need much planning and communication; only then would our church family embrace it. We believed this model would facilitate assimilation and provide a structure through which each leader of each age group could shepherd his own people. The purpose of the Sunday school hour would be twofold: (1) to build relationships through fellowship and prayer and (2) to study the Bible.

We identified two main areas on which to concentrate in implementing the program: communication and leadership development. We devoted eighteen months to preparing for "D-Day." We named this whole process Operation Jethro (O.J.) because ultimately we were delegating ministry in this new model as Jethro exhorted his son-in-law, Moses, to do with his responsibilities as judge over the people of Israel.

We presented our initial proposal to the senior pastor, then to the deacons, and then to the church board and received their approval and encouragement to proceed with O.J. Later we came back to these same people with our final draft for implementation. We wanted to be sure that we had the full backing of the leadership of the church. The leaders were supportive and appreciated having the opportunity for input.

We had been offering up to fourteen electives each quarter, so the idea of strictly age-graded classes represented a major change for our adult students. We began publishing brief articles in the church newsletter about eight months before O.J. began, trying to introduce the whole concept to the church family. In the final six months leading to D-Day we had two meetings (about sixty days apart) on Sunday evenings after church to explain the philosophy, structure, and function of the new Sunday morning program. Participants were able to ask questions and make suggestions. In addition, we distributed several sample brochures explaining Operation Jethro during the final nine months.

Besides communication, the C.E. committee and I realized that leadership development was critical to building a strong foundation and ongoing direction for O.J. The chairman, chairman-elect, and I met twice a month to pray and plan for O.J. We identified potential people from each age group and began praying for God to raise up those leaders who were gifted and would be committed. Ten months before O.J. began, we knew the key leaders who would coordinate and teach each class. With these leaders, we further defined the vision and clarified the job descriptions. We then worked with them in putting together the rest of their ministry team.

In preparation for D-Day, each age-group ministry team designed an event of some kind to initiate O.J. Team members contacted personally each individual in their age category to invite them to Sunday school. In involving them, the ministry team was asked to further explain or answer questions about O.J.

D-Day has come and gone, and we believe Operation Jethro has yielded a quality ministry and greater, deeper friendships than our church family knew before. Initial adult attendance in Sunday school increased more than 30 percent, and we have sustained most of that growth. On average, our Sunday school grows about 8 percent a year and runs about 75 percent of our worship attendance.

The process of implementing Operation Jethro and its subsequent success did not come easily. A major shift in Sunday school programming requires a church family willing to try something new; we had such a family. In addition, the Christian education committee must exert strong, creative leadership. We had that too. Some adults strongly opposed O.J. and some still do; yet we have seen God do a mighty work in our midst. As a result of this program, I believe we are much better positioned to assimilate new people and guide the flock than before. In the final analysis, God has been behind this successful effort, and He deserves much praise.

AT A MEDIUM CHURCH

Black Rock Congregational Church
Fairfield, Connecticut
Sunday school size: 500

by Doug Christgau
Minister of Christian Education/Missions

The impact of the local church on the community must begin where it is most likely to succeed, in specific programming to reach the community. Christian education ministries have played a significant role in community outreach at Black Rock Community Church (BRCC). I have found that two ministry principles are fundamental to having an impact in the community. We teach these principles to our volunteer staff at BRCC, and the principles enhance the effectiveness of our programs.

Principle one: Realistic children's outreach always involves parents. Certain children's programs can draw significant numbers of community children when conducted properly; however, without a ministry to parents, the chances of nurturing a child who is evangelized through these programs is small. Volunteers who staff outreach programs must recognize this. In fact, training in the skills of relating to parents, not just children, is essential. Christians usually need to overcome a fear of relating to adults who are outside the Christian subculture. Of course, the CES should be a model in reaching the community. Merely encouraging volunteer workers from the sidelines is not enough to motivate them to action.

BRCC has been able to develop relationships with parents through several conventional children's programs, including nursery school, vacation Bible school, and children's clubs. In each program we encourage staff to invite and involve parents, who are the critical influence of our students.

Two-thirds of our nursery school students are from non–Black Rock families. Nursery school mothers have many questions about parenting, and we are able to integrate the gospel as we teach parenting skills in a mother's class. Organized by our nursery school director, the mother's class meets during school hours, though in the past we have offered evening classes when working mothers requested it in sufficient numbers.

Traditionally a father has limited contact with a nursery school. However, we have found that fathers can be attracted to one-hour father/child programming in the early evening. Game nights and cookouts have been effective in drawing the fathers and children together. At our cookouts, for instance, one of the most popular events is a wheelbarrow ride in which the father drives the child through a simple obstacle course. During indoor game night the father/child pairs enjoy working together for five minutes to build a tower from Tinker Toys®.

At Black Rock about 75 percent of the potential dads and children attend these events. That's a high percentage in any program, especially considering that most of these men view our church as merely the sponsoring institution of their child's nursery school. Because our priority is reaching dads, the programs usually include a fifteen-minute period during which the dads are separated from the children. As the children prepare a craft for Dad or play games under the supervision of regular nursery school staff, the fathers hear a testimony from a man whose relationship to God has made a difference in his fathering. Sometimes we have used dads in the nursery school program. We have also used "experts," such as members of our pastoral staff and elder board. The strong gospel messages usually are well received. We do not give an invitation, but we make clear that Jesus Christ makes the critical difference in effective parenting.

Although some fathers have expressed a personal interest in the gospel, the nursery school fathers' programs have yielded little direct fruit. On the other hand, few programs of any kind at BRCC draw as high a proportion of nonchurch men. We believe our outreach expectations are realistic and biblical. No single C.E. program can be expected to yield the entire evangelistic harvest. Our theology emphasizes the proclamation of the gospel, trusting the Holy Spirit to do the convicting work of regeneration.

We hope to strengthen the fathers' program by putting a lay

person in charge. As the CES, I have had overall leadership, while drawing on Black Rock dads to give testimonies and to teach the simple Bible lessons on occasional "club nights," using Christian Service Brigade material. This year, for the first time, I will have a lay assistant. The example of a layman reaching out to the non-Black Rock men attending should encourage the other Christian men present to do the same. The program moves quickly, and the opportunities to build relationships with these unchurched men are usually missed unless the BRCC men initiate contact.

Vacation Bible school also offers a vital outreach to parents. Each year we include a "mothers' class" as part of the VBS program. Evangelism is its priority, and class leaders have the evangelistic vision to bring women to Christ. The only mothers allowed to attend mothers' class are from outside the church. Meanwhile, Black Rock church attenders are expected to serve in one of the many roles required to make a VBS for five hundred children effective.

The mothers' class receives special publicity, and during registration, VBS staff members encourage mothers to stay for the class rather than leave only to have to pick up their children in a few hours. The size of the women's class averages ten, yet it is a fruitful time. One year the entire mothers' class made professions of faith. Most were not from Protestant backgrounds. The class is held in a relatively isolated room, away from the distraction of the children's classes.

The mothers' class begins immediately after the opening exercise. About seventy-five minutes are spent in presentation and discussion of five gospel-oriented lessons during the week. The last section of class time is spent doing either an adult-oriented craft or in helping VBS children with crafts.

Decisions for Christ are a joyful result of VBS. Typically we see about 15 percent of the children respond to the salvation message. When a nonchurched child accepts Jesus as Savior, we follow up with a home visit, both to encourage the child and to make a personal contact with the parents. The teacher who led the child to Christ makes a phone call to parents asking to place a children's

Bible in their home. In their visits with parents, our staff discuss the child's response to VBS and Jesus without using confusing church jargon. If a staff person feels insecure about making the contact, the department head or the VBS director will accompany him.

Parent/child activities often are a regular part of children's club programs. We use Christian Service Brigade materials and have found the more activities, the better the participation of non-Christian parents. Of course, the activities also build friendly relationships with Christian parents, which can help the program, especially in recruiting volunteer workers. Sometimes we complement the traditional father/son and mother/daughter functions with less common father/daughter and mother/son programming. The goal in these activities is to provide many opportunities for leader-parent contacts. The number of parents responding may not always be large, but with prayer and persistence these can lead to evangelism among community families.

Principle 2: Effective community outreach requires a cooperative attitude among children's program leaders. A multifaceted Christian education ministry can cause program leaders to engage in an uneasy, competitive tug for children, facilities, and budget support. Therefore the C.E. specialist must take a balanced approach to administrating the various programs. An active CES will help the lay directors of each ministry to protect the overall Christian education program. If the CES allows some programs to "run themselves" while reserving his efforts for personal favorites, much of the innovation described above will be impossible. The energies of lay staff will instead be absorbed in trying to recruit from the same pool of people. Having a fair share of storage space will become more important than cooperating for the sake of effective evangelistic outreach. Unbiased leadership from the CES will critically influence the positive spirit that is required to have effective parent outreach integrated into all the programs, not just a few.

Many people will not come to a church of any kind. Also, there are community needs a church should address that require leaving the security of their building. Typically these efforts will not draw large numbers of volunteers. But the fervor of those involved, and the distinctiveness of the needs they meet, contribute significantly to the church's impact on its community. The church can become involved with secular agencies to demonstrate Christian compassion. There can be an evangelistic impact as well.

BRCC has four programs in the community helping four needy segments with physical, emotional, and social needs. However, their greatest needs are spiritual. These ministries are to the homeless, the mentally and emotionally disturbed, the prisoners, and those recovering from drug addiction. Each ministry offers wholeness to the person. We will look at two of these programs.

The focus of our prison ministry is the local jail, where BRCC has led worship services for several years. The program encourages Christian prisoners, and ministry leaders also present the gospel to the men who express their need for spiritual salvation. We see professions of faith at every service.

The prison ministry can extend further. Meeting and counseling prisoners during the week requires significant personal commitment of volunteers. Some prison chaplains offer training courses to sharpen skills. Our ministry volunteers help prisoners find jobs, residences, and transportation after they are released. Those tasks can be at once the most rewarding and the most frustrating aspect of prison ministry. Regardless, these efforts demonstrate that the church is concerned with more than simply selling "jailhouse religion."

Those struggling to recover from drug addiction are in dire need of role models who have successfully conducted a conventional, drug-free lifestyle. Secular rehabilitation centers are usually open to involvement of Christians who are content to let their actions be their testimony. Black Rock has found, however, that some secular rehabilitation centers will allow weekly discussions involving spiritual concepts and values. Each Sunday evening two of our best lay evangelists spend an hour discussing spiritual and moral issues of interest to the clients at the rehab center. Whenever an authority source is needed, the Bible is brought into the discussion.

One Sunday a month the entire group attends the "Second Sunday" service at BRCC. This is a "seeker" service designed for the secular person who does not attend church regularly. The clients thoroughly enjoy these services and respond to their messages with enthusiasm. In fact, the services have become so well received that the center's leadership have made their attendance a mandatory part of the center's program. A social event often follows the service to promote contacts with people from our church outside of the few who conduct the weekly discussions.

The rehabilitation center typically keeps clients for thirty to sixty days. Dozens have accepted Christ as their Savior during this time. A great effort is made to disciple new converts, especially since many of them move out of the rehabilitation center and into bad home environments just weeks after they make commitments to Christ.

We have seen a much higher percentage of these clients grow in their faith than those in the prison ministry. It's likely that the highly personalized weekly discussion format is a stronger means of teaching Scripture than the monthly worship services of the jail. It has also been a miraculous encouragement to see the program leader at the rehab center accept Christ along with his wife after an initial attitude that was begrudging at best.

Authenticity and longevity must characterize church outreach into the community. The CES must work at keeping the evangelical priorities of his church in the forefront while having flexibility to relate to the felt needs of the community. Although we are thankful for the community ministry of Black Rock, we recognize that it has been developed carefully with much prayer over a five-year period.

AT A LARGE CHURCH

First Evangelical Free Church
Wichita, Kansas
Sunday school size: 900

by Joy Domen
Director of Children's Ministries

The need for the CES to be an effective change agent is great at our church. As the person responsible for assigning rooms to various Sunday school classes, I often help in the moving of tables, chairs, and cupboards. One day after one of these changes occurred, someone told me that one of the small cupboards I had moved was built specifically for the previous classroom. Although it was not needed in the previous class, I moved it back to the original room. I have learned that people become very attached to rooms, furniture, and tradition.

Fortunately, most people are willing to change if (1) given sufficient notice that a change is necessary, (2) given specific reasons to prove the change is necessary, and (3) their advice is listened to carefully, even if it later must be overruled. Those who are affected by a change must have a voice in the decision. If I had realized how important that cupboard was to the members of the previous class and that one of the members had built it himself, I would never have moved it! I learned that no matter how small a matter seems, I should consult with everyone involved, or at least with the leader of every group involved.

Recently our pastors and elders have been developing a mission statement. As we evaluate the various church ministries to see how they fit our mission, we involved many people in the process. As a result of their input we will be reorganizing our adult Sunday school. We want to be sure that people who attend are really discipled, so we will be starting special classes to orientate new believers to the Christian life, as well as making certain that older Christians are continually stimulated to grow and learn.

We also want to organize classes to help develop selected

individuals into leaders. As we began to chart our course toward establishing such classes, we learned that one of our members had realized that the church was not effectively discipling new people and had taken private initiative. He was actively setting up a series of Bible study groups for discipleship. The only problem was that he was trying to establish a program without going to the church leadership. Once we discovered what "Henry" was doing, we approached him and have encouraged him to work with the model already approved by the church board. The church needs such gifted, Spirit-sensitive people. They must never be discouraged. They must, however, be channeled to work within the authority of the church leadership.

Knowing and satisfying the needs of the congregation is important. We have responded to the needs of specific groups of individuals by establishing classes or support groups for such areas as mothers of preschool children, adults who were abused as children, parents of teenagers, single parents, and couples without children. These groups are a formal part of the church ministry, and we try to provide various resources when we are asked.

Our church members also have been active in outreach to the community. We initiate and support a growing mission church in an economically deprived area of the city. Some of our members participate in leading a children's weekday club, others help with private tutoring, teaching GED classes (for high school graduation requirements), running a thrift clothing store, and so on. Our newest project is helping to plant a black ethnic church. In addition, a Chinese Bible study group has used our facility for years.

All these groups and projects have been largely initiated and maintained by people in the church with God-given vision and gifts to do these ministries. A fundamental axiom at First Evangelical Free is "A ministry must be done by that person (or those persons) whom God burdens for that ministry." The C.E. staff can facilitate that process, but only God can burden and motivate people to want to do it.

The Female Christian Education Specialist

By Lynn Gannett

In the summer of 1980, Debbie was interviewing for the position of director of Christian education in a church on the East Coast. She was having lunch with the woman who had held that position for many years, and Debbie will never forget her words. "Your role as DCE will be limited to women's and children's ministries. They will never allow you to work with men." Since these words did not reflect all that Debbie had heard from the leadership of the church, she accepted the job. For six years her role as CES was all encompassing, from the nursery to senior adult ministry.

The words of the former DCE reflected her own experience in that church. However, times are changing in women's ministries. Debbie and many other women are finding greater freedom as Christian education specialists, and women often participate in the full scope of Christian education ministry.

Historically, women hired as C.E. specialists were limited to children's ministries and given part-time employment with less pay.

Before the Depression an equal number of laymen and laywomen participated in religious education. However, by 1938 only 26 percent of religious educators were men. After World War II, men assumed formal leadership as C.E. directors, and women, in evangelical circles, served in the more traditional volunteer role behind the scenes or part-time with lower pay.[1]

Henrietta Mears (1890-1963) helped women by breaking the mold. As a C.E. director for thirty-three years, she trained many men for the ministry and wrote curriculum resources for what would later become Gospel Light Publishing, a company she helped found.[2] Two other Christian education evangelical role models for women are Mary LeBar and Lois LeBar, professors in the Christian Education Department at Wheaton College and Graduate School from 1949 to 1975. The LeBar sisters contributed to today's philosophy of Christian education through their writings and by training men and women who now implement their philosophy in local churches. Women such as Henrietta Mears and Mary and Lois LeBar helped open the door for women to serve in the fullest capacity as Christian education specialists.

Several factors are contributing to the expanding role of women in the church. The feminist movement has made several evangelical groups more willing to reach beyond the traditional role and to challenge limits in ministry. In addition, many denominational groups are ordaining women as pastors and ministers of Christian education. The feminist movement may have helped women in the church to use their gifts more extensively; however, it also has created a backlash. Churches with a conservative theological view of the woman's role find it easier to hire a man than risk any role conflict, thus closing the door for women.[3]

The availability of seminary education for women has also helped to expand the woman's role in Christian education. In 1972 women constituted only 10.2 percent of the total enrollment in American and Canadian seminaries. In 1986, women constituted 26.4 percent of the seminary population.[4] This professional training opens the door for professional positions in the local church.

What does the future hold for women serving in local

churches in the role of Christian education specialist? As more women become ordained, fewer will enter the field of Christian education in order to seek the pastorate. The field of Christian education is becoming more professional and credentialing for ministry is on the upswing. A seminary education is desirable, but for many women it is difficult to attain because of family responsibilities. Yet many women are serving in denominational and independent churches today and are blazing a trail for women in the future. For many their role in a traditionally male-oriented church has not been easy, yet men and women are learning to work with each other to further the ministry of the church.

ATTITUDES OF CHURCH LEADERS

In 1938, though 75 percent of the CESs were women, pastors still reported that they preferred a man for the position.[5] This attitude is still true for some pastors; many, however, intentionally hire women. The attitude of a church, which most often reflects the attitude of the senior pastor, usually falls into one of three categories: preference for a woman as CES, no preference for a man or woman, or opposition to a woman.

Churches That Prefer a Woman

A church that prefers a woman CES may do so for traditional stereotypical reasons. It may perceive her as more nurturing, better with details, willing to do secretarial work, willing to be paid less or work part-time.[6] A long-standing theory, which may still hold true, is that some pastors prefer a woman because they see her as less threatening than an equally qualified man. Women are not perceived to be as competitive as men.[7] If a pastor wants a person committed to Christian education who is not using the role as a career stepping-stone to the pastorate, he may look for a woman who is not seeking ordination. But many churches today are recruiting women to serve on their church staff because they understand that a woman has unique contributions to make that may or may not fit the historical stereotype.

There have been numerous studies in the area of male and female differences. These studies go beyond physical differences to examine such areas as socialization, psychoanalysis, brain research, moral development, and cognitive learning styles.[8] It is generally accepted that differences do exist. More important, experts are recognizing that these differences are beneficial and should be valued equally. Words used to describe women, such as vulnerable, generous, flexible, and cooperative, are no longer being seen as liabilities in the workplace but rather as contributions.[9]

As individuals, each person sees the world from a unique perspective based on one's culture, home background, education, and many other factors. In addition to individual variances, we see things differently as men and women. If a church staff is totally male, who is representing the female perspective? Consider one woman's contribution on a church staff during a staff meeting. The men decided to have a potluck dinner to honor the wives of the elders and deacons. The CES, a woman, quickly pointed out who would do the cooking in most of the households and suggested this did not quite accomplish what they intended! As a result, the staff decided to have the event catered. The woman's input can bring a balanced, fair perspective.

Of course, the woman's perspective is not limited to the planning of church dinners; it is vital in all areas of Christian education. Children's ministries, family enrichment, women's programs, facilities, curriculum, and the needs of new mothers are just a few examples of issues that would profit from the input of a woman.

The presence of women on traditionally male church staffs serves to broaden perspectives and enhance creativity. An examination of business meetings revealed that it is not uncommon for an all-male meeting to be described as lifeless or dull. Yet when men and women meet together there is more energy and buoyancy.[10] Differences between men and women can complement and enhance one another. A church that desires a woman on its staff usually understands this.

Churches Looking for a Person

Many churches do not believe that one's gender is an issue; they just want to hire the best person for the job. The concern is focused on a person's gifts in relation to the demands of the position. This attitude reflects a belief that both men and women can be effective as C.E. specialists. The issue is not male or female but individual. When asked what qualities they look for in a potential staff member, pastors identified most often: character, intelligence, flexibility, excitement about learning, being a team player, and comfortableness with review.[11] These qualities know no gender.

Churches That Will Not Hire a Woman

Some churches will not consider a woman for their staff. There are two basic reasons: Either they believe a woman has limitations that will hinder her effectiveness, or they have theological convictions that restrict a woman's role in the church.

In spite of the strides women have made in the workplace, many people still don't think women can make it. Many refuse to acknowledge a woman's obvious success or attribute it to chance. Some women even doubt their own ability to lead and the ability of women in general. This was illustrated in a recent study in which five hundred managers, both men and women, were asked to describe men, women, and successful managers in a single word. Men and successful managers were described as having the same characteristics: leadership, ability, competitiveness, self-confidence, objectivity, aggressiveness, forcefulness, and a desire for responsibility. The conclusion was clear. Both men and women have strong preferences for a "masculine" manager.[12] If men and women prefer male leadership in the business world, it is likely to be true in many churches, and a woman may not be seen as a candidate for the leadership of the educational ministires in these churches.

Some churches will not consider a woman because of their interpretation of Scripture. Most of what is written regarding women in ministry deals with the exegesis of passages speaking to the authority issue and the role of women in the church. We need not enter the debate to conclude that a church that holds to the traditional hierarchical position will probably not consider a woman for C.E. specialist if it regards the position as granting spiritual authority over men. The church leadership may hold to the hierarchical view, as opposed to the egalitarian position, and still hire a woman as a CES because it does not view the position as one of spiritual authority but as an educational specialty.

AN EXPANDING ROLE

As seen in chapter 3, the role of the Christian education specialist is ever-expanding. It includes meeting the needs of people in the nursery to senior adult ministries. A woman serving as a CES in a local church may find that her role is also expanding and growing. No longer is she seen as a "children's specialist" but as one who can manage the entire scope of educational ministries in the church.

In preparing this chapter, I interviewed women CESs across the country in order to compare their experiences in churches. Their position descriptions varied, but all reflected the wide scope of Christian education. Women are developing and overseeing adult educational ministries, youth programs, teacher training, family centers, Sunday school, vacation Bible school, club programs, and libraries. Women are assessing the needs of the church, initiating new programs, overseeing large budgets, and motivating, recruiting, and training people.

Many respondents believe that as women they have a special contribution to make in the area of women's and children's ministries. Women have been socialized in our society to be the primary nurturer of the family. Many women CESs consider children's ministry as their strong area. But we must be careful not to assume that this is true for all women CESs. Most CESs today have attended colleges, seminaries, and graduate schools and are trained in a full gamut of Christian education. They may have taken only one or two courses on children's education. A woman CES may feel more competent in the area of youth, adults, or administration.

Women serving in churches today usually act as part of a team. With the pastor and staff, they are part of a composite ministry, as they contribute to the total church program by planning and participating in worship services, hospital visitation, counseling, and working with families. They are involved with other staff members in the ongoing evaluation of the church and its ministry. During our survey we asked women, "How would the role be changed if a man were hired to replace you?" Most said there would be little or no change.

Are women giving up their femininity in order to fulfill this expanding role and fit into the male-dominated leadership structure of the church? Many women in the workplace do struggle to maintain congruence between their work and nonwork behaviors. But as women realize the validity of their "masculine" and "feminine" traits within themselves their careers are enhanced.[13] In the study of male and female differences, androgyny is the theory that "it is both possible and desirable . . . for both males and females to possess both what are traditionally known as masculine virtues and feminine virtues." Although the validity of androgyny is in debate, the concept has helped us better understand the differences between males and females, the validity and strengths of those differences, and the ways we can learn and grow from each other and complement one another.[14]

The "feminine" traits of vulnerability, nurturing, sensitivity, caregiving, cooperation, and commitment to family are needed in the church. They are values we want to see in the people of our churches. These qualities provide opportunities for a woman to minister. Church members who would never approach a male staff member will be drawn to a woman for support, counseling, and discipling. A woman will motivate and reach men and women who have never responded to the ministry of a man, just as her male counterparts will reach people she will never reach.

THE FEMALE CES AND CHURCH RELATIONSHIPS

The church can be defined as people in relationship with God and each other. The quality of both of these relationships affects the work of the church. The Christian education specialist deals with people on all levels of church involvement: the church board, pastor, the pastoral team, committee members, ministry leaders, teachers, helpers, active participants, and visitors. Quality relationships are essential for the CES to be effective in mobilizing people into ministry. The female CES brings not only her training and experience to these relationships but also her femaleness, which may enhance or deter her work with various groups in the church. For the most part, she will interact with people who perceive the church leadership as male-dominated.

With the Pastor

A good working relationship with the pastor is crucial for any CES. A female CES vitally needs the support of her leader. His attitude toward her abilities and leadership will set the tone for the entire church. It is not unusual for a female CES to be the first full-time professional woman on a given church staff. By providing personal and public support, the pastor can help her become established as a capable professional.

Two-way communication is crucial to a supportive relationship. The pastor should communicate what he expects, clearly define the CES's position description, and give feedback. In turn, the CES needs to keep the pastor updated on the status of the various educational ministries. This sounds basic, yet finding the time to communicate with each other can become difficult. Both minister to the same group of people and have offices under the same roof, yet may only pass quickly in the hall.

In interviews with women across the country serving as CESs, two statements kept being repeated: "I have a lot of responsibility and little authority" and "I expect more time from the senior pastor than I get." These two statements emphasize the importance of keeping the pastor informed. If every decision is subject to his approval, the CES must let him know what those decisions are. This may change as trust develops or it may never change, depending on the leadership style of the pastor. If the pastor is not taking the initiative to relate to the CES, she should take the initiative to relate to him. Remember, he is overseeing the total ministry of the church, and the CES is one of many people reporting to him. It is natural to expect the leader to do the reaching out, but it may not happen. As a staff member you may have to initiate open communication.

Although many women CESs enjoy genuine friendship, care, support, and open communication with their senior pastors, this is not always the case. Many male senior pastors are still learning to relate to a woman on staff. Most male senior pastors have attended a male-dominated seminary and may have never worked with a woman in the church. During staff meetings the pastor at one church often would say, "Now, men . . ." and then as an afterthought add, ". . . and lady."

Problems in adjustment can range from insignificant ones like that to those that are more complex. There may be subtle, even subconscious, sexist attitudes that may cause problems between a pastor and his female staff member. If a pastor has never worked with a woman, he may find himself being overly protective of her, not allowing her to represent herself on issues. He may patronize, use innocent flirtation to persuade, or be openly hostile.[15] It is vital that the woman help him by communicating in a calm, assertive way how she wants him to relate to her. This approach should be used for all male staff members. Many men will respond to this and will want to relate to her in a way that is respectful and professional. This kind of communication can help all parties from overreacting and becoming hostile and abrasive.

With Colleagues

One of the benefits of working in a church is the opportunity to be part of a team. Many women CESs speak of these relationships as rewarding and supportive. Male and female church staff can be colleagues in the truest sense of the word. This usually occurs because everyone is on the same line reporting to the pastor. A woman may find that she has a closer, more supportive and encouraging relationship with male associates than the men have with each other. This is due in part to men's perceptions of women as being less competitive or threatening than other men.

The situation may change if the woman CES is supervising another staff member, such as an adult minister or youth pastor. Typically the dynamics change when she is supervising men. This often reflects the discomfort many men in our society feel in reporting to a woman. Built-in factors that may affect this attitude include age, seniority, experience, tenure, and the educational levels of the people involved.[16] Here are six rules of relationships for the woman who supervises a man.[17]

1. Be careful that the relationship does not become a power struggle. Focus on establishing the kind of relationship with your subordinate that you desire from your superior. Little things, such as not being separated by a big desk when talking and meeting in his office or over coffee, will go a long way toward putting him at ease with your authority.
2. Never reprimand him in public. If a problem occurs, discuss it in a firm manner in private.
3. Anticipate situations that may become a problem. Try to give input "before the fact" to prevent painful critiques. For instance, you may have a question about the appropriateness or quality of the music, a testimony, or skit for Youth Night. Ask the youth pastor to discuss the program with you ahead of time.
4. You are his manager; don't be defensive about that. If his behavior or words lack respect, communicate what you expect clearly, calmly, and nondefensively.
5. Don't allow either one of you to use flirtatious remarks or flattery for the purpose of manipulation. It is easy to fall into the trap of using whatever will work when all else has failed. Keep the relationship friendly but professional.

6. Ask the Lord to give you wisdom in the relationship and to help you to allow His love to be consistently shown toward this individual.

One woman responding to our survey tells of a male youth pastor who would get angry and defensive in every encounter. After getting nowhere she discussed it with the pastor who, to her surprise, was having the same problem. What she interpreted as a problem with women was an authority problem in general. When the female CES encounters problems with subordinates she should keep the pastor informed. She also should allow others to give input and guidance. Eventually the CES and her subordinate may need to sit down with the pastor or an elder and discuss the problems. The CES would benefit by having detailed documentation of past problems.

With the Church Board

A CES's relationship with the church board varies from church to church. Some CESs attend every meeting, and others may send only written reports. One female CES was invited to the board meeting only twice a year. After her report during one of these meetings, the elders invited her to attend every meeting, saying, "You know more about what's going on in this church than any of us, and we need to hear it." She may not have actually known more than anyone else, but the statement reflected their realization that she saw things from a different and valuable perspective.

A CES needs visibility with the church board. The CES who does not communicate regularly to the board can quickly become upset when other staff members go to the board and come out with personal and financial support for programs that seem less strategic than those of the CES. When the CES is a woman, she may assume this support for others reflects an inattentiveness to C.E. programs because the specialist is a woman. Instead, the female CES may need to acknowledge she is not presenting on a regular basis the needs of educational ministries. The woman who does her job effectively will practice the art of assertive diplomacy.

Church boards are usually concerned with budgets, and rightly so. One way for a woman to establish herself as a professional is to counteract the stereotype that women cannot handle money well. She must prepare, present, and handle her budget carefully. If she must exceed her budget, she should convince the board beforehand that it is essential.

With Secretaries and Support Staff

In most, if not all, churches the secretaries are women. How do these women respond to a woman on the pastoral team? In many cases there is no problem. Some women, however, do not want to see a woman in leadership; according to Howe, they do not want to work for another woman, and they do not think that a woman can do as good a job as a man.[18] In our survey, several CESs expressed a problem with secretaries putting their work as last priority.

The female CES may tend to develop such open friendships with the secretaries that a professional relationship no longer exists. This tendency is especially strong if the CES is the only woman on staff. Of course, the CES should be cordial and friendly, but professional decorum must be maintained. A woman CES should always be identified as a member of the ministry team.

Other support staff also can regard the female CES with less respect than they should. If this occurs, the CES may have to help others understand her role and help them treat that role with respect. One woman CES had just joined the church staff and kept finding the custodian at her desk eating his lunch and talking on the phone. He would have never thought of using one of the other staff member's offices, but he was the father of several adult daughters and regarded this CES as just one more woman. One day he began to ask her about the evaluation of a program she had made that was lying on her desk. She finally realized she had to put an end to this situation. The female CES must recognize such situations and deal with them quickly.

With Committees and Teachers

A CES relates to committee members, ministry leaders, and teachers. She is involved in managing, planning, organizing, leading, controlling, recruiting, and training. Her leadership style is reflected in how she approaches all of the above.

How does a woman in church ministry lead? A study of clergywomen found that they most often operate with a more collegial style of leadership than do their male counterparts. Rather than being "directive," most clergywomen have found that a "participatory" style of leadership tends to alleviate the male/female authority conflict and establishes positive and supportive relationships.[19] Most of the women CESs interviewed do not chair the Christian education committee or program committees, but they do work closely with the chairperson.

Unfortunately, not everyone responds to a woman in leadership, regardless of style. It is not unusual for a woman CES to have her position questioned on a "scriptural basis." When this happens, the concerned parties need to meet with the pastor and the CES to address the questions and issues. It is important that the CES have the pastor's support. Not everyone will agree on the interpretation of Scripture on this issue, but the pastor working with the woman CES must be convinced of the validity of her leadership or he would not have hired her.

With the Congregation

The CES is constantly building relationships in the church and helping people use their gifts within the body. As discussed earlier in the chapter, the female CES has numerous opportunities to minister to the individual needs of people in the congregation. Her availability to know and be known will be the heart of her ministry.

Like any staff member, the CES needs to be visible to the whole congregation. She should discuss with the pastor ways this can happen. Many CESs participate in some aspect of the worship service by reading Scripture, praying, giving announcements or a report on some aspect of ministry. If the CES is not active on the platform some people in the church will not know who she is.

A woman on a church staff becomes a role model for the congregation, especially to the women. They will observe how her Christian faith is translated into daily life. The woman CES who is modeling an alive, vibrant faith will challenge women to grow spiritually. Her involvement in ministry will be an encouragement to others to use their spiritual gifts and perhaps even to pursue professional training.

All church leaders, both men and women, need to exercise care in their relationships with members of the opposite sex. Within the congregation are some women who can become emotionally attached to the pastor and pursue a sexual relationship with him. Similarly, some men in the church can become emotionally attached to the woman CES and may pursue a sexual relationship with her. Anthony Campolo explains the attraction this way:

> In a very real sense, the nature of being a church leader is to become a sex object. It is very naive to assume that the only thing that turns people on is good looks. The truth is that power, influence, and prestige have a tremendous capacity to stimulate sexual excitement. Church leaders often find themselves unwittingly eliciting powerful sexual responses.[20]

The warnings to male staff members about women in the church also apply to female staff members in dealing with men. Nothing will destroy a ministry faster.

SPECIAL CONCERNS FOR THE WOMAN CES

The first seven chapters of this book discussed issues that are relevant for every Christian education specialist. The woman CES has special areas of concern that relate to her effectiveness in fulfilling her role. The concerns here are not limited solely to women but are especially crucial to that group of educators.

Marriage Versus Singleness

Women account for 45 percent of the labor force in the United States. In 1986 two out of five of these women had children under the age of eighteen. One out of five was a single mother.[21] The debate over whether mothers of young children should work is still fierce.

Everyone has an opinion about which is the better choice. While the debate continues, married women with children are working in the church, some with more success than others.

For the female CES, ministry pressures will affect her marriage in distinct ways. Mid-life seminarians and clergywomen and their husbands were interviewed regarding the stress seminary and ministry put on their marriages. Of the fifteen couples, five were already divorced or divorcing, three marriages were strained to the breaking point, and seven of the marriages were stable. From the study Mehl found six stress points that all working married women should take note of: (1) the use of time (caused by deadline pressures), (2) the care of home and children, (3) the lack of sharing and communication, (4) the husband's relationship to the church, (5) the lack of time spent together, and (6) understanding that the husband's work has as much validity as the wife's.[22]

In spite of these pressures, married women CESs will find built-in support systems at the church. A woman in church ministry may be out nights, but she also may be free in the morning or afternoon to take care of home responsibilities. Her family will most likely be involved in the church and will attend many functions with her. In addition, most women in ministry who are mothers of young children have built-in nursery care at work.

The single woman can have more time for ministry, without a husband and children consuming her attention. But singleness poses its own problems for the female CES. A single woman may become so caught up in the job that she forgets to balance her work with needed recreation and rest. Usually she has no built-in support structure at home, no one to care for her needs after a hard day. Church ministry can be demanding physically, mentally, emotionally, and spiritually. The single woman must take the time to develop quality friendships in and outside the church that are supportive, stimulating, and encouraging.

Salary

Historically, a primary reason churches hired women to serve as CESs was financial: they could pay women less. This began when married laywomen took the job on a part-time basis and were not considered the primary breadwinners. This is still true today. For the most part, women in our survey, working as CESs, perceived themselves as making less money than a man would in the same position.

Talking about money and ministry in the same breath can be awkward. We all know that one does not go into the ministry to retire a millionaire. Yet money is a fact of life. We need it to live. The Bible teaches us that "the love of money is a root of all kinds of evil." It also teaches us that "the worker deserves his wages" (1 Tim. 6:10; 5:18). Like their male counterparts, women desire to be paid for the job they do. When people are not compensated properly for their work, their motivation and self-esteem often suffer.

Pay structures in churches vary as much as the physical structures. Even in denominational situations individual church pay scales vary. Salaries may be determined by such factors as the average income of the community, size of the church, responsibility level, educational background, marital status, number of dependents, need, and experience, or a combination of these. Obviously, not all of these involve bias based on sexual discrimination.

The CES should not expect to make the same salary as the senior pastor and associates with more responsibility, education, and experience. But what happens when the gap is unreasonable? Should a woman be paid less because she has a husband who is employed? How are men in a similar position paid? Should a single woman's salary be lower because she has no dependents? Are the salaries of single men on staff lower for this reason? If these questions are not answered adequately, they can cause bitterness and low motivation in ministry.

When a female CES wrestles with these difficult issues she should remember the reason for ministry is not to make money. We are in it to serve God. Many men and women are in the ministry at a great financial sacrifice. If the principle of sacrifice is employed at a church, it should be across the board.

How important is a financial package to the Christian? It is important but hopefully not the deciding factor. The real questions are: Is this a place where I can minister effectively? Do this church and the people I'll work with motivate me? Will I be able to challenge them in ministry? If the answer to these questions is affirmative, then the financial package often becomes secondary.[23] Day by day job satisfaction for many people is more important in the long run than the paycheck twice a month.

Conflict

All CESs operate as change agents at some time in their ministries. As the needs of the people in the church change, the ministry must change to meet those needs. The female CES may very well be effecting change in attitudes toward women in ministry as she affects attitudes toward programs. Any time change takes place there will be resistance and possibly conflict.

Conflict in a church and among church staff at some point is a given. The church and staff are composed of individuals who (thankfully) do not all think alike. No matter how congenial a group is, the day will come when they will disagree on some aspect of the ministry. It is imperative for the woman on staff (especially if she is the only woman) to understand the sources of conflict. This will keep her from the tendency to see everything as either discrimination or personal resistance.

When conflict does occur, how do people deal with it? Men are taught to confront, to "stand up and take it like a man." Women, on the other hand, have been taught that "it's not ladylike to fight." In a situation involving conflict, men are valued for being competitive. Women are valued for being receptive, which includes accommodation, giving in, or smoothing over the conflict. Handling conflict in a healthy manner is vital to the dignity and productivity of both men and women.[24]

For both men and women, collaboration and negotiating skills are essential in dealing with conflict. This means coming to a problem ready to resolve conflict and recognizing that people have vested interests and legitimate differences that are to be respected. Bonnie Kasten, who has trained thousands of managers in complex negotiation strategy and influence skills, studied the behavior of men and women dealing with conflict and found that each had distinct negotiating skills. Women listen attentively and often clarify the other's position, use logic to support their ideas, comment on areas of agreement, and avoid provoking the other person. In contrast, men make firm proposals and demands, make few concessions and hold their position, use time as their ally, and bargain to get what they want. She concludes that all eight behaviors are necessary to come to lasting agreements. Both men and women would have a full complement of skills if they would learn to develop the other's strengths.[25] There are times when a woman CES's position is correct and the change she proposes, which is causing the conflict, would be best for the ministry. She needs to learn to develop the skills necessary to negotiate with men.

Power often becomes an issue in conflict. Men have had the power base in our culture. A woman can balance the power in a conflict situation by using her perceptual skills, gathering all the facts, being trustworthy, and communicating clearly.[24] Christians have another source of power in conflict resolution—the power of the Holy Spirit, whose fruit is seen in our lives as love, joy, peace, patience, kindness, goodness, faithfulness, gentleness, and self-control. What helpful tools these are in conflict situations! A church should never forget that we are all headed toward the same goal of reaching the world for Christ and building up the Body of Christ. With this in mind we should approach conflict not from a personal standpoint but with a desire to work together in carrying forward God's will.

Women in ministry should prioritize issues before airing disagreements. Four good questions of priority are: (1) How important is this issue, really? (2) Does it reach to the depths of my philosophy of ministry, my theological convictions that cannot be compromised, or my personal priorities? (3) Is this issue worth the price, or are there other more important issues that must be resolved? (4) What price must be paid to fight this battle?[27] Some women tend to fight for whatever issue they think is important at the time. Instead, women must recognize when to keep mouths shut and when to unleash thunder. Save the thunder for the big ones.

Stress

Pick up a magazine, turn on the television, or attend a business seminar and you can read or hear something on the topic of stress. Unfortunately, stress and its effects are not limited to secular society. A visit to the local Christian bookstore will reveal that volumes have been written to Christians on the subject; yes, even to Christian leaders.

For the woman CES, stress has many forms: the normal demands of ministry; the pressure from society to be a superwoman who combines career, marriage, and motherhood; and the special stresses of being a woman in ministry. Among those special stress issues, the female CES may be the first woman on staff, feeling the pressure of proving that a woman can have an effective ministry. Or she could be facing conflicts from those who do not accept her leadership role. As alleged "superwomen," many women CESs are juggling the erratic schedule of ministry with raising children and maintaining a strong marriage. Meanwhile, single women in C.E. ministry may be internalizing many of their frustrations because of the lack of a confidant and encourager.

The effects of stress on an individual vary. Stress stifles a person's creativity, drains energy, and can lead to depression. Several women CESs reported going to the doctor with various symptoms, such as chest pains and difficulty in breathing. All were diagnosed as suffering from stress. The bottom line is that stress robs a person of joy and peace.

When facing stress, we need to know how much is too much. A degree of pressure in our lives can be exhilarating. Then suddenly all the demands seem overwhelming. What once brought fulfillment now is a drain. The following basic strategies will help the woman in ministry to keep her life manageable:

1. Clearly understand what your superiors expect of you. Remember, the expectations of your superiors count; those of the entire congregation do not. (Often the congregation

has unrealistic expectations.)

2. Set priorities. They will need to be evaluated and changed periodically. The realistic CES recognizes that she cannot give every ministry area her full attention at all times.

3. Pray that God will teach you how to trust Him with the results of your ministry and that you will learn not to be anxious.

4. Realize your own limitations. Only God is omnipresent, omniscient, and omnipotent. You can attend only one meeting at a time, you cannot be an expert on all areas of ministry, and you cannot solve every problem. You are gifted and created in the image of God, but you have limitations.

5. Maintain honest communication with those with whom you work and live. Talk to those who can do something about the things that are causing you stress. If a situation is a problem for you, don't ignore it—deal with it.

6. Find a good friend with whom you can be brutally honest. Such a friend will love and accept you, will listen to and encourage you, and will hold your words in strict confidence.

7. Take care of yourself. God designed our bodies to need regular sleep; don't feel guilty about that. Exercise helps our bodies relax. It is worth the time it takes.

8. Be aware of the power of hormonal changes in your body. For many women, premenstrual syndrome plays a big part in their ability or inability to cope with stressful situations. Know when not to schedule crucial meetings or make major decisions. Being aware of our bodies can help us understand our thoughts, feelings, and responses to otherwise normal events in our lives.

Church ministry is demanding on everyone involved—men, women, professionals, and lay people. The issues of family adjustment, financial difficulties, conflict, and stress can affect us all. It is important to remember that these difficulties are not insurmountable. God is faithful. By His grace we can learn to effectively handle each concern, thus adding to the productivity of ministry.

THE SUCCESSFUL WOMAN CES

In the literature dealing with women in the workplace and in the church, one word keeps reappearing: *anger.* Women are describing themselves as angry at the closed doors and lack of freedom to minister. I do not believe women have to be angry. Certainly their ministry is ineffective when they are.

More and more women are enjoying the growing field of Christian education to its fullest. To do so, they are seeing ministry as an opportunity and a profession given by God. To insure this attitude, here are three crucial determinants for women who desire a successful ministry characterized by faithfulness and obedience to our Lord. First, be a competent leader. Keep learning, growing, and working hard. Competence in the area of Christian education has no gender. Second, try to avoid seeing everything through the eyes of discrimination. Realize that everyone in a career—male and female, black or white—must pay his dues and earn the trust of his superiors and those he seeks to lead.

Finally, approach the ministry with the servant attitude of our Lord Jesus Christ. He modeled this by washing the disciples' feet and then taught us that "many who are first will be last," "he who is least among you, this is the one who is great," and "the greatest among you will be your servant" (Matt. 19:30; Luke 9:48; and Matt. 23:11).

— NOTES —

1. Dorothy Jean Furnish, "Pioneers for Women in Professional Ministry," in *Women and Religion in America*, ed. Rosemary Radford Reuther and Rosemary Skinner Killer (San Francisco: Harper & Row, 1986), 3:312.
2. Ibid., pp. 311-15.
3. Roberta Hestenes, "Women in Leadership: Finding Ways to Serve the Church," *Christianity Today*, 3 October 1986, pp. 10-11.
4. Constant H. Jacquet, Jr., ed., *Yearbook of American and Canadian Churches* (Nashville: Abindgon, 1987), p. 271.

5. Furnish, p. 312.
6. Kenneth O. Gangel, *Leadership for Church Education* (Chicago: Moody, 1970), pp. 90-91.
7. Clarence H. Benson, *Techniques of a Working Church* (Chicago: Moody, 1946), p. 104; as cited in Vernon R. Kraft, *The Director of Christian Education in the Local Church* (Chicago: Moody, 1957), p. 49.
8. Irene E. Schroeder, "The Source of Male/Female Differences and Their Implications for Christian Nurture," *Christian Education Journal* 8 (Autumn 1987): 73-84.
9. Janet L. Kobobel, *But Can She Type?* (Downers Grove, Ill.: InterVarsity, 1986), p. 79.
10. Bonnie R. Kasten, "Separate Strengths: How Men and Women Manage Conflict and Competition," in *Not as Far as You Think,* ed. Lynda L. Moore (Lexington: D.C. Heath, 1986), p. 124.
11. Fred Smith, "Building the Church Staff," *Leadership* 7 (Winter 1986): 99-104.
12. Mark Lipton, "Successful Women in a Man's World: The Myth of Managerial Androgyny," in *Not as Far as You Think,* ed. Lynda L. Moore (Lexington: D.C. Heath, 1986), p. 165.
13. Kobobel, pp. 59-60.
14. Ibid., pp. 53-54.
15. E. Margaret Howe, *Women and Church Leadership* (Grand Rapids: Zondervan, 1982), pp. 196-97.
16. Lyle E. Schaller, *The Multiple Staff and the Large Church* (Nashville: Abingdon, 1980), pp. 126-27.
17. The first five rules are based on Marilyn Bendu, "When the Boss Is a Woman," *Esquire,* 28 March 1978, p. 41, as cited in Kobobel, p. 167.
18. Howe, p. 22.
19. Nadine M. Luhutsky, "Women and Ministry: Changes in the Future," *Lexington Theological Quarterly* 20 (Spring 1985): 37-38.
20. Anthony Campolo, "Sexual Temptation and the Church Leader," *Innovations* 1 (Spring 1985): 36.
21. Rosalyn B. Will and Steven D. Lydenberg, "20 Corporations That Listen to Women," *MS Magazine,* November 1987, p. 45.
22. L. Guy Mehl, "Marriage and Ministry in Mid-Life Women," *Journal of Religion and Health* 23 (Winter 1984): 293-98.
23. Jerry Hayner, "The Uneasy Marriage of Money and Ministry," *Leadership* 8 (Winter 1987): 14-15.
24. Kasten, pp. 122-29.
25. Ibid., pp. 130-31.
26. Ibid., p. 132.
27. Ernest Beevers, "Is It Worth the Battle?" *Leadership* 7 (Fall 1986): 39.

Principles in Practice

AT A MEDIUM CHURCH

Central Community Church
Wichita, Kansas
Sunday school size: 1,000

by Sydney McPeak
Minister of Christian Education

My overall experience as a woman in ministry has been positive. I was in public education for fourteen years as a classroom teacher before accepting the position of minister of Christian education. I was not seeking other employment but doing much volunteer work in Christian education when the pastor approached me with this opportunity. He insisted (and I agreed) that I begin to pursue a license; he also recommended that I seek ordination in our denomination within three years. The pastor gave me much support from the pulpit, recognizing the need for public exposure to develop the credibility of the CES to perform the tasks properly.

In those early years I joined an all-male staff. We have since added one female associate; so among the ten ministers on staff, two are women. In relationships with both senior staff and the congregation I receive much affirmation. The pastor has a keen awareness of the value of women in ministry positions. He would agree with the statement "The issue is not male or female, but the individual." When questioned regarding women on a pastoral staff, he refers to the declaration in Galatians 3:28, "There is neither Jew nor Greek, slave nor free, male nor female, for you are all one in Christ Jesus." I definitely feel a part of the team, a valuable, contributing member, and highly respected by my coworkers.

My pastor's management style is not unlike that of many persons who are visionary. He tends to expect a staff member to complete his or her duties, exhibit initiative, and finish each task with little thumb-pressing from him. He must have a self-starter and an independent worker with a creative mind. This is not to say he does not listen or advise when he deems it necessary or pertinent. This approach gives rise to an untethered sense of mission and creates in me a confirmation that he has the utmost confidence in my decisions and what I do in Christian education.

The pastor's treatment of me is no different from his treatment of the male members of the staff. I do feel that relationally I tend to be the catalyst that builds community within the staff, and I have a closer relationship with most of the male staff than they do with each other.

Being female does lend a different perspective on issues that are broader than my own ministry area and churchwide in scope. I have encountered some obstacles, but I do not believe they are a result of my being a woman. I think they are the same obstacles male ministers face with the exception of responsibilities in the home.

In the early years when my children were home and I was also scrambling to establish my credibility in ministry, much energy had to be expended to keep pace with the male pastors and also function in the role of a wife and mother. My husband and I have always shared the responsibilities at home, but the nurturer in a mother will usually take on additional responsibilities. As a result, as I attended most church functions and also fulfilled the many responsibilities within Christian education, I became very busy and somewhat frustrated. I placed most of the expectations in both areas upon myself, feeling I had to keep pace in my ministry to establish myself in an appreciated position. In the beginning of my ministry, I had to accept the fact and deal with the ramifications of the work as a lifestyle and not simply a job. I learned that my work touched every area of my life. I also learned that my life is no longer my own but belongs to God and the work in His kingdom. When a CES or any minister is unable to accept or adjust to this reality, discontent may result.

Since I entered the ministry, my husband has been wholeheartedly supportive of the hours and energy I need to accomplish the task. He is self-sufficient and has an excellent concept of his own manhood. This is apparent in the manner in which he accepts my accolades, visibility, and stature. The church I am affiliated with is the largest in a city of 300,000, and holds a prestigious place within the community and metroplex. I would not be able to do this work with the same zest and fervor without this godly man as my supporter, friend, and husband.

I have participated in the Kansas state Sunday school convention and have served as its president for seven years. The board of eight members is predominantly male. These men, some of whom are senior pastors of churches from various denominations, have never resisted my authority or my leadership because I am a woman. This group encompasses denominations that strictly adhere to the conservative position limiting women in leadership within their congregations; yet they seem to accept my leadership gratefully.

The author illustrates her points with several women whose experiences parallel my own personal ministry. I take heart that I'm not the only woman having these struggles and feelings. I disagree, however, with the author's observation that anger is a recurring theme among women in ministry. My exposure is not as broad, nor is it based on any scientific census, but I do not perceive such an attitude in my associations. I think if women are angry or upset because they are women in a man's world, it would stem from a belief of gender discrimination or from women who possess a self-serving nature. I do agree, however, with Gannett's conclusion: Gender must not be an issue if the women in ministry are to find fulfillment, satisfaction, and have the liberty to respond to the ministry to which they have been called.

AT A LARGE CHURCH

First Presbyterian Church
Greenville, South Carolina
Sunday school size: 2,000

by Karen Van Galder
Director of Children's Ministries

Most evangelical churches are sincerely struggling with the role of women. As I have talked with churches in many denominations, the leaders have asked me repeatedly, "What do you think of women being . . . ?" (Fill in the blank according to your denomination's position.) Often these issues have been settled by denominational leaders years ago, but local churches only now seem to be dealing with them. As leaders in local churches discuss such issues, they may become more open to women's being on staff.

Already I see several advances for women in ministry:

- More age specialists (especially children's workers) are women.
- Fewer CESs are male, especially as ordination is possible with additional, but not necessarily extensive, course work. Ordination in many denominations leads to specific benefits and greater salaries. A nonordained woman may be more feasible financially.
- More women are being hired as staff from within the ranks of the congregation.

As a CES for more than ten years, I have seen myself filling a unique role on the church staff. I have listened to concerns from women in the congregation that would deeply embarrass them if heard by a male colleague. Women who have had personal crises, such as miscarriages, have warmly received me after they greeted coolly the obligatory pastoral call. I have also realized that young girls in the congregation see me as a role model, a humbling thought. One Sunday after reading Scripture in the worship service, I received a note in the offering from an eight-year-old girl, telling me how much she enjoyed my being in the pulpit.

One's relationship with the senior minister is not an issue unique to women CESs. Program staff, male and female, wrestle with dealing with the senior minister. Much of the literature available is equally applicable to male or female. I have often found, though, much variance among pastors in their dealing with women staff. On one hand, I know of senior ministers who have expressed eagerness to have a woman on staff but who have exhibited sexist behavior, often with the best intentions. A dozen red roses is wonderful, but a dozen red roses on Secretaries' Day with the card "Happy Secretaries' Day" is not! On the other hand, one minister, shortly after hiring me, announced, "I am a male chauvinist. I do not think that women should do certain things." Yet in my years of working with him, I saw an openness to a broader involvement and a willingness to let me develop as a staff person. His self-awareness and honesty were keys to a strong working relationship.

I have often done an exercise in which I ask groups (men and women) to visualize the physical appearance of the ideal boss. Adjectives such as "kindly," "smiling," "gray-haired" always come. After a pause, and often prodding for more details, they admit their ideal boss as being a male—an assumption so obvious they have deemed it not worth mentioning.

I can thus echo the author's comments about supervising males. Her points in dealing with the situation are excellent. I have found it essential to have support from the senior minister for my role, and also from the Christian education committee. At the time of conflict I can use the official structure to support me if necessary.

Supervising women can also be tricky. Although some secretaries have responded well to a lower-key approach, others may either ignore work or do it very poorly. On the other hand, I have been friends with several of my secretaries, who have not taken advantage of that relationship. After all, our Christian sisterhood precedes and undergirds our other relationships.

As an evangelical, a Presbyterian in a mainline denomination, and a staff member in some large congregations, I have had the unique opportunity to function in settings where women's leadership is officially and actively encouraged. I have found, however, that my experience has varied widely between the Midwest, West, and South. Though some of this can be directly traced to the senior ministers' attitudes, some is definitely due to regional differences. Not surprisingly, both the staff and congregation in the Southern church have perceived my role as far more traditional and much less collegial than those in other churches. In the South, where more traditional roles are important, I have found that many women will not consider teaching a mixed group of adult men and women. One of my finest adult teachers resigned as a teacher of a mixed Bible study. I found it fascinating that her husband made a point of telling me that it was not his idea at all!

Perhaps, too, because of the more traditional attitudes toward women, I have had to deal with more inappropriate behavior from men in the South than elsewhere. From the pat on the rear by a single man as he was being ushered to a new Sunday school class to the subtle and flattering attentions of an older male member, which left me feeling intuitively uncomfortable, I have found that I must be vigilant in my behavior and must work to be seen as a professional.

Crucial to a woman's success as a CES is visibility in the congregation. Affirming comments from the pulpit are significant aids to a CES, as are simple things such as being included in a staff listing in the bulletin. I have had the opportunity of being part of the regular rotation assisting in worship. My appearance itself is a positive philosophical statement by the pastoral staff.

Competence is another key to success. When I first became a CES, I thought I had to be perfect. An irritated parent, an unhappy child, an omission in a supply order all seemed to indicate that I was incompetent. As I began to develop professionally, I realized that perfection was not expected.

We do have a perfect Model for leadership, however, in Jesus Christ. In His washing of the disciples' feet we have a powerful and radical image of Christian leadership—servanthood. And yet, especially for women, this can be a two-edged sword. We may be so eager to be a servant that we lose our perspective. Servants are not slaves.

Christ *chose* to wash those dusty feet; too often we begrudge the services we perform, therefore not meeting real needs and not being genuine.

Anyone in the ministry must at some point come to grips with forgiveness for hurts inflicted, either intentionally or accidentally. If one does not deal with these, I am convinced that one is not only missing an opportunity for spiritual growth, but one is also being disobedient to Scripture. Forgiveness is the key to building an ongoing, loving ministry that will influence many lives with the message that God can change and heal us.

A Future Look:
Three Views from the Front

AT A SMALL CHURCH

Bethel Evangelical Free Church
Fargo, North Dakota
Sunday school size: 300

by Carol Miller
Director of Christian Education

For the past sixteen years I have enjoyed the task of serving Christ and His church as a C.E. specialist. While a college student, I served in two churches on a part-time basis. The senior pastors of those churches, with too many duties for their time, could not complete all the tasks, and I believed God had given me the ability to make a difference in these areas and especially in the lives of the volunteer workers. Later in seminary, I served on another staff as a part-time CES and discovered that I enjoyed this aspect of the ministry more than the responsibilities of other staff members. This confirmed my calling to Christian education as ministry. When I sometimes feel discouraged today, I still have the assurance that the Lord has called me to serve as a staff member in Christian education.

For me it has been fun serving Christ. In spite of the frustrations that every CES faces in ministry, we can have genuine enjoyment watching lives being changed and problems solved as people take little steps or giant leaps in their personal walks with God. In my ministry I have seen problems overcome, impossible situations salvaged and restored, outstanding answers to prayer, and people made new as they put their faith in Christ. In addition, my family (Becky and our three sons) and I have made great friends in the locations where we served and have had good times in training people and then seeing them reproduce themselves in the lives of others. We have watched young children become teens, then become adults and later marry, making us feel as if we are part of many nuclear families.

Being real! That best describes what makes ministry a joy. The greatest fulfillment in my ministry as a CES has come when coworkers have been open with us and allowed us to be open and honest with them. As we laugh together, cry together, seek counsel from each other, and share the nitty-gritty of our lives and ministry, my colaborers and I have each benefited. The difference comes when teachers and other volunteer staff learn, teach, and live openly before each other.

Like most seminary graduates, I was too idealistic about how to do the work of the ministry when it came to dealing with people. Since I had the training and they didn't, if they would just listen to me and do it my way, I believed a particular ministry or class would proceed correctly and efficiently. What I failed to do was consider their training (good, bad, or lacking) for the position, their personality, their expectations, their recent history in the position, and whether they saw me as friend or foe. I have learned (and am still learning) that I need to trust people. Trust means I must solicit input from my volunteers to understand their concerns, rather than dictating how they will perform based on the job descriptions alone.

The vast majority of Christian people really want to do what is right. Once I clearly communicate what I sense is needed in a given instance, I should give them an opportunity to express their convictions and expectations about the position. Then, once we have reached agreement on what is to be done and how it is to be done, service for Christ will be far more encouraging and comfortable for both of us. In my early years I was not able to have that kind of an open dialogue because I feared appearing as "weak" to people if I didn't have all the answers or that I was being a poor leader if I sought input from them.

One big mistake I made concerns the expectations I had of myself and those the church had of me. In my first two years in ministry, I gave myself to the "job" so much that I neglected Becky and our small son. I did this because there was so much to do and I was having a good time doing it. But I also thought that this is what the people in the church expected me to do. I knew that the Lord had called me to be a husband and a father before He had given me the call to this church, but I had deceived myself into thinking that investing my best time and energy in the ministry was pleasing to God and absolutely necessary to be faithful to the church. Becky came to hate the fact that I gave my best to the church. When I came home late for supper and then left for a evening meeting only to return exhausted, I would give the leftovers of my time, energy, and attention to her and David.

Several sessions with a counselor helped me to see the unrealistic expectations I had for myself and the damage I was doing to our marriage and ministry by not giving some prime time to the family. Becoming accountable to another man in the church as to whether I am taking my days off, spending quality and quantity time with the family, helped me ensure I was giving the proper attention to my family.

All of us make mistakes in life. Tom Peters in his book *Thriving on Chaos* gives some great advice when he says it is better to make lots of little mistakes, admit them, and then change through them rather than continually trying to protect ourselves by hiding them. The Bible depicts many men and women who grew best when they recognized that they had made mistakes. My mistake in priorities occurred when I neglected my family. By acknowledging my mistake I became more effective as a servant at my church. Most people will allow us to grow through the mistakes we make if we will be genuine enough to admit the mistakes early and show that we are willing to let the Lord mature us as we work through the problem. The church—its leadership and membership—is looking for authentic role models who will be open and mature enough to admit mistakes, seek help, and change.

Another area where people have greatly helped me has been in confrontation. For me, "telling the truth in love" meant meeting any church problem with 90 percent love and 10 percent truth. Because I didn't want to hurt the person who was causing problems for others, I always did the loving thing (or so I thought) and erred on the side of "love." I refused to clearly tell him the truth about the negative impact his attitude or actions were having. I found it difficult to practice the balance that the Scripture calls for in Ephesians 4:15. Through the involvement of people who loved me enough to tell me the truth, I have learned that telling the truth first, but also telling it in love, works best in all relationships. As C.E. specialists, we must consistently demonstate such honest love in our words before the volunteer staff.

I think these are great days to be involved in local church ministry as a Christian education specialist. During the remainder of the 1990s, we should witness a door opening even wider to bring Christ to a world that is tired, confused, and looking for meaning in life. Due to the increased crisis in our country morally, economically, spiritually, and politically, many people have given up on these systems and are looking for the reality that believers have to offer as we point them to Christ. The methods with which we make Christ known to the nonbeliever and the methods that we will use in discipling the believer will need to be more low-key and personal than what we were able to use in the 1970s and 1980s.

To evangelize people by "telling" them about Christ and teaching disciples by "telling" them how to grow in Christ will not be as readily received in the 1990s. We are told that the average American is bombarded with 2,000 messages a day. Each message tells him or her to do something, buy something, or consider something. Due to the oversaturation with messages that the people in our culture must process each day, they are hesitant about being told anything. The implications for us in church leadership are: (1) The nonbeliever, rather than being "told" about God's love, wants to be shown God's love; (2) the growing believer, rather than to be "told" how to live for Christ, wants to be shown how to live for Christ. This means our time and energy must be invested in people through close involvement where they can see the difference Christ makes rather than just hear us tell them about the difference He makes in our lives. The command is still the same as it was nearly 2,000 years ago, "Make disciples."

As servant-leader in the church the CES will need to lead as well as serve. These days will require effective and Holy Spirit-inspired leading. I need to become a risk-taker for the Lord rather than playing it safe, as is my natural tendency. One way I'm trying to stay sharp is by returning to seminary for another degree that should help me understand how to better minister to the diverse needs represented in our church and culture today. I grew up in a fine traditional home, had a great time being raised in a traditional church, and received excellent training in a seminary that prepared me to serve in a traditional fashion. Now I find myself giving leadership in a church where many of the people have nontraditional problems and, like myself, are living in a nontraditional world. How encouraging it is to know Christ, who has great plans for the traditionalist and the nontraditionalist.

I have set before me, as a means of evaluating my involvement with people for the 1990s, Philippians 1:25-26: "Convinced of this, I know that I will remain, and I will continue with all of you for your progress and joy in the faith, so that through my being with you again your joy in Christ Jesus will overflow on account of me." As a CES, I want our people to know that I will continue to work with them, lead them, and serve them so that their progress and joy in Christ will continue; and that their joy, and my joy, in Christ will overflow into the lives of others. As CESs, we must follow the leading of the Holy Spirit and seek to faithfully apply the

Word to the world and to the church. I trust that together we will see God continue to do great things through His church and with you and me.

AT A MEDIUM CHURCH

Shenandoah Baptist Church
Roanoke, Virginia
Sunday school size: 700

by Phil Humphries
Director of Christian Education

When Jesus Christ was brought before Pontius Pilate the question the Roman procurator posed was one that has echoed through the years.[1] "What is truth?" Pilate asked. As a Christian education specialist I have, from God Himself, the opportunity and the strategic task of providing an answer to that question through the local church. And of each CES I must ask another question: What could be more exciting and challenging than leading children and adults to a thorough understanding and greater commitment to God's truth? The answer, of course, is "Nothing." Therefore, the role of the CES is not only important but is becoming essential as the church approaches the twenty-first century.

In recent years I have had many highlights in my role as a CES. I remember the glow of one young mother as she proudly announced that her daughter had just trusted Christ in Sunday school. There was the day that our newly formed class for mentally handicapped adults asked me to come hear them sing "Jesus Loves Me." And they just didn't sing it—they *knew* it. Nor will I forget the day that an adult approached his Sunday school teacher and said, "Thanks for showing me how God's Word was written in order to change my life." This is the joy of Christian education—knowing that individuals are being educated in the *truth* of God's Word with eternal results. The CES is privileged to be on the cutting edge of such a task.

But joy is often accompanied by challenge. And the CES faces many. One of the greatest for me personally is that of recruiting volunteers. I find it interesting that so much has been written on "The Art of Pulling Teeth," otherwise known as volunteer recruitment. Educational programs manifest life-changing results based upon the truth of the Word, and the CES must locate volunteers who are most qualified, rather than simply trying to find available bodies to shape into teachers. Recruitment was not a first-century task, but serving the Lord on behalf of His truth was.

Another challenge for the 1990s will remain interpersonal relationships. At my church more than 200 lay volunteers each week participate in numerous ministries; therefore I must ensure cooperation and unity. To a CES this can, at times, be disconcerting. The CES, however, holds the key to harmony. It is called *vision*. What great joy it is to see our nursery workers changing diapers in keeping with the common vision of the educational program. The CES is not only an educator but also a visionary.

In some unexplained way, vision has a tendency to be contagious. And when it is, those individuals doing the work of the ministry, whether paid or nonpaid, become infected to the point of shared vision and cooperative participation. The CES is the catalyst for vision that unites and brings harmony.

With challenge comes growth—personal growth. I must admit that being a CES does not bring the accolades accorded to those men God has placed in the pulpit or other high profile positions within the church. In fact, most attenders are unaware that many spiritual things are happening throughout the church building at the same time they are participating in the worship service. Yet the children's church, nursery, children's choirs, and club programs do just that. The CES is first and foremost a servant of Christ and His people. Though the CES adopts a philosophy that contradicts that of the culture in which we live, so did Christ. A CES must minister as Christ ministered, with a servant's heart.

In addition, being a CES has given me an acute understanding of the term *administration*. I have had to develop skills in such areas as budgets, delegation, prioritization of tasks, scheduling, logistics, maintenance, purchase orders, physical plant utilization, job descriptions, and handbooks. Though not always exciting, these tasks are important and vital to the success of the education program. A good CES will be a good administrator.

In his book *Future Shock,* Alvin Toffler made the following statement that can be applied directly to the task of the CES: "Unless changes are made there will be adaptional breakdown."[2] As the CES implements the educational program within his or her context, one influencing factor will always be in a state of change—*culture*—and another will always remain constant—the Word of God. Therefore the CES must oversee an educational program that creatively and aggressively applies the constant truth of God to a dynamic society. The CES must regularly ask the question, "Is our program designed to provide God's unchanging truth to today's culture?" This requires reevalution of the *method,* not the message. Just take a look at today's changing family structure, job market, and the differing philosophies of the Baby Boomers and post Boomers, compared to the lifestyle of earlier generations. Does the education program meet the personal needs of today's whirlwind society?

Schaller concludes that 85 percent of new people entering churches today come for relational reasons, and 15 percent attend for functional reasons.[3] This desire for personal relationships, along with a growing decentralized, less personal, high-tech society of the future, means the CES has a tremendous responsibility to provide a solution. And it is obvious that the solution is found by returning to one of the central messages of the first-century church: Christianity is a relationship between man and Christ.

There could be nothing more vital and exciting than to be a CES in today's church involved in the critical task of operating the vehicle that offers instruction of the truth of God's Word to a world in desperate need of it. I thank God that He has called me to such a task.

AT A LARGE CHURCH

First Baptist Church
Hendersonville, North Carolina
Sunday school size: 1,800

by Steve Briggs
Minister of Children

In my role as a C.E. specialist, specifically as a minister of children's education in two large churches, I've felt joy, frustration, and challenge. The joys have been numerous. They are God's reward for service. Reflecting on them keeps me going in the difficult days.

First, I think of all the special friendships and working relationships with the creative, committed, and talented people God has brought into my life. In both churches where I've served, God has provided deep personal friendships and a core of people dedicated to working with children. They have provided the support and encouragement often needed. Their commitment and insight have motivated me; their compassion has challenged me.

A second area of great joy centers on the opportunity to effectively use my spiritual gifts in ministry. Children's ministry demands administrative abilities and teaching skills. These are the two areas in which I consistently score the highest in any spiritual gifts inventory. Most of my ministry revolves around organizing and administering ongoing programs and training volunteer leadership. When I entered seminary I had no thought of ministry with children, but God has led me in that direction in order that I might use these gifts and have joy from doing so.

Closely related is the joy that comes from discerning a need and meeting it. There is a great satisfaction in recognizing a need in the church or the community and developing a ministry program to meet that need. In my first church I developed a computer camp for children and a week-long resident camp as part of our existing day camp. Both have a strong Christian emphasis. I implemented Awana to give new life to our sagging midweek program for children. In my current church, I've developed a children's worship, a moms' support group, and other family life programs.

Like many of my colleagues, I also have enjoyed linking my spiritual gifts with the gifts and support of my wife. We are teammates in ministry. Her commitment to teaching preschoolers in Sunday school originally steered me in the direction of children's ministry. Together we have served. She has been my sounding board, my confidante, my encourager, my nursery coordinator, a kindergarten teacher, a children's worship leader, moms' support group director, and helper in many other ways. I thank God for the way we complement each other in the work of ministering to children and their parents.

Of course, no joy could be greater in children's ministry than to be involved in the process of helping individual children come to a personal relationship with Christ. Over the years God has allowed me the privilege of guiding children in their conversion experience. This is the ultimate reason for ministry to children—to lay a foundation for faith in the preschool and younger childhood years and to see it blossom into personal trust as they mature into middle and older childhood.

Though the joys have been many, I confess to several challenges during the past ten years of ministry. Some have been short-lived, others are continuous. The greatest challenge continues to be volunteer staff recruitment, especially for Sunday school ministry. I believe that to be effective, Sunday school must have small teacher-to-student ratios, yet maintaining an adequate staff in all departments is an ongoing challenge. Many would-be teachers claim busy schedules, and the rapid pace of daily life means more and more adults are unwilling to commit to a regular teaching responsibility. I face a continuous challenge to maintain a full staff of volunteers for all the programs offered for children.

A second, related challenge comes in trying to motivate volunteers for ongoing training to refresh and improve their skills. Many simply do not acknowledge the need. Either they have been teaching for years and have set methods and routines, or they are just beginning and think, "What could be simpler than teaching children a Bible story?" Effective ministry requires understanding the children—their needs, their characteristics, and their abilities. It requires understanding how God has designed children to learn and therefore the role of the teacher as guide, motivator, example, and friend. I must convince our teachers that continual improvement of skills and knowledge base is important. Motivating leaders to participate is a constant challenge.

Working on a multiple staff also poses a challenge. I'm thankful to serve together with other men and women whose gifts and abilities complement each other. In some areas of ministry that I am less comfortable with they do well, so we are able to effectively carry out the ministry together. But often frustrations do arise. Trying to blend different philosophies of ministry, setting priorities, and establishing goals often brings tension to relationships.

I have attended meetings where supervisors had no agenda; we lost valuable time and energy. I've experienced lack of vision and coordination from the top. This brings frustration in trying to be a ministry team working together to lead the church. A few times I have faced the "pecking order" issue in such small things as who offers the welcome and announcements in the worship service. Such tensions pose an ongoing challenge and become a prayer concern.

One challenge has brought both blessing and frustration to my ministry: finances. Dealing with a shortfall in the church budget provides both an opportunity to be creative and the tendency to be disappointed and frustrated. The ministry of the church must continue whether the funds are there or not. A quality educational environment requires programs, materials to train leaders, curriculum, and equipment. Somehow the minister must find a way to make it happen even when funds are short or nonexistent. I remember years when the church supplied such a large budget that I was unable to spend it all. I also remember one year when the offerings were sufficient to meet only the fixed costs of the church. No program funds were available. God was faithful and met our needs through other sources, and the children's ministries were able to flourish.

During the 1990s, the task of the Christian educator must remain constant. The goal of the C.E. specialist must be to nurture

Christian knowledge, attitudes, and behavior. That goal, however, will be fulfilled in the context of a changing world. The pace of life will continue to speed up, strong families will be more protective of their time together, and the number of single parent and blended families will increase. More people coming to know Christ will have no biblical foundation. Therefore, although the task will remain the same, the methods and focus will change to accommodate the culture.

Although the concern is great now, family life education will receive even greater emphasis in the church. Churches will need to provide better and more practical premarital help, beginning to lay foundations as early as with the preschool child. The church will need to provide more electives, seminars, small groups, and possibly even mentor-type relationships to help young adults understand what God desires in a marriage relationship.

A second emphasis will be on basic biblical knowledge. More new converts will come from non-Christian families. They will not have had the benefit of "having known the scriptures since childhood." Their minds will be full of New Age and secular humanist thought without even being aware of it. The Christian education process will need to devise programs, classes, and groups that will foster a knowledge of the Scriptures. This will have to be done in a world where people want information and services faster, in a world that has little time for reading and meditating. Self-guided instruction through workbooks, videotapes, and possibly computer billboards and networks may become increasingly important as educational tools.

Finally, I believe the computer will become an important tool of Christian education. Computers now exist in one of every four American homes, according to researcher George Barna. By the year 2000 one of every two Americans will have a computer, as younger adults who have been raised on computers in school come of age. Students will submit homework on computer disks; the teacher will use a master computer to check the work. Encyclopedias will be on computer systems, and libraries will circulate more materials on computer diskettes.[4] I believe churches will need to provide computer stations in the elementary department for Bible learning projects, research, and individual instruction.

Already church media centers (or libraries) can locate materials on computer diskettes, such as concordances, Bible dictionaries, and other study resources. Media centers should provide more of these for students, young and old alike, to use in the classroom or at home. Of course, teachers will need training in the proper use of these resources. In addition, simple desktop publishing software could give interesting learning opportunities to students.

The future for Christian education ministry will have many challenges. It will require talented, creative leaders who are discerning and willing to take risks. I believe that God will supply the leadership necessary to keep His church strong, faithful, relevant, and growing.

— NOTES —

1. Frank E. Gaebelein, *The Pattern of God's Truth* (Moody: Chicago, 1954), p. 3.
2. Alvin Toffler, *Future Shock* (New York: Random House, 1970), p. 32.
3. Lyle E. Schaller, *Assimilating New Members* (Nashville: Abingdon, 1978), p. 55.
4. George Barna, *The Frog in the Kettle: What Christians Need to Know About Life in the Year 2000* (Ventura, Calif.: Regal, 1990), p. 55.

Bibliography

Ames, Louise Bates, and Ilg, Frances L. *Your Five Year Old.* New York: Delta, 1979.

———. *Your Four Year Old.* New York: Delta, 1976.

———. *Your One Year Old.* New York: Delta, 1982.

———. *Your Seven Year Old.* New York: Delta, 1985.

———. *Your Six Year Old.* New York: Delta, 1980.

———. *Your Three Year Old.* New York: Delta, 1976.

———. *Your Two Year Old.* New York: Delta, 1976.

Anderson, Leith. *Dying for Change.* Minneapolis: Bethany House, 1990.

Benson, Warren S., and Senter, Mark H. *The Complete Book of Youth Ministry.* Chicago: Moody, 1987.

Blanchard, Kenneth, and Johnson, Spencer. *The One Minute Manager.* New York: William Morrow, 1982.

Borthwick, Paul. *Organizing Your Youth Ministry.* Grand Rapids: Zondervan/Youth Specialties, 1988.

Brown, Lowell D. *Sunday School Standards.* Ventura, Calif.: Gospel Light, 1986.

Burns, Jim. *The Youth Builder.* Eugene, Oreg.: Harvest House, 1988.

Burns, Ridge, and Campbell, Pam. *Create in Me a Youth Ministry.* Wheaton, Ill.: Victor, 1986.

Bushnell, Horace. *Christian Nurture.* New Haven, Conn.: Yale U., 1916.

Campbell, Donald K. *Nehemiah: Man in Charge.* Wheaton, Ill.: Victor, 1979.

Campbell, Ross. *How to Really Love Your Teenager.* Wheaton, Ill.: Victor, 1983.

Dayton, Edward R., and Engstrom, Ted W. *Strategy for Leadership.* Old Tappan, N.J.: Revell, 1979.

Dewey, John. *Experience and Education.* New York: Macmillan, 1973.

Dobson, James. *Hide or Seek.* Old Tappan, N.J.: Revell, 1975.

_____. *Dare to Discipline.* Wheaton, Ill.: Tyndale, 1977.

_____. *Love Must Be Tough.* Waco, Tex.: Word, 1983.

_____. *Love for a Lifetime.* Waco, Tex.: Word, 1987.

_____. *Preparing for Adolescence.* New York: Bantam, 1980.

_____. *What Wives Wish Their Husbands Knew About Women.* Wheaton, Ill.: Tyndale, 1975.

Eims, Leroy. *Be the Leader You Were Meant to Be.* Wheaton, Ill.: Victor, 1975.

_____. *Be a Motivational Leader.* Wheaton, Ill.: Victor, 1982.

Elkind, David. *All Grown Up and No Place to Go.* Reading, Mass.: Addison-Wesley, 1984.

_____. *A Sympathetic Understanding of the Child Six to Sixteen.* Boston, Mass.: Allyn and Bacon, 1971.

_____. *Children and Adolescents: Interpretative Essays on Jean Piaget.* New York: Oxford U., 1970.

_____. *The Hurried Child.* Reading, Mass.: Addison-Wesley, 1981.

Engstrom, Ted. W., and Dayton, Edward R. *60-Second Management Guide.* Waco, Tex.: Word, 1984.

Gangel, Kenneth O. *Building Leaders for Church Education.* Chicago: Moody, 1981.

_____. *Church Education Handbook.* Wheaton, Ill.: Victor, 1985.

_____. *Lessons in Leadership from the Bible.* Winona Lake, Ind.: BMH Books, 1980.

Kesler, Jay. *Family Forum.* Wheaton, Ill.: Victor, 1984.

_____. *Parents & Teenagers.* Wheaton, Ill.: Victor, 1985.

Ketterman, Grace H., and Ketterman, Herbert L. *The Complete Book of Baby and Child Care for Christian Parents.* Old Tappan, N.J.: Revell, 1982.

Lefever, Marlene D. *Creative Teaching Methods.* Elgin, Ill.: David C. Cook, 1985.

McDowell, Josh, and Day, Dick. *Why Wait?* San Bernardino, Calif.: Here's Life, 1987.

Myers, Marvin. *Managing the Business Affairs of the Church.* Nashville: Convention, 1981.

Myra, Harold. *Leaders: Learning Leadership from Some of Christianity's Best.* Waco, Tex.: Word, 1987.

Naisbitt, John. *Megatrends.* New York: Warner, 1982.

Piaget, Jean. *Origins of Intelligence.* New York: International Universities, 1964.

_____. *Science of Education and the Psychology of the Child.* New York: Orion, 1970.

_____. *The Moral Judgment of the Child.* Glencoe, Ill.: Free Press, 1948.

_____. *To Understand Is to Invent: The Future of Education.* New York: Grossman, 1973.

_____, and Inhelder, Barbel. *The Psychology of the Child.* New York: Basic, 1969.

Pitcher, Evelyn G., et al. *Helping Young Children Learn.* Columbus, Ohio: Charles E. Merrill, 1966.

Rice, Wayne. *Junior High Ministry.* Grand Rapids: Zondervan, 1978.

Richards, Lawrence O. *A Theology of Children's Ministry.* Grand Rapids: Zondervan, 1983.

_____. *A Theology of Church Leadership.* Grand Rapids: Zondervan, 1980.

_____. *Youth Ministry.* Grand Rapids: Zondervan, 1985.

Schaller, Lyle E. *Activating the Passive Church.* Nashville: Abingdon, 1981.

_____. *Effective Church Planning.* Nashville: Abingdon, 1979.

_____. *The Change Agent.* Nashville: Abingdon, 1972.

_____. *The Decision-Makers.* Nashville: Abingdon, 1972.

_____. *The Multiple Staff and the Larger Church.* Nashville: Abingdon, 1980.

_____. *The Pastor and the People.* Nashville: Abingdon, 1973.

Schaller, Lyle E., and Tidwell, Charles A. *Creative Church Administration.* Nashville: Abingdon, 1975.

Sell, Charles M. *Achieving the Impossible: Intimate Marriage.* Portland, Oreg.: Multnomah, 1982.

_____. *Family Ministry.* Grand Rapids: Zondervan, 1981.

_____. *Unfinished Business.* Portland, Oreg.: Multnomah, 1989.

Small, Dwight H. *After You've Said I Do.* Old Tappan, N.J.: Revell, 1968.

_____. *Design for Christian Marriage.* Old Tappan, N.J.: Revell, 1975.

_____. *The Right to Remarry.* Old Tappan, N.J.: Revell, 1975.

Smalley, Gary, and Trent, John. *Language of Love.* Pomona, Calif.: Focus on the Family, 1988.

Westing, Harold J. *Evaluate and Grow.* Wheaton, Ill.: Victor, 1984.

_____. *Multiple Church Staff Handbook.* Grand Rapids: Kregel, 1985.

White, Burton L. *The First Three Years of Life.* Englewood Cliffs, N.J.: Prentice-Hall, 1975.

Wilhoit, Jim, and Ryken, Leland. *Effective Bible Teaching.* Grand Rapids: Baker, 1988.

Zuck, Roy B. *The Holy Spirit in Your Teaching.* Wheaton, Ill.: Victor, 1984.

Resource List

Christian Education Organizations
State Conferences/Conventions

Alaska

Alaska Christian Education Convention
Assoc.
2440 E. Tudor Rd., Box 150
Anchorage, AK 99507
907-272-8760

Arizona

Greater Arizona Christian Education
Association (GRACE)
P.O. Box 12686
Tucson, AZ 85732-2218
602-297-7283

Leaders in Growing, Helping, Training
(LIGHT)
P.O. Box 51342
Phoenix, AZ 85076-1342

California

Bay Area Sunday School Assoc. (BASS)
Box 2829
Castro Valley, CA 94546
415-537-2041

San Bernardino, Riverside Area SS
Assoc. (BRASS)
1787 Prince Albert Dr.
Riverside, CA 92507
714-683-1009 (evenings)

Central Valley Christian Ed. Conv.
P.O. Box 5730
Fresno, CA 93755
209-226-0541

Church Leadership & Sunday School
Convention of Sacramento (CLASS)
4400 - 58th St.
Sacramento, CA 95820
916-344-7966

Greater Los Angeles S.S. Assoc. (GLASS)
P.O. Box 296
Rosemead, CA 91770-0296
818-288-8720

GRACE (Greater Redding Area Christian
Ed.)
P.O. Box 494794
Redding, CA 96049
916-221-4275

Greater San Jose S.S. Assoc.
P.O. Box 6111
San Jose, CA 95150-6111
408-293-9441

Kern County Sunday School Assoc.
P.O. Box 275
Bakersfield, CA 93309
805-832-5757

San Diego Sunday School Assoc.
  (SANDS)
P.O. Box 1776
Spring Valley, CA 92077
619-670-6657

Youth Specialties Ministries
1224 Greenfield Dr.
El Cajon, CA 92021
619-440-2333

Colorado
Mountain Area Sunday School Assoc.
  (MASS)
P.O. Box 5881
Denver, CO 80217
303-696-6277

Illinois
Central Illinois Sunday School Conv.
4100 War Memorial Dr.
Peoria, IL 61614
309-688-0625

Greater Chicago Sunday School Assoc.
202 Chicago Ave.
Oak Park, IL 60302
708-383-7550

Greater Rockford Area Sunday School
  Assoc.
P.O. Box 4005
Rockford, IL 61110
815-877-5769

Tri-State Sunday School Conference
  (Missouri, Iowa, Illinois)
Lighthouse Ministries
1440 Highland Lane
Quincy, IL 62301
217-222-1440

Indiana
Three Rivers Sunday School Assoc.
Douglas Barealow, Chairman
Summit Christian College
1025 W. Rudisill Blvd.
Ft. Wayne, IN 46807
219-456-2111

Iowa
Iowa State Sunday School Assoc.
First Assembly of God
2725 Merle Hay Rd.
Des Moines, IA 50310
515-279-9766

Kansas
Christian Education Conference
c/o Bible Supply & Gift Co.
Mark Holmgren
1020 Kansas Ave.
Topeka, KS 66612
913-233-4219

Kansas Leadership & Sunday School
  Assoc.
P.O. Box 9184
Wichita, KS 67277-0184
316-943-1800

Mid-America Church Leadership Conf.
c/o Manhattan Christian College
Kenneth Cable
1415 Anderson Ave.
Manhattan, KS 66502
913-539-3571

Kentucky
Good News
308 E. Main St.
Wilmore, KY 40390
606-858-4661

Maine
Maine Assoc. of Christian Educators
  (MACE)
P.O. Box 154
Palermo, ME 04354
207-993-2357

Maryland
Baltimore Area Sunday School Assoc.
P.O. Box 24008
Baltimore, MD 21227
301-789-1438

Greater Washington Christian Education Association
2130 E. Randolph Rd.
Silver Springs, MD 20904
301-431-4141

Massachusetts
Evangelistic Assoc. of New England
279 Cambridge St.
Burlington, MA 01803
617-229-1990

New England Association for Christian
  Education
279 Cambridge St.
Burlington, MA 01803
617-229-1990

Michigan
International Christian Education
  Assoc.
13165 Cloverdale, Suite #1
Oak Park, MI 48237
313-399-6500

Midwest Christian Sunday School
  Assoc.
Marvin Bolt, Exec. Sec.
3222 Johnson Ct.
Grandville, MI 49418
616-531-4713

Minnesota
Minnesota Sunday School Assoc.
Timothy Johnson, Pres.
3745 - 26th Ave. S.
Minneapolis, MN 55406
612-729-4384

Nebraska
Central Nebraska Sunday School Assoc.
c/o Rev. Paul Harkness, Chairman
Box 275
Firth, NE 68358
402-791-5112 evenings
402-791-5598 days

New Jersey
Northern New Jersey Sunday School
  Assoc.
Mr. Ken Sewall, Pres.
44 Lakewood Terr.
Bloomfield, NJ 07003-3722
201-743-0650

New York
Greater New York Sunday School Assoc.
Paul Lenz
3015 Morgan Dr.
Wantagh, NY 11793
516-221-0231

New York State Sunday School Assoc.
P.O. Box 1848
Buffalo, NY 14231-1848
716-631-3221

North Carolina
Mid-Atlantic Sunday School Assoc.
(North and South Carolina, Virginia,
Tennessee, and Georgia)
P.O. Box 29045
Charlotte, NC 28229-9045
800-532-6221 (Elizabeth Burchett)

North Dakota
North Dakota State Sunday School
Assoc.
P.O. Box 1093
Minot, ND 58701
701-839-1544

Ohio
Central Ohio Christian Ed. Confer.
Heritage Christian Books & Supply
173 Cline Ave.
Mansfield, OH 44907
419-526-3166

North American Christian Convention
Box 39456
Cincinnati, OH 45239
513-385-2470

Ohio Christian Education Assoc.
2130 31st St. NW
Canton, OH 44709
216-492-9162; 492-6333

Oklahoma
Northeast Oklahoma Christian Ed.
Assoc.
13426 S. 123 E. Pl.
Broken Arrow, OK 74011
918-252-3166; 455-2476

Oklahoma Christian Ed. Assoc. (OCEA)
Box 457
Bethany, OK 73008

Oregon
Greater Salem Assoc. of Christian Edu-
cators
P.O. Box 7354
Salem, OR 97301
503-581-2129

Pennsylvania
Delaware Valley Christian Ed. Conv.
c/o Philadelphia College of Bible
200 Manor Ave.
Langhorne, PA 19047-2992
215-752-5800, ext. 286

Central Pennsylvania Christian Ed.
Conf.
901 Eden Rd.
Lancaster, PA 17601
717-569-7071

Pennsylvania State S.S. Assoc.
5915 Fox St.
Harrisburg, PA 17112
717-752-1930

Greater Philadelphia Area S.S. Assoc.
P.O. Box 28882
Philadelphia, PA 19151
215-748-8568 (church number)

South Dakota
South Dakota Sunday School Assoc.
Crossroads Book & Music Store
Darrel Modica
3817 S. Western
Sioux Falls, SD 57105
605-338-5951

Texas
Texas State Sunday School Conv.
P.O. Box 153767
Irving, TX 75015
817-481-4949

Utah
Intermountain Christian Ed. Assoc.
P.O. Box 57714
Salt Lake City, UT 84157
801-328-0768

Washington
Christian Growth Conference
Greater Yakima Assoc. of Evangelicals
P.O. Box 989
Yakima, WA 98907

Spokane Christian Workers Conf.
Daryl Bursch, Chairman
3527 E. Sprague
Spokane, WA 99202
509-534-8575

Greater Tacoma Christian Ed. Conf.
P.O. Box 110548
Tacoma, WA 98411-0548
206-564-6118; 352-9044

Wisconsin
Wisconsin Sunday School Assoc.
For information, contact:
Evangel Ministries, Inc.
Attn: Diane Bishop
1909 W. Second St.
Appleton, WI 54914
414-749-9456

Source: National Christian Education Association (a commission of the National Association of Evangelicals), May 1990 edition.

Telephone Hotlines (1-800) for Assistance

Abuse of People
Abuse Hotline   800-252-5400
(Report abuse of children, elderly, or handicapped)
Alcohol
Abuse Hotline   800-444-9999
(For counsel and treatment center)
Cigarettes
Smokenders   800-828-4357
Crisis Hotlines
Abuse Hotline   800-252-54000
(Report abuse of children, elderly, or the handicapped, either physical or emotional)
Alcohol Abuse Hotline and
Treatment Center   800-444-9999
Child Find Hotline   800-426-5678
(Locating missing children)
Cocaine Hotline   800-COCAINE

National Institute on Drug Abuse
(Info. & referral)   800-662-4357
Parents Anonymous 800-421-0353
Disease
American Cancer Society
800-ACS-2354
Why Me? (Breast cancer)
800-221-2141
Endometriosis Association
800-992-3636
Food
Eating Disorders Program
800-792-8713
Landlord-Tenant Relations
Women's Legal Hotline (Counseling, referrals)   800-777-3247
Suicide
Suicide Prevention Helpline
800-333-4444

Appendix A

Sample Job Descriptions

The eight job descriptions show the diversity of positions and duties for full-time Christian education specialists. The descriptions are provided by CESs from a variety of denominations and sizes of educational programs.

JOB DESCRIPTION #1
PASTOR OF CHRISTIAN EDUCATION

Job Summary

Supervise and give daily direction to the educational ministry of the church. The mission of the pastor of Christian education is to see to it that the philosophy of ministry is carried out in each educational ministry of the church. His goal will thus be to assist every Christian in achieving his maximum growth as a disciple of Jesus Christ. He will also assist the senior pastor by relieving him of administrative responsibilities relative to the educational ministry of the church. Accomplishing this will require the performance of the following job duties.

(All objectives are "recurring, long-term objectives" unless otherwise noted as "short-term objectives" by the letters "ST".)

Job Duties

1. *Teacher Training*

Develop and maintain a recurring program of teacher training for the Sunday school and children's church. Institute a systematic apprenticeship of new teachers so that they have on-the-job training prior to assuming Sunday school teaching responsibilities.

   a. Assess training needs for the teaching staff in each of the age group ministries.
   b. Develop a basic orientation training curriculum for each staff member. (ST)
   c. Develop a rotating two-year teacher training curriculum for use in department staff meetings. (ST)
   d. Plan for quarterly teaching staff meetings.
   e. Chair quarterly teaching staff meetings.
   f. Meet with preschool, elementary, and adult teaching staff member's departments quarterly.
   g. Implement an ongoing plan to express appreciation to all teaching staff members.

2. *Teacher Selection*

Assume responsibility for the selection of all teachers for the Sunday school and children's church at the following levels: preschool, elementary, and adult. This requires establishing standards teachers must meet in order to become part of our Christian education team.

   a. Devise a requirement standards policy which will need to be met by every potential teaching staff member. (ST)
   b. Brief each age group ministry coordinator regarding these standards and monitor their utilization of these standards in the selection of potential teaching staff members.
   c. Devise a policy which would need to be invoked in the case of a teaching staff member who might no longer meet the required standards. (ST)

  d. Determine what type of adult Sunday school classes should be formed and their number.

3. *Teacher Recruitment*

Assume responsibility for the recruitment of Sunday school and children's church teachers. This necessitates approaching prospective teachers far enough in advance that the Sunday school and children's church leaders and the teacher may plan their schedules to the best advantage. Long term (one year or longer) commitments are to be obtained wherever possible to insure positive teacher-student relationships.

  a. Develop a recruitment philosophy.
  b. Serve as the recruitment monitor to avoid cross recruiting by various ministries.
  c. Assemble a recruitment team for all Sunday morning ministries.
  d. Request a four quarter commitment from each teaching staff member, but secure at least a two consecutive quarter commitment.
  e. Publicize needs for teaching staff positions to the general congregation.

4. *Regular Teaching Ministry*

Maintain a regular teaching ministry for the benefit of the church as a whole. This would include teaching an adult class on Sunday mornings, occasional preaching on Sunday nights, and oversight teaching with the Women's Discipling Group.

  a. Develop curriculum necessary for the needs of the particular learner group.
  b. Prepare lessons for the learning experience.
  c. Perform pastoral duties for these learners.

5. *Vacation Bible School*

Act as director of the annual vacation Bible school. Recruit, train, and supervise all teachers, teacher's assistants, crafts leaders, and recreation leaders. Select curriculum and meet with department supervisors to plan vacation Bible school.

a. Select VBS curriculum each year.

b. Order VBS curriculum each year.

c. Select a VBS assistant director each year.

d. Recruit coordinators in the areas of preschool, elementary, crafts, recreation, music, and refreshments.

e. Plan with each coordinator regarding the specifics of their ministries.

f. Train the teaching staff with the specifics necessary for their particular ministries.

g. Set up the facilities for the VBS week and re-set for the following Sunday morning.

h. Supervise each day's activities.

i. Express appreciation to all VBS workers.

6. *Christian Education Team*

Develop a Christian education team composed of department coordinators, key teachers, the vacation Bible school assistant director, and other pivotal leaders, to meet quarterly to review progress in all areas of Christian education. Brief the Board of Elders via memo and/or in person on the results of these evaluations.

a. Meet with preschool, elementary, and adult age group coordinators on a monthly basis to evaluate the current status of the Sunday morning ministry.

b. Contact by telephone the various coordinators during the week and at other crucial junctures regarding particulars of their ministries.

7. *Evangelism*

The pastor of Christian education will see to it that teachers are equipped to share the good news of Jesus Christ with students in various educational ministries of the church.

a. Incorporate into the teacher training program a course on the evangelism of children.

b. Provide for the teachers, at the church's cost, children's evangelism material.

c. See that each child in children's church is presented with the gospel twice a year.

d. See that each child in VBS is presented with the gospel each year.

8. *Library/Media Center*

Develop the church library/media center to its full potential. Initiate and implement a system of publicizing and making available high quality Christian literature and teaching aids which will augment the educational ministries of the church.

    a. Enlist library ministry coordinators who will carry out the ongoing maintenance of the library ministry.

    b. Provide counsel to the library staff regarding their ministry.

    c. Provide encouragement to the library staff regarding their ministry.

    d. Work with the library staff in the securing of literature for the library.

    e. Keep abreast with current books to be incorporated into the library.

    f. Personally review, as many as possible, prospective books and tapes to be entered into the library.

    g. Develop a Christian Education Resource Center for use by the teaching staff.

    h. Continue to supply the CERC with teacher's reference material.

    i. Monitor the suppy needs for the CERC.

    j. Continue to supply the CERC with teaching supplies, at the church's expense, to be used by the teaching staff for the ministry.

9. *Curriculum Supervision*

Choose and supervise the curriculum used in the Sunday school and children's church. This requires a continuing familiarity with every major line of Sunday school and children's church curriculum: Gospel Light, David C. Cook, Scripture Press, and others.

    a. Discuss with other Christian education colleagues and teachers what curriculm resources are best suited for the church's needs.

    b. Keep abreast with current curriculum changes and resources available through magazines, catalogs, and journals.

c. Continue to evaluate our current curriculum to determine whether any changes need to be made.

d. Approve all adult curriculum that might be taught.

10. *Departmentalization*

Develop a departmental system of administration for the Sunday school with a minimum of four levels: nursery, preschool, elementary, and adult departments. Add departments as necessary as the Sunday school expands. Recruit, train, and meet regularly with department superintendents to assure quality control of all teaching and activities.

a. Select coordinators for the above categories.

b. Meet with the above coordinators periodically for communication purposes and assist them in any direction needed.

c. Establish a written ministry description for each coordinator, complete with an explanation of necessary ministry tasks to be carried out. (ST)

11. *Church Retreat Children's Program*

Assume the overall administration of the children's program for the church retreat.

a. Develop the program.

b. Write lesson plans for the college staff.

c. Determine the number of staff needed.

d. Assemble all supplies necessary.

e. Orient the staff.

f. Supervise the program for the weekend.

12. *Discipleship Training*

Develop and expand discipleship training at various levels within the church family. This includes responsibility for existing programs (Women's Discipling Groups, ladies' Bible study, etc.) and prospective new programs (Navigators 2:7, Masterlife, or others).

a. Select coordinators for the various discipleship ministries.

b. Select curriculum for the various discipleship ministries.

c. Meet with various coordinators to plan for their ministries.

d. Train any leaders within the ministries regarding their leadership.

e. Lead the various ministries at certain times, such as WDG or LBS.

f. Supervise the activities as they are in process.

g. Meet with the ministry coordinators to evaluate their programs so that changes can be implemented to strengthen each ministry for the future.

h. Develop a men's discipleship ministry.

i. Develop a children's discipleship ministry.

j. Develop a wholistic approach to family ministry at the church, and implement it.

13. *Curriculum Integration*

Over time, develop the curriculum of the Christian education program so that it is consistent throughout. Have children's church materials and (to the extent practicable) the worship service reinforce Sunday school.

a. Determine how feasible a plan would be to use the same children's church curriculum publishers' material along with their Sunday school material. (ST)

b. Determine whether a plan could be utilized regarding development of worship service message and any children's material.

14. *Standards and Direction*

The pastor of Christian education will establish overall direction and set standards for the Sunday school, using as a guide the ICL Leadership Resource, *Sunday School Standards,* by Lowell Brown. Periodic reports on progress will be made to the Board of Elders and will be made part of the Annual Report.

a. Facilities standards must be evaluated.

b. Staffing standards must be evaluated.

c. Procedural standards must be evaluated.

d. Sunday morning coordinators must be made aware of the standards so that they can assist in the evaluation process.

e. Maintain accurate attendance records of all Sunday morning ministry groups.

   f. Make progress reports to the Christian Education Council on a periodic basis.

15. *Communication*

Keep the leadership and congregation informed of special events which have bearing on the Christian education program of the church (e.g., Navigators' Conferences, Family Life Conference, etc.). Integrate these into the church's Christian education program to the extent compatible with our goals and doctrinal position.

   a. Maintain a Christian education bulletin board.

   b. Post flyers on the Christian education bulletin boards.

   c. Keep the Christian education bulletin boards current.

   d. Place information in the bulletin.

   e. Ask the pastoral staff to announce these events within their areas of ministry.

   f. Ask the Sunday school staff to announce these events to their classes.

16. *Christian Education Facilities*

Inform the Board of Elders of future needs of the church Christian education program so that the building will not be prematurely obsolescent.

   a. Evaluate current educational facilities needs.

   b. Evaluate potential future educational facilities needs.

   c. Make recommendations to the Board of Elders which measure up with *Sunday School Standards,* by Lowell Brown.

17. *Miscellaneous Christian Education Duties*

JOB DESCRIPTION #2
PASTOR OF EDUCATION MINISTRIES

Responsibilities

1. *To the Congregation:*
   a. He shall bring an awareness of its educational ministries from a biblical basis and spell out its aims.
   b. He shall encourage, counsel, and instruct lay workers in all phases of educational ministries of the church through such services as visitation, observation, personal conferences, workers' conferences, and the provision of leadership classes.
   c. He shall develop and plan for the discovery, enlisting, and training of other leaders for the total education ministries of the church in cooperation with other staff and ministry areas, keeping as a primary goal the development of the spiritual gifts of the members of the congregation.
   d. He shall see that programs are developed for age designated groups, including adults, students, and children, and for special groups, including but not limited to singles, seniors, men, women, single parents, etc.
   e. He shall coordinate and act as liaison with other organizations whose primary function is within education ministries, including but not limited to preschool and church Bible studies.

2. *To the Elders:*
   a. With the assistance and counsel of the Education Ministries Elders and committees, he shall:
      (1) Lead the development of and supervise balanced education ministries in the church.
      (2) Provide for an ongoing evaluation of the education ministries programs.
      (3) Evaluate and see to proper approval of curriculum taught in the various education ministries of the church.
      (4) Coordinate and unify the education ministries of the

church.

(5) See that decisions are interpreted to the appropriate people and that programs are carried through effectively.

(6) Develop, train, evaluate, and coordinate a corps of teachers and helpers.

(7) Develop, maintain, equip, and staff church libraries.

(8) Submit an annual budget for education ministries.

b. Participate in special councils, task forces, and committees at the request of the elders.

3. *To the Staff:*

a. He shall share with other members of the pastoral staff general pastoral duties as delegated by the senior pastor.

b. He shall supervise other staff assigned to education ministries.

c. He shall suggest needs of building, equipment, methods, and materials.

4. *General:*

a. He shall cooperate with denomination education ministries and shall be encouraged to participate in the denominational educational ministries with first priority to the local body.

b. He shall be responsible for keeping himself and staff supervised, current with trends and developments in his area(s) of ministry, and will be given the opportunity to further his training, education, and personal career development.

JOB DESCRIPTION #3
DIRECTOR OF CHRISTIAN EDUCATION

1. *Supervision of Total Christian Education Program*

   Serves as chairman of Christian education committee, meeting monthly with it for planning and developing the Christian education program of the church.

2. *Supervision of All Departments of the Sunday School*
   a. Recruits and maintains total Sunday school staff.
   b. Arranges for substitute staff as needed.
   c. Conducts quarterly teacher training sessions.
   d. Observes and evaluates classroom teachers.
   e. Assigns classrooms.
   f. Plans for and purchases classroom equipment.
   g. Purchases classroom materials and supplies.
   h. Supervises special events and emphases such as:
      (1) Children's Day
      (2) Children's Christmas Party
      (3) MARCH to Sunday School
      (4) Christian Education Month
         —Rally Day
         —Teacher appreciation banquet
         —Open house
         —Book Fair

3. *Library Organization and Maintenance*
   a. Purchases materials.
   b. Supervises processing of materials.
   c. Promotes library.
   d. Supervises tape ministry
      (1) Oversees ordering and duplication of tapes.
      (2) Oversees organization of sound room as related to tape ministry.

4. *Organization of Vacation Bible School*
   a. Recruits VBS coordinators.
   b. Develops and oversees program with coordinators:

(1) Selection and purchase of curriculum and supplies.
(2) Recruitment of staff.
(3) Coordination of crafts.
(4) Scheduling of classes.
(5) Registration of students.
   c. Trains VBS staff.

5. *Organization and Supervision of Nursery Ministry*
   a. Recruits nursery coordinators.
   b. Selects materials for teaching.
   c. Oversees purchase of equipment and supplies.
   d. Trains leaders and teachers.
   e. Oversees continuation of cradle roll ministry.

6. *Organization and Supervision of Junior Church*
   a. Selects curriculum.
   b. Recruits leaders.
   c. Trains leaders.

7. *David's School of Christian Growth*
   a. Plans and schedules classes for fall and winter semesters.
   b. Teaches a class.
   c. Publicizes program through newspaper advertisng and bulk mailings.

8. *Advisory Capacity to Women's Ministry*
   a. Meets with officers.
   b. Serves as liaison between consistory and women's ministry.

9. *Sunday Evening Youth Ministry (Children)*
   a. Selects curriculum.
   b. Recruits leaders.
   c. Trains leaders.

10. *Supervision of Secretarial Staff*
   a. Coordinates work load between administration and secretarial staff in absence of pastor-teacher.
   b. Serves as liaison between consistory and secretarial staff.
   c. Serves as supervisor of secretarial staff.

d. Conducts job evaluations of secretarial staff.
e. Approves arrangements for time off from work.
f. Approves arrangements for volunteer help.
g. Answers phone in secretary's absence.
h. Arranges for office work to be conducted in secretary's absence.

11. *Other Responsibilities*
    a. Writes midweek and bulletin items pertaining to areas of Christian education.
    b. Meets with staff weekly to plan and develop program.
    c. Plans the annual calendar along with staff.
    d. Organizes and develops special programs and seminars:
       (1) College fair
       (2) Saturday seminars
    e. Serves as senior pastor's administrative assistant.

JOB DESCRIPTION #4
MINISTER OF EDUCATION AND DISCIPLESHIP

Responsible to: The senior pastor and the Staff Parish Relations Committee

The Minister of Education and Discipleship shall be responsible for the following areas and receive the following benefits:

Education

The Minister of Education shall work in conjunction with the Education Committee in carrying out the ministries of the church. The primary responsibilities for this work area include:

1. *Sunday School*
   The recruitment of teachers, selection of curriculum, management of the Sunday school department, development of new Sunday school classes, assessing the needs of the Sunday school classes, recruitment and contacting substitute teachers as necessary, coordinate intergenerational ministries (i.e. nursery, preschool, children,

youth, and adults), and equipping teachers for their ministry of teaching.

2. *Preschool*

Assess the need for development of a preschool through the following means: projection of date to begin (if and when depending on assessment), promotion of fund-raising for the opening, survey to the congregation, and serve as a liaison between the congregation and the preschool committee.

3. *Resource Center*

Supervise the cataloging of existing books and audio/visual resources into a library system (Dewey decimal) functional for use by the church, selection of new books, media, and equipment for the center, purchase and manage supplies for classroom instruction.

4. *Vacation Bible School*

Recruit co-directors, assist in the recruitment of teaching staff and support staff (kitchen, recreation, refreshments), provide recommendations for curriculum, supervise registration, supervise the entire VBS program, enhance the child's physical, social, intellectual, and spiritual developments, with an emphasis on the spiritual development.

5. *Parent's Day Out*

Serve as a support to the director of the PDO program and a liaison between the PDO program and the congregation, assist in problem solving and decision making, supervise the entire PDO program, meet with the PDO board of directors.

6. *Singles' Ministries*

Serve as a support of existing singles' ministries, develop and implement future singles' ministries programs, develop leadership within the singles' program, resource small groups and Sunday school classes as needed, plan and implement special retreats, camps, and other ministries for singles.

Evangelism and Discipleship

The Minister of Education and Discipleship shall work in conjunction with the Evangelism and Discipleship Committee in carrying out the ministries of the church. The primary areas of responsibility are as follows:

1. *Visitation of Prospective Members*

Recruit and train visitation team, assist in the training of the team, manage and organize the team's efforts, call each first-time visitor the week following his initial visit, or arrange a call from a group within the church (i.e., a Sunday school class, small group, etc.), answer any questions that visitors may have.

2. *Visitation of New Members*

Assist in the recruitment of members for the assimilation team, update the questionnaire as needed, implement the gifts and talents of new members.

3. *Visitation of Inactive Members*

Plan and implement a lay visitation team to minister to and care for inactive members, assist other staff members in the recruitment and training of follow-up for members who have not attended worship for 4 consecutive Sundays, assess the needs of the inactive members and evaluate how those needs can be met effectively through existing ministries and in the planning of future ministries of the church.

4. *Prayer Chains*

Recruit persons interested in being on the prayer chain to pray for the needs of the congregation each week, develop and annually revise prayer cards that are distributed throughout the congregation to pray for the church's needs and ministries.

5. *Time and Talent Commitments*

Annually re-administer and update the time and talent commitments for the congregation, allowing each member to actively exercise his gifts and talents within this body.

6. *GRACE Groups/LEAD Programs*

Recruit, train, resource, and encourage persons interested in leading a grace group to be trained through the LEAD program (L—

laity, E—education, A—and, D—development), update the list of available grace groups (their leaders, focus, meeting times, new groups, and members), making this information available to the congregation.

JOB DESCRIPTION #5
EDUCATION DIRECTOR

General Responsibilities

1. To assist the elders and pulpit minister in developing the desired Bible school class structure for the Sunday A.M. and Wednesday P.M. class periods in the areas of subject matter, age and sex, or other special purpose classification of classes.
2. To assist with, advise, and/or develop curriculum for each established class, including respective time frames for each, and to develop written objectives for each class.
3. Select departmental supervisors from among those approved to teach. Develop and set forth in writing the responsibilities of each supervisor, and communicate those responsibilites.
4. Select, from among those approved to teach, teachers qualified for respective classes, including assistant teachers. Constantly solicit prospective teachers that will meet our established qualifications for Bible teachers, and otherwise assist prospective teachers to qualify.
5. Develop, organize, and direct teacher training programs and seminars as the elders shall judge necessary from time to time.
6. Promote our Bible school, the virtues of and honor due our teachers, publicly from the pulpit, through the *Bulletin,* and on special occasions.
7. Teach regular and/or special classes from time to time as he or the elders may consider necessary.
8. Preach on occasions in absence of pulpit minister.
9. Promote and organize annual teachers' appreciation banquet, including obtaining special speakers therefore.
10. Investigate, review, test, and procure various items of visual

aids and/or equipment that may make teaching programs more effective.

11. Review, screen, select, and procure various items of literature for teaching aids.

12. Assist in the development and maintenance of a record-keeping system for each class.

13. Participate in personal and mission evangelism efforts as conscience dictates and time permits.

14. Supervise the operation of the church library, including supervision of the librarians.

JOB DESCRIPTION #6
MINISTER OF CHRISTIAN EDUCATION

Job Summary

The Minister of Christian Education shall have the responsibility for the children, youth, and adult programs of the church, to develop educational programs through people that will touch lives for Christ in evangelism and contribute to the growth of lives through discipleship. The Minister of Christian Education will be a member of the church staff, selected by the pastor in cooperation with the Church Board and called by the congregation for a nonspecific period of time, and be in agreement with the doctrinal statements of the church and be willing to abide by the constitution and bylaws.

Salary and other benefits will be commensurate with other staff members. This will be reviewed and recommended by the general board and voted upon each year by the congregation at the annual church business meeting. Vacation periods, insurance coverage, retirement, and other benefits will be indicated in the Church's Administrative Policy.

Job Responsibilities

1. *Administration*

a. Aid the Christian education committee and the church staff in determining philosophy, goals, policies, and programs for the total Christian education program.

b. Administer the children and adult education programs and the youth program, being responsible to organize, supervise, and coordinate the programs for these groups.

c. Administer the policies of the Christian education committee and assist in advising program leaders.

d. Plan with the Christian education committee and lead in the establishment of programs and projects.

e. Develop conferences and other means for family life education with the program committee of that conference or specific ministry.

f. Administer the maintenance of a filing system in Christian education personnel, programs, materials, and equipment.

g. Periodically oversee the review of the use of the church library (books, audiovisuals, maps, teaching aids, etc.) in cooperation with the library committee and the Christian education committee.

2. *Coordination*

a. Coordinate and give direction and purpose to the year-round program of education.

b. Supervise the youth director and coordinate the youth program.

c. Coordinate the year-round education ministry with the church calendar.

d. Oversee the camping program of the church for children, youth, and adults.

e. Cooperate with the missions committee in planning the missions emphasis throughout the educational programs of the church.

3. *Training and Leadership*

a. See that an effective leadership training program is maintained in keeping with the assessed needs of the church.

b. Supervise any activities considered essential to the development of present and prospective workers.

c. Select and give guidance and training to workers and teachers in the children, youth, and adult departments.

4. *Evaluation*

a. Evaluate the total program and recommend changes so that a unified, progressive, biblical program of outreach, spiritual growth, training, and service may be accomplished for all ages.

b. Study the church program, resources, building facilities, and equipment, formulating plans and recommendations for improvements.

c. Observe the work of teachers, leaders, and sponsors, in order to evaluate the total program.

Organization Relationship

1. *To the Pastor*

a. Be responsible to and work under the direct supervision of the senior pastor.

b. Consult with the pastor on all major plans and policies related to the Christian education ministry.

2. *To the Church Staff*

a. Attend meetings and conferences of the staff as scheduled.

b. Work in close cooperation with other church staff, the youth director, and all Christian education personnel.

c. Supervise and coordinate all activities of the youth director.

3. *To the Christian Education Committee*

a. Be the administrator of the committee and responsible to carry out its policies.

b. Work closely with the chairman, giving direction and input for committee action.

c. Act as a liaison between program leaders and the committee.

d. Give guidance and leadership to the committee as a resource person.

    e. Give direction to the committee and guide them in selection of teaching materials and curriculum for the children, youth, and adult programs.

    f. Attend all meetings and report monthly on activities for the previous month and review plans and schedules for the coming month.

4. *To the General Board*

    a. Be an ex-officio member of the general board and all church committees.

Qualifications

    a. A born-again believer, in accord with the church's constitution.

    b. Spiritually mature, maintaining personal Bible study and prayer.

    c. A pastoral heart with a burden for local church ministries.

    d. Gifts and abilities in the area of Christian education and youth; preferably a seminary graduate.

    e. Ability to work with people.

    f. Supports the total church program of stewardship, worship, missions, fellowship, and education.

Training and Development

    a. Be concerned with self-improvement in order to continue to improve the quality of his/her work, and seek educational opportunities when possible.

    b. Attend conferences and conventions as recommended by the pastor and Christian education committee and approved by the church board. These must be coordinated with the senior pastor.

JOB DESCRIPTION #7
PASTOR OF LAY MINISTRIES

Purpose

To advance the ministry of Christ's kingdom by effectively managing, as a servant leader, the vital ministries of lay involvement, adult, and single adults of the church. In accomplishing this purpose the pastor will conform to biblical principles and will maintain the highest ethical and professional standards in relating to members of the church family and community.

Scope

To give overall leadership to the ministries of lay involvement, adult, and single adults in and through the staff and members of the church.

Duties, Responsibilities, Authorities

1. *Planning*
   a. To be sensitive to God's leading through prayer, godly counsel, and the guidance of Scripture in the development and implementation of a planning system and plans for the lay adult ministries of the church.
   b. To assist the executive pastor of nurture in the development of long-range plans (3-5 year) through working with the lay involvement, adult, and single adults.
   c. To ensure that annual operation plans (1-2 years) and budget for the lay involvement, adult, and single adults committees will lead to the achievement of the established ministry objectives.
   d. To assist the executive pastor of nurture in the preparation of the annual vision statement, which will be presented to the board of nurture in March of each year.
   e. To keep abreast of current trends and information related to his area of ministry.

2. *Organizing*

a. To provide a staffing structure that efficiently achieves ministry objectives and creates an environment in which each staff member can grow to his fullest potential.

b. To direct the development of a lay adult ministry that will help the Body to care for one another.

c. To ensure that all pastoral team members, staff members, and committees under his area of responsibility understand, accept, and perform their responsibilities within the authority they have been given.

d. To assume responsibility for the hiring and dismissing of all personnel under his supervision in consultation with the executive pastor of nurture and appropriate committee.

e. To oversee the small group ministry of the church, including the equipping of small group leaders.

3. *Leading*

a. To maintain a formal system of communication that ensures that each individual has a thorough understanding of the philosophy of ministry including the three priorities and the "seven guidelines of spiritual maturity," history, character, and vision statement of the church and is able to relate that understanding to his or her personal ministry responsibilities.

b. To ensure that laity possessing appropriate skills and spiritual gifts are identified, equipped, given opportunity for exercise of their skills and gifts, strengthened, and retained.

c. To give leadership to the adult classes in equipping the laity for specific ministries that are needed in order for the classes to nurture, shepherd, and care for each other.

d. To give leadership to the total body in equipping laity for specific ministries which will function both within the church family and out in the community and world.

4. *Managing*

a. To meet regularly with staff reporting directly to him; to at least quarterly appraise the performance of these staff members (appraisal will include discussion of each individual's personal, spiritual, and professional development).

b. To provide the executive pastor of nurture on a regular basis with written reports that accurately reflect the status of all key ministry areas against established budget and ministry objectives.

c. To identify needed changes in established committee/departmental strategies that allow the church to take advantage of new opportunities for growth or increase ministry effectiveness.

d. To be responsible for the management of a lay involvement, adult, and single adults ministry.

e. To assist in the recruiting, equipping, and deploying of pastor-teachers for adult classes within the church and to coordinate their ministry in cooperation with the adult committee and Sunday school classes.

f. To assist the executive committees of the adult classes in coordinating class activities and ministries in a manner which is faithful to the objectives and ministries of the total body of the church.

g. To coordinate various equipping seminars and/or training programs designed to equip our people for special ministries.

5. *Operating*

a. To provide direct, day-to-day leadership to the departments under his supervision.

b. To hold regular meetings with those reporting to him for the purpose of planning, coordinating, problem solving, decision making, and performance evaluation—organizational and personal.

c. To contribute to the strengthening and edifying of other ministry groups within the church by providing appropriate communication and coordination.

d. To work closely with the senior pastor in forming a ministry team of the pastor-teachers.

JOB DESCRIPTION #8
DIRECTOR OF CHURCH MINISTRIES

1. *The Person*
    a. Should enjoy a vital, personal relationship with Christ and be a growing Christian, whose life is exemplary as a spiritual leader. (His spouse should share this relationship.)
    b. Should identify with Christ and the local church in membership, the fulfillment of the Great Commission, and in the doctrinal commitments of the church. Similar support is expected of the spouse.
    c. Should have appropriate formal training from an accredited theological seminary or educational institution deemed appropriate for practical experience in the field of Christian education, youth ministry, and home visitation.
    d. Should believe in a multiple *staff team ministry* in which employed and/or volunteer staff persons are mutually concerned for the overall ministry of the church within the Body, in the community, and in the world.
    e. Should cooperate with the churches with which the church is affiliated, and with its other commitments to local organizations.
    f. Should cultivate and develop relationships with the staff and congregation that will be marked by a spirit of unity, cooperation, and understanding.

2. *Principal Functions*
    a. The director will provide leadership in developing, implementing, overseeing, and evaluating a comprehensive ministry of *Christian education.* This will consist of the following duties:
    (1) Assist in organizing, recruiting, planning, training, and promoting a growing church school ministry.

(2) Weekday children's club program

(3) Annual summer ministry (vacation Bible school, day camps, etc.)

(4) Youth camps

b. The director will use approximately 30 percent of the week to give leadership in developing, implementing, overseeing, and evaluating the ministry with young persons:

(1) High school youth (Omegans)

(2) Junior highs

(3) Proposed college and career youth (singles)

The director and the senior pastor will arrange for their high visibility and involvement in youth ministry.

c. The director will, under the direction of the senior pastor, be involved in home visitation and personal evangelism, primarily as it relates to the aforementioned work responsibilities, and will participate in the busing ministry.

d. The director will participate in team planning to develop the larger ministry of the church with both the church staff and church boards and committees.

e. The director will participate in growth groups, discovery groups, and/or home Bible study groups where appropriate.

f. The director will participate in and assist in the organizing, recruiting, planning, and training of volunteer staff (and/or paid persons) for preschool, primary church, and child care during regular worship services.

g. The director will, in consultation with the senior pastor, supervisory boards, and committees of the congregation, perform additional functions as may be deemed temporarily essential.

3. *Organizational and Administrative Relationships*

a. *Senior Pastor.* The director will receive guidance from and be primarily accountable to the senior pastor.

b. *Church Secretary.* The director will give direction to the work of the church secretary in the absence of the senior pastor, and as it relates to his areas of responsibilities.

c. *Church Board and Congregation.* The director will give monthly and quarterly reports, and counsel to the boards and congregation as pertain to his primary responsibilities.

d. *Board of Christian Education.* The director will be an ex-officio member of the church board and be responsible for guiding, developing, implementing, overseeing, and evaluating the ministry of Christian education. Assignments of additional responsibilities by the Board may be made in consultation with the senior pastor. The director will encourage, support, train, and cooperate with the various staffs and leaders within the area of Christian education ministry.

e. *Deacon Board.* The director will attend the meetings of the deacon board and be prepared to report to them at their request. The deacon board will have the responsibility of determining the salary and other compensation. He will, with the senior pastor, seek to expedite all policies and programs approved by this board.

4. *General Considerations*

a. Salary, allowances, and other compensation will be commensurate with churches of comparable size and will be negotiated with the director prior to acceptance of employment, considering the education and experience of the applicant.

b. Assistance to make arrangements for housing will be provided.

c. Weekdays off will be determined in consultation with the senior pastor. The director shall keep regular office hours to be determined in consultation with the senior pastor.

d. A three-week annual vacation will be granted, the time to be determined in consultation with the senior pastor.

e. Expenses to permit attendance at approved conferences, seminars, and/or continuing education events will be provided at the discretion of the deacon board.

f. The following holidays will be allowed:
(1) New Year's Day

(2) Good Friday afternoon

(3) Memorial Day

(4) Fourth of July

(5) Labor Day

(6) Veteran's Day

(7) Thanksgiving Day

(8) Afternoons of December 24th and 31st

(9) Christmas Day (When New Year's Day and Christmas fall on Sunday, the holiday will be on Monday.)

g. Participation in community affairs is not discouraged but shall not be given precedence over the work at the church. The senior pastor should be made aware of such activities.

h. Participation in funerals and weddings will be only in response to a special request or need.

i. Participation in worship services or other public services shall be determined at the discretion of the senior pastor and the board of deacons.

j. Reimbursement will be provided for youth activities.

Appendix B

A Schedule Planner for the CES

by Gary Prehn
Northview Bible Church
Spokane, Washington

The duties of most C.E. specialists can easily form a long list of monthly "Things to Do." It's wearisome to try to work through the whole list. Too often items are forgotten or left undone, or the month passes without completing what we want to do.

To lessen the problem, I've taken my month's list of things to do and divided it over four weeks. Then I further divided each week's list by spreading activities over five or six days. Now I have a manageable list of one or two things to be done each day.

There are two benefits to this method. Tasks are spread over an entire month, which makes them easier to accomplish. Second, it serves as a reminder system of what needs to be done. One does not need to depend on his memory.

Every three months there is a fifth week; this is a bonus week for catching up on work and for doing quarterly tasks. I seldom accomplish everything on each week's list, but at least I have systematically reminded myself what needs to be done or what I would like to do.

The two reminder systems on the following pages accomplish different purposes. The master monthly calendar reminds me of things that need to be done quarterly or annually. I have included January through June as a model. The five-week system reminds me of things I want or need to do each month.

JANUARY REMINDERS
CALENDAR QUARTER

Church Board Staff/Elder

> The staff should request that the church board designate part of their salary as house allowance for tax purposes.
>
> Prepare for annual business meeting on the fourth Thursday. Need film for the kids and sitters for babies. Ask non-members to sit.

S.S.   Order S.S. curriculum for the next quarter by the 21st. Start to line up adult classes and teachers.

C.E.   Provide a master calendar of C.E. events for all C.E. commission members for the next six months.

Camp   Turn in stats for winter camps.

Mid-Week Clubs

Misc.   Promote the Couple's Conference

Personal   Determine what conference materials to review for the next quarter.

FEBRUARY REMINDERS
MIDDLE QUARTER

Church Board Staff/Elder

S.S.   Distribute Sunday school materials to the teachers. Send note informing them to read the teaching sections and plan to attend teachers' meetings the last Sunday of February. Review your quarter teachers' and missions' goals. Promote the membership and discovery classes that start next month.

Write adult Sunday school class descriptions for the bulletin.

(1) Redo the visitor's handout map.

(2) Redo the large maps in foyers.

(3) Redo reader board.

(4) Inserts in the visitors' packets.

(5) Put up new door signs for the adult Sunday school classes.

(6) Make sure handouts are prepared and distributed for the membership class.

Sunday school clerk should check S.S. supplies and A.V. inventory for the quarter. Inform S.S. secretary of all inventory changes.

Plan the Sunday school teachers' meeting for last Sunday of the month. Be sure teachers are well-stocked for the new quarter.

C.E.   Evaluate couple's conference. Set date for next year, location, and speaker.

Camp   Committee to decide on bus departure and arrival times and fees.

Turn in speakers' names for summer camp.

Work on camp for next summer—date and speaker.

Mid-Week Clubs

Misc.   Promote the Christian Workers' Conference coming in March. Encourage registration.

Personal   Check oil, tires, general condition of car. Plan spring family activities.

MARCH REMINDERS
SEASONAL QUARTER

*** _____ is Daylight Savings Time***

Church Board Staff/Elder

S.S.   Send memo to teachers reminding them to collect and return for credit all unused S.S. literature by the 15th. Record what was returned and clip it to the current curriculum order.

S.S./AWANA Collect and summarize attendance and registration information for winter quarter.

Quarter Report:

(1) Summarize list of teachers for S.S.

(2) Summarize list of new people recruited for S.S., Awana, camp, etc.

(3) Record their names and positions.

(4) If any changes, correct the reader board.

Remind each department head of regular matters over the next quarter.

Review goals for next quarter with C.E. commission.

Plan and prepare for and publicize teacher training opportunities for the upcoming quarter. C.E.F./ CWC/Curriculum Workshop/Teacher's Meetings.

C.E. Ask C.E. members to have prayer requests for the week of prayer ready for the April meeting.

Camp Committee to decide on dates and directors for summer camp for the following year. Work on camp planning packet for summer camp.

Mid-Week Clubs

Misc. Summarize workshop notes from CWC. Contact people who attended and ask what they learned. Challenge them to implement 2 or 3 ideas. Check back for evidence of implementation. Save list of registrants for CWC and sample of the year's promotional inserts.

Personal

APRIL REMINDERS
CALENDAR QUARTER

*** _____ is National Secretaries' Week***

Church Board Staff/Elder

S.S.   Order S.S. curriculum for the next quarter. Order by 21st.
Start to line up adult classes and teachers for the next quarter.

Begin recruiting S.S. and Awana teachers for next fall.

Plan for baby dedication service on Mother's Day next month. See form in April file. Decide which service it will be in.

Begin preparations for the Week of Prayer.

C.E.

Evangelism/Outreach

Promote 5-Day Clubs and training.

Camp   Work on camp planning packet for summer camp. Run dates of camp in the bulletin.

Mid-Week Clubs

Run in the bulletin in late April the last day of clubs and the nursery.

Misc.   Determine what conference materials to review and read for the next quarter. Schedule it.

Announcements/Bulletin: Run appreciation cards in the bulletin for S.S. teachers.

Make an announcement and ask people to write a note and send it to a S.S. teacher this week. Do the same week as S.S. Appreciation Dinner.

Personal

MAY REMINDERS
MIDDLE QUARTER

Church Board Staff/Elder

S.S.   Have S.S. materials distributed to the teachers.
Send note informing them to read the teaching sec-

tions and plan to attend teacher's meeting the last Sunday of May. Promote discovery and membership classes.

Write adult S.S. class descriptions for the bulletin. Promote the New Members' class.

(1) Redo the visitor's handout map.

(2) Redo the large maps in foyers.

(3) Redo reader board.

(4) Inserts in the visitors' packets.

(5) Put up new door signs for the adult S.S. classes.

(6) Make sure handouts are prepared and distributed for the membership class.

S.S. clerk should check S.S. supplies and A.V. inventory for the quarter. Inform S.S. secretary of all inventory changes.

Plan for the S.S. teachers' meeting for last Sunday of the month. Be sure teachers are well-stocked for the new quarter.

Continue lining up clubs and S.S. teachers for next fall.

C.E.

Camp   Work with camp elder to promote camps.

Schedule a Sunday night to take an offering for camp scholarships. Notify ushers to take the offering.

Work on a camp planning packet for summer camp.

Turn in requests for summer camp devotional material.

Run bulletin request for camp workers and counselors.

Mid-Week Clubs

Skating party. Remember to bring tapes for music to skate to.

Misc.   Write thank you notes to whoever coordinates the Week of Prayer. Schedule a graduation evening service. Make sure it's not the same month as a school graduation function.

Personal   Check/change motor oil in car. Check tires. Plan sum-
            mer family activities.

JUNE REMINDERS
SEASONAL QUARTER

Church Board Staff/Elder
S.S.   Collect and return for credit all unused S.S. literature
            by the 15th.
            Record what was returned and clip it to the current
            quarter curriculum order.
            Check on date of S.S. promotion for junior and senior
            high school.
S.S./AWANA Collect and summarize attendance and registration in-
            formation for winter quarter.
            Quarter Report:
            (1) Summarize list of teachers for S.S.
            (2) Summarize list of new people recruited for Sunday
                school/AWANA/camp/etc.
            (3) Record their names and positions.
            Remind each department head of regular matters
            over the next quarter.
            Review goals for next quarter with C.E. commission.
            Plan and prepare for and publicize teacher training
            opportunities for the upcoming quarter.
C.E.   Provide the C.E. commission with a calendar of events.
Camp   Pass out forms for NBC camp statistics.
            Turn in summer camp director planning sheets with
            attachments.
VBS   Send a thank you note to the VBS director.
Mid-Week Clubs
Misc.   Send thank you notes to Women's Bible Study leaders
            and MOPS president.
Personal

Monthly Responsibilities

WEEK ONE

Monday

Tuesday   Gather information on last month's accomplishments and activities. Summarize. List who was recruited for what.

Wednesday Continue to gather and summarize information.
Work on S.S. 2-3 hours.
Talk with Sunday school superintendent. Set up C.E. meeting and work through the progress report form.
Request attendance figures and S.S. and Awana new registrations.

Thursday   Compare and evaluate accomplishments and activities with last month's goals.
Give a summary report and evaluation.
Fill out monthly report sheets.
Set goals for the next month.

Friday   Set goals for the next month. Call or meet with _____
_____. Dictation of notes.

Saturday

Sunday   Call or meet with _____.

WEEK TWO

Monday   Personal bills and budget.

Tuesday   Plan to take someone out to lunch and meet with him.
Review next month's activities.

Wednesday Work on Awana 3 hours.
Trash for an hour.
Set time to meet with Awana commander and work through the progress report form.

Thursday   Review conference materials and notes. Give notes to others to read and think about.

Friday   Prepare for camp meeting one hour.
          Send an encouragement card to someone.
Saturday Read.
Sunday

WEEK THREE

Monday   Write letters.
Tuesday   Determine what church/personal projects I want to work
          on for next month.
          Study on improving message preparations/church
          growth, etc.
Wednesday Go through *Daily Walk* and summarize key teaching
          insights.
          File illustrations.
          Contact nursery superintendents and work through
          the progress report forms.
Thursday Check up on _____ ministries.
          Call _____. How is S.S. going?
Friday   Dictate notes.
Saturday Plan family devotions/missions emphasis/mission-
          ary and family letters/family prayer items for the next
          month.
          Write letters.
          Read/prepare for S.S. lesson.
Sunday   Meet or call _____.

WEEK FOUR

Monday   Personal/bills/budget or letter.
Tuesday   Go to library.
          Recognize a C.E. group in the bulletin.
          Schedule day and hour for routine meetings for the
          next month:
          1st Thurs.—C.E. meeting (evening)
          2d Tues.—GSAE pastor's luncheon (12:00-1:30 P.M.)

3d Thurs.. _____ Meeting (8-10 P.M.)
4th Thurs.—Elder's meeting
Weekly—recruitment, visitation
Periodic—DCE, Staff luncheon, CEW meeting

Wednesday Recognize a S.S. class on Sunday night.

Contact children's church superintendent and work through program report form.

Work on Keys for Kids. Summarize and file.

Thursday Do the financial report for the month.

Review philosophy of ministry statement and C.E. goals.

Set goals and deadlines for the next month.

Friday Determine what I want to read for the next month.

Saturday Read/prepare for S.S. lesson.

Sunday Coordinate my calendar with _____.

Schedule school/piano/church functions.

Schedule two family outreach/fellowship socials.

Determine what house/yard/car projects to do.

Set family plans for the coming month, e.g., outings/trips/treats/meals, reading (missionary stories and good literature).

Library trip.

Something special with _____.

Devotions and singing.

WEEK FIVE

Monday

Tuesday Schedule dates for seasonal events coming up.

Inform C.E. commission.

Identify items for special prayer and planning for Friday.

Study recruitment.

Wednesday Screen books for church library. Recommend and order books. Ask C.E. commission members for suggestions.

Trash and file (3-5 hours).

	Review my annual goals and my job description.
Thursday	Catch-up day. Dictate notes, review lay leadership developments.
Friday	Use the entire day for creative thinking and long-range planning and prayer.
Saturday	Plan family calendar for the upcoming quarter/season. List, select, set dates.
Sunday	See Saturday.

PROGRESS REPORT
COLOSSIANS 1:28-29

Ministry _____ Name _____

Your Position _____ Date _____

1. *Blessings* we are experiencing in our ministry:

2. *Progress* we are making toward our *goals:*

3. *Problems* or needs requiring attention:

4. *Questions* that come to mind:

5. *Ideas* we want to suggest:

GOALS AND ACTION STEPS
COLOSSIANS 1:28-29

1. List 2 or 3 goals you would like to work toward over the next month or quarter.

    a.

    b.

    c.

2. Write out a plan of action for teaching one of your goals listed above.

3. List items to be taken care of by our next meeting.

4. Prayer requests:

5. Date and time of next meeting:

Appendix C

When Should A Church Hire a CES?

"When do we hire a CES?" is a question that takes a complex answer. No two churches are exactly alike. We have isolated four major factors for evaluating the need: potential, proportion, program, and pastor. By providing a series of questions, church leaders may be able to find the correct answer for their church.

POTENTIAL

Four questions will help in evaluating the potential of having a CES on staff.

1. What is the size of your congregation? Many experts believe that a staff member should be added for every 150-200 people in a congregation.
2. Does the church (leadership, pastor, people) desire to grow to the next size level?
3. What is the size of your community in relationship to the size of your church? Are there enough people available to substantially increase the size of your church?

4. In what kind of community is the church? Different kinds of communities may call for different strategies. Does the church mainly service suburbs, retirement areas, resort communities? Clearly the needs of the inner city differ from those of rural areas. A CES may not be the best choice in every case.

5. What is the financial strength of your church? Can you afford to adequately support another person (and his/her family if married)? Will an additional salary and benefits stretch the resources of the church where they will eventually resent the extra burden?

PROPORTION

Before answering these questions, you will need to do a little research. Determine the demographic elements of the church in three categories: adults, youth, children. Then, collect a copy of the church budget and a set of plans for the church building showing square footage for all classroom and sanctuary spaces. Next, prepare an hourly breakdown of the average workweek for each member of the professional staff. Finally, determine whether the answers to the following questions reveal any glaring weaknesses. You may put your answers into the following chart.

	Children	Youth	Adult
Staff			
Dollars			
Space			

1. Approximately how much professional staff time is devoted to each age group? (Remember, each believer, regardless of age, deserves professional attention.) Could this be modified by reallocating present staff priorities, or is another person really needed?

2. Approximately how much actual space is devoted to each age group? The sanctuary counts as a facility for adults, but youth should not be considered unless they can use it regularly for something besides the worship service. If you subtract the sanctuary space, are there still major differences between the ideal and the available space? Generally, allocate 35 square feet per child, 25 square feet per youth, and 15 square feet per adult. For how many people in each category have you provided? Do you really need a person to help you reallocate old space or design new space based upon your statistics?

3. Can you categorize your operating budget according to dollars spent on each of the three age groups? Be fair. For example, staff salaries ought to be assigned to the group where they have direct contact and ministry. Activities that primarily benefit adults should be assigned to adults. Does this analysis provide any insights about the priorities of your church? Do you need someone to lead you in shifting any of these priorities?

PROGRAM

Examine your present program and what you want educationally for your church. List all your programs and then those you wish to have. Be realistic. Then ask two key questions about the leadership of these programs:

1. How many volunteer leaders will this programming require? Like followers, leaders need some person to whom to report and with whom they can plan. A church with a vacation Bible school, Sunday school, and children's church that wants to add a shepherding ministry, home Bible studies, and a media center eventually would have six leaders. Who will give these people the support they need to provide the ministry you desire?

2. Does your leadership have any qualitative improvements they wish to make? If so, this may require leadership de-

velopment. Is this realistically more than a volunteer can do? Is any specialized training necessary to help achieve these improvements?

PASTOR

The current problems with short-term associate staff reminds us that this is not a marginal factor. Two people won't fit in a one-man show. In considering an additional staff member, the pastor should honestly answer these questions:

1. Am I ready to share the loyalties of the people?
2. Am I prepared for the fact that some people will actually prefer my associate?
3. Do I truly want to spend time planning the ministry with someone else?
4. Could I accept a better idea and give credit?
5. Would I want this person to succeed?
6. Can I enjoy watching financial resources going to this new person and his area of ministry?
7. Would I protect this person from undue criticism?
8. Can I like someone who disagrees with me?
9. Can I work well in collegial relationships?
10. Would others feel I handle different opinions well?

Should A Church Hire A C.E. Consultant?

For decades some denominations have provided their smaller churches with regional C.E. consultants. But a more entrepeneurial appproach has been pioneered in the last twenty years. In this model, one CES serves four to six churches in a single area. Because the CES's role is highly administrative, he can meet one night each week with the leadership of a different church. The churches reimburse the CES on a negotiated-contract basis. By spreading the cost over several churches, even very small churches could budget expert weekly counsel and receive help in strategizing and evaluating their ministries.

What would the actual cost be? In 1988 dollars, if six churches divided equally a $39,000 annual salary, the cost would be only $6,500 each. The overall salary may appear to be high, but the CES would need to bear all hospitalization and retirement costs and his or her social security. A seasoned veteran might be worth even more.

At $6,500 a year, or approximately $550 a month per church, many churches would benefit and could afford a CES. Moreover, small churches might move beyond that "little church" hump that finds them small but unable to grow to another size without expert help. Conversely, CESs could stabilize their family geography as they would be less subject to the whims of a church board or a single pastor.

Larry Hutt developed this concept as a consultant CES. For more information contact: Christian Education Leadership Service, P.O. Box 706, Palo Cedro, CA 96073.

Appendix D

Results of the CES Survey

The survey respondents totaled 146, but not all responded to every question. Each question has a different base on which percentages are fixed.

Regional Replies

Three-fourths of the responses came from the Northeast, Southwest, and West. There were no responses from seventeen states.

Respondents are members of the Professional Association of Christian Educators, and the authors are grateful for the assistance of PACE in this study. For more information about the study or PACE, write: Professional Association of Christian Educators, 8405 N. Rockwell, 5 Plaza Square Suite 222, Oklahoma City, OK 73132 (telephone 405-841-1712).

Northeast	39 replies (9 women)
Southeast	21 replies (7 women)
Southwest	32 replies (1 woman)
West	36 replies (5 women)
Central	16 replies (4 women)

Ages

20-24:	2	25-29:	11
30-34:	33	35-39:	28
30-44:	27	45-49:	18
50-54:	10	55-59:	7
60-64:	2	65-69:	1

73% of responders were 30-50 years old.

Church Size

Number in Attendance	At Worship	At Sunday School
25-49		1
50-74	1	1
75-99		2
100-199	6	13
200-299	5	16
300-399	11	15
400-499	13	10
500-599	12	16
600-699	19	6
700-799	6	7
800-899	5	8
900-999	3	8
1000-1499	22	9
1500-1999	8	10
2000-2499	9	1
2500-2999	3	2
3000-3499	3	3
3500-3999	1	
4000-4499		
4500-4999	1	
5000+	1	

Most had larger attendance at worship than S.S. Two had larger S.S. Nine percent of those reporting both figures had less than one-half worshipers also attending S.S.

Titles/Responsibilities

Pastor	4	Associate Pastor	8
Dir. of Discipleship	2	Assistant Pastor	3
Dir./Min./Pstr. of C.E.	69	Asst./Assoc. of C.E.	2
Dir./Min to Children	15	Asst. Dir./Min. to Children	1
Min. of Youth	2	Pstr of Adult Ed./Music	1

Multiple Titles

Visitation	1	Family	2
Outreach	1	Children & Families	1
Children	1	Youth & Families	2
Youth	3	Youth & College	1
Adults	1	Singles & Discipleship	1
Music	1	Adults/Discipleship	4
Administration	3	Nurture	1

Other: (one each)
> Assoc. Pastor Ministry Development
> Minister of Christian Development
> Minister of Education and Programs
> Minister of Programs
> Director of Learning Center
> Assoc. Pastor Shepherding
> Director of Church Growth
> Pastor of Families, Pastoral Care
> Assoc. Pastor of Care Ministries

Half of those responding held title of Dir./Min. or Pastor of C.E. The next largest group represented were Dir./Min to Children. As later responses showed, the title was not always a reliable indication of responsibilities.

Major Role

62% coordinator/administrator
27% recruiter/trainer
16% planner

14% leader/director
12% encourager
12% equipper/enabler

Smaller percentages of responders indicated their role included: new-program developer, motivator, resource person, discipler, teacher, counselor, adviser, partner, modeler, pastor, manager of staff relationships, communicator, dreamer, conciliator, and consultant.

Experience

Years at 1st Church	No. of Responses
0-4	39
5-9	39
10-14	17
15-19	4
more	3

Figures above do not include 44 responders (30% of survey) still in the first four years of their first church ministry. One-fourth of those who had served at more than one church served less than five years at the first.

Total years experience represented by survey: 1425

Affiliation

31 Independent/non-demon./inter-denom.
15 Evangelical Free Church
11 Church of Christ
6 PC US, Conserv. Bapt., Amer. Bapt., Bible churches
5 Methodist
4 Church of God, Assemblies of God, Ind. Christian
3 Presbyterian, Evan. Pres., Ind. Bapt., Bapt. Gen. Conf.
2 PC America, Baptist, Salvation Army, IFCA, Christian
1 each, thirteen other denominations

Work Schedule

One-half of full-time workers (40 hrs. +) said one-third of

their time was devoted to administrative matters.

Bible study and prayer: One-half reported this at #1 or #2 in hours, but this question was worded so that some of the responders may have interpreted it as including time spent teaching.

Average weekly time allocation for full-time workers:

6½ hours   teacher meetings, staff meetings, board meetings
4 hours   on the phone
5¾ hours   planning
3 hours   teaching
2¼ hours   training

Educational Background

  4   no degree
35   bachelor's degree (one-quarter of responders)
89   master's degree (about two-thirds of responders)
  5   doctor's degree

Total respondents: 133. These figures include seventeen responders with degrees in secular areas.

Of the 116 reporting completion of a master's degree:

M.A.	13	M.A.C.E.	26	M.Div.	17
M.R.E.	17	M.A.R.	4	Th.M.	23
M.Ed.	5	M.S.	8	M.A.B.S.	1
M.C.M.	1	M.B.A.	1		

46% of master's degrees reported specified education.

Salaries

Full Time (includes all benefits)		Part Time (7)	
Under $20,000	7	Under $20,000	5
Under $30,000	42	$20,000+	2
Under $40,000	56		
Under $50,000	24		
$50,000+	8		

Of full-timers, 40% were paid less than $40,000 including benefits; 30% less than $30,000.

Age Respondent Decided to Enter Full-time Ministry

5-9	(2)	10-14	(11)	15-19	(40)	20-24	(45)
25-29	(19)	30-34	(13)	35-39	(5)	40-44	(6)
45-49	(0)	50-54	(1)				

28% of responders had decided on vocational ministry as a teen; 45% made the decision in their 20s.

Who Influenced Decision?

Pastor	46	Success in lay ministry	5
Family	18	Teachers/profs	13
Youth leader	11	Coworkers in lay min.	8
Felt called	26	Discipler	2
Role models	4	Campus Crusade	2
Friends	9	Young Life	1
Camp experiences	6	CSB	2
Missionaries	5	Classes in C.E.	1
Church members	1	Director of C.E.	3

Two-thirds were influenced by vocational ministers, one-third specified their pastor; 13% were influenced by family/spouse.

Previous Vocation

Approximately 35% of responses indicated no previous vocation other than that of student. Of those reporting previous vocations:
25% education
44% business/management/sales, white collar/blue collar, science, medicine, engineering
28% ministry-related vocation
(Total percentage includes overlap in some categories.)

Parachurch/Community Involvement

16% very involved
36% limited involvement
32% little or no involvement
16% did not respond to this question, which may have been an indication of little or no involvement.

Those who reported involvement listed: school system, athletic leagues, hospital work, ministries to homeless/abused.

Parachurch organizations mentioned specifically included: Young Life, Campus Crusade, Intervarsity, Navigators, NADCE.

Most who reported involvement beyond the local church specified denominationally related boards and committees. These were sometimes reported as parachurch, so figures may be inflated regarding active involvement in community affairs outside the local church.

Staff Relationships

28% on multi-staff churches reported that they got along better with the congregation than they did with the senior pastor.

18% on multi-staff felt their relationship with the congregation and lay boards/committees was better than their relationship with other vocational staff.

5% reported a better relationship with other vocational staff than with congregation and lay boards/committees.

For the most part, the relationships between various elements was too similar to make distinctions.

Programming Responsibilities

Total responses: 141. Of those reporting direct, specific responsibilities:

92%   Sunday School
75%   Weekday Clubs
73%   VBS
70%   Children's Church
61%   Camping

Specific Programs

Weekday clubs	99	Family	5
Pioneer Girls	19	Senior Adults	5
Awana	13	Media/Resource Center	80
Pioneer Boys	11	Membership	3
CSB	12	Library	5
Boy Scouts	1	Weekday studies	18
Adventure	1	Handicapped program	3
Whirlybirds	1	Weekday Sch./Child care	13
MOPS	16	Women's min.	6
Missions	3		

No specific responsibilities
(for some, this meant in charge of everything)   5
Oversee entire program but do not direct   4

Specific Age Group Responsibilities

47 reported that they oversee entire C.E. ministry
 4 oversee youth exclusively
25 oversee children exclusively
34 oversee children and adults only
25 oversee adults exclusively

36% of those reporting specific age group responsibilities indicated children and adults with the exclusion of youth.
27% indicated children exclusively.

Secretarial Help

63 no secretary or shared a secretary
78 exclusive use of secretary (55%). Of these, 26 were full-time secretaries; 52 were part time; 21% had exclusive use of a full-time secretary

Problems of Women CESs

(21 of the 26 responded to this question)
Twice as many reported problems as reported supportive, encouraging situations with opportunities to use gifts. The five most

common problems (not listed in order of frequency) are:
1. Difficulty of working with an all-male staff
2. Accorded less credibility or respect
3. Lower salary
4. Lack of acceptance or support
5. Balancing church/home responsibilities

Problems/Frustrations

One-third reported worker recruitment problems (highest number of complaints). Comments on recruiting: apathy, low motivation, hard to match right people to right job, low commitment level, never-ending job.

Other problems listed in order of frequency reported:

1. Apathetic laity with lack of vision (20%) often due to a low priority for C.E. ministry (25%)
2. Problems with other staff, including senior pastor (17%). Half making this complaint specified problem was with senior pastor. Half cited lack of support/teamwork from other staff members.
3. Not enough time (13%)
4. Too much time devoted to administrative details (9%)
5. Family pressures, personal problems (8%; includes stress ministry placed on family, little time for personal spiritual growth or social needs, and illness)
6. Too many tasks, spread too thin (6%); too little money for ministry (6%); too little space for programs (6%)
7. Problems with teacher training (5%)

There were as many complaints about staff relationships as about the combined problems of too many responsibilities, too little money, and too little space.

Recruitment Problems

Reported people not willing to commit to a period of six months to one year (25%)

General apathy (10%)

People had no time available to volunteer (9%)

Recruiters did not know prospects' gifts or spiritual maturity (5%)

CES had no time for recruitment or felt uncomfortable with the task (5%)

Job makes extra demands on working parent, longer weeks, travel (5%)

CES did not know people in large congregation (4%)

Lay people do not want to act as recruiters (4%)

Other complaints received from the CES:

1. The job is continual, perpetual.
2. Recruitment effort not backed by other staff.
3. Overprogramming creates stiff competition for workers.
4. Church policies limit who can serve.
5. Hard to get a person out of a position for which he or she is not qualified.
6. How to match workers to jobs.
7. No recruitment strategy.
8. Surprised by sudden staff needs.
9. Recruits would need training before serving.
10. Recruits suffer rapid burnout.

Recruitment Strategies

39% of those offering responses specified personal contact. Other recruitment strategies include:

1. Make appointments to interview all prospective teachers/ leaders
2. Involve the C.E. committee and ministerial staff in recruitment
3. Enlist people to pray for recruitment of workers
4. A yearly talent ministry survey on which people indicate their skills
5. Personal one-on-one approach

6. Recruitment booth in foyer
7. Teacher testimonies
8. Children's parade in worship service
9. Inform those in membership classes about service opportunities
10. Keep in close communication, show appreciation of workers
11. A class on discovering spiritual gifts
12. Teachers "perks," recognition, banquet, paid conference attendance
13. Teacher covenant
14. Provide training pre-service and in-service
15. Specify length of service
16. Encourage, support, direct, and develop
17. Work with other staff for referrals
18. Suit duties to the gifts of the recruit
19. Move VBS workers into S.S. positions
20. Anticipate needs, have plenty of lead time
21. Slide or video presentation in worship
22. Recruit from adult S.S. classes
23. Raise perception of the work by professional strategy of recruitment
24. Share the vision of the educational ministry
25. Recruit couples as teaching teams

11% of surveys had no answer or responded: "Looking for one" or "I don't have one."

Teacher Training Strategies

Monthly (or a short series of) training/planning meetings (15%)

Age-graded groups trained separately to make material relevant (13%)

Team new teachers with experienced hands for observation and teams (11%)

Quarterly training/planning meetings (10%)

Personal attention (7%)

Professionally prepared resource materials (6%)

Outside speaker (5%)

Others: meetings with mealtime, CES as model, weekend retreats, encourage attendance at regional or denominational events, teachers choose topics for training and help plan sessions, newsletters/mailings, written job descriptions, teens trained for ministry. 18% had no answer to "successful training strategy," which could be interpreted as simply not having such a strategy.

Teacher Training Problems

(In order of frequency reported)
1. Can't get people to attend
2. People don't feel the need for training
3. Can't find a convenient time slot
4. Can't find good materials/resources
5. Only ones who attend are the ones who need the training the least

Advice on Hiring a Church's First CES

(In order of frequency)
1. Clear, concise job description (38% requested this)
2. Evaluate the needs of your church
3. Make sure the pastor supports the call of a CES
4. Have a philosophy of Christian education
5. Provide adequate budget/salary
6. Provide support of board and congregation (communicate the role expectations to the congregation)
7. Ask searching questions of the candidate and references
8. Raise status of the position
9. Ask CES to be enabler, not a one-man show
10. Support with resources, training, and personnel
11. Determine lines of authority and responsibility
12. Provide room for creativity

Desirable Characteristics

(Listed in order of frequency mentioned by responders):
1. People-oriented
2. Organizer/administrator
3. Servant's heart
4. Experience
5. Pastor
6. Educator
7. Equipper
8. Persevering
9. Loves children
10. Well-trained
11. Visionary
12. Satisfied with assistant position, not using C.E. as stepping-stone

Others included: problem solver, creative, motivator, mature, sound philosophy of C.E., communicator, Bible knowledge, flexible, planner, team worker, sense of humor.

Appendix E

Developing a Church in Response to Aids

SAMPLE POLICIES AND PROCEDURES

As a gathering place for the hurting and the seeking, the local church should welcome those of the community and within the church family itself who have communicable diseases. Despite fears about the human immunodeficiency virus (HIV) that causes AIDS, the church must open its doors to those with this disease as well. The church staff, especially the CES, must be concerned about the interactions of students with their teachers and one another in the classroom setting. Therefore, a thoughtful AIDS policy is needed for most churches.

The following two sample policies are good models that can guide volunteer workers with procedures and philosophy regarding students and church attenders with AIDS and other communicable diseases.

COMMUNICABLE DISEASE POLICY

It is the policy of Black Rock Congregational Church to seek to meet the spiritual needs of each individual who comes to the church honestly seeking worship, fellowship, and spiritual growth. In keeping with such, there will be no exceptions to this policy. This would apply to those with communicable diseases. For those whose diagnosis would require isolation, a proper referral will be made. For those whose diagnosis allows for integration, this will be effected with discretion and sensitivity.

Procedure: Guidelines Relating to Persons with Infectious Diseases

These guidelines apply to infectious diseases transmitted through contact with blood, blood products, excretions, secretions, tissues (including open skin lesions, urine, saliva, vomitus, feces, tears, sweat), drainage from any orifice.

1. *General*
   a. Careful handwashing before and after contact with all individuals and his/her belongings (i.e., clothing) is the most important personal hygiene practice. Pay particular attention to around and under fingernails and between the fingers.
   b. Disposable gloves should be used any time there will be contact with blood or body fluids (i.e., urine, bowel movements, disposable diapers, gauze pads, or dressings). Gloves need not be worn in ordinary contact.
   c. Surfaces contaminated with blood or body fluids should be promptly cleaned and disinfected with a solution of household bleach. The solution should be left on the surface to be disinfected for at least ten minutes before it is rinsed or wiped off. The surface should be wiped with a disposable cloth and then rinsed with another disposable cloth containing warm water.

2. *Personal Contact*
   a. Affection is an important part of care, especially for chil-

dren. Cuddling, hugging, feeding, and kissing on non-mucous membranes (e.g., cheek) are considered perfectly safe.

  b. Care providers who are accidentally exposed to blood or body fluids (i.e., urine) should wear gloves when removing their soiled clothing and wash with soap and water. Contaminated garments should be handled as in D.2. "Laundry." When accidental skin exposure occurs, remove blood or body substances by washing exposed areas with soap and water.

  c. Any display of an orientation toward biting, i.e., child v. child, child v. adult, should be immediately and firmly discouraged. This activity should then be brought to the attention of the parents by the staff person involved.

3. *Contact with Blood*
  a. Skin Breaks
     Persons providing care should attempt to minimize breaks in their skin. (Chapping of hands can be prevented by the use of hand lotion.) If the ill person has breaks in the skin, the care giver should use gloves when touching those areas. Good handwashing should be used before and after any direct contact.

  b. Bleeding Lesions
     Bleeding or oozing cuts or abrasions (either the care giver or the ill person) should be covered with gauze or adhesive bandages whenever possible. The care giver's fingernails should be kept trimmed and clean to prevent scratching or cutting the patient.

4. *Items that May Be Contaminated with Secretions and Excretions*
  a. Food, Dishes, and Utensils
     Mouth to mouth sharing of food and other objects (i.e., pencils, toys) should be discouraged. Utensils (spoons, forks, knives) should not be shared. Otherwise, special precautions related to food, dishes, and utensils are unnecessary; e.g., separate dishwashing for the dishes and utensils used

by the ill person is unnecessary. Regular dishwashing with soap and hot water is all that is necessary before use by others.

b. Laundry

As with dishes, washing with soap and hot water, followed by thorough rinsing, is suggested. If available, a washing machine and dryer should be utilized. In general, separate laundering is not needed for items used by the ill person.

Before washing, body-fluid-contaminated items only should be stored in plastic bags and washed separately in the hottest water setting for at least 25 minutes. A standard laundry soap and ½ cup of bleach should be added per wash load. Gloves should be worn when handling contaminated items.

In order to prevent staining of blood-soiled clothing, laundry may be soaked immediately in one cup of bleach to one gallon cold water solution for at least ten minutes, then wash as stated above.

c. Disposable Items

(1) Used gloves, gauze pads, disposable diapers, disposable washcloths, or any other disposable materials from the patient should be carefully and promptly discarded in sealed trash bags or containers.

(2) Do not share toothbrushes, towels, combs, or other personal items.

Disinfect with bleach solution after use.

5. *Disinfectants*

a. The most commonly used disinfectant is a solution of household bleach, such as Clorox or Purex. The recommended strength is one cup of bleach per gallon of water. This solution should be prepared fresh daily. Commercially prepared solutions in spray bottles are also acceptable for use.

b. Spilled blood or other body fluids should be disinfected with bleach solution. Contaminated surfaces should then be cleaned with soap and water.

c. In order for disinfectants to work, they should be left on areas for at least ten minutes before rinsing with water.

Source: Black Rock Community Church, Fairfield, Connecticut. Used by permission.

A STATEMENT FROM THE ELDERS ON HIV
(THE AIDS VIRUS)
AND
OUR CHURCH'S RESPONSE TO THOSE INFECTED

It is the responsibility of First Evangelical Free Church to encourage righteousness in the way that we corporately and individually demonstrate the breadth and length and height and depth of Christ's love to all of God's creation (Eph. 3:14-19). Because of the presence of growing numbers of persons with AIDS in our society and the fears that many have about having casual contact with such persons, the board of elders of First Evangelical Free Church has adopted the following policy on AIDS to apply to the life of the church.

Regardless of the factors that may have led to the contracting of a particular disease, Christians are called to have compassion on all persons in need. Because we are followers of Jesus Christ, we must follow His example and teaching, as well as those of the Old and New Testament writers in showing comfort and compassion to those who suffer from HIV disease. Just as Jesus showed compassion on those with leprosy (the HIV disease of His day), so must we show concern, compassion, and Christ's love and attempt to comfort those who may have this equally dreaded disease of our day and society. Colossians 3:12 urges us as God's chosen ones to be full of compassion, kindness, and gentleness to those afflicted ones about us.

Acquired Immune Deficiency Syndrome (AIDS) is a serious, life-threatening condition that is not transmissible by casual contact. The best scientific evidence indicates that AIDS is caused by a virus known as HIV (human immunodeficiency virus), which is transmitted through the exchange of blood or semen by infected sexual partners, contaminated needles, contaminated blood, or by infected mothers to their infants.

Medical knowledge about AIDS is developing, and thus is incomplete. It is almost certainly true that infection with the HIV virus takes a multiplicity of forms, some disabling and some not, varying not only from individual to individual, but also from one phase to another within the same individual. From what is known today, AIDS reduces the body's immune response, leaving the infected person vulnerable to life-threatening infections and malignancies.

In responding to the knowledge that someone attending FEFC has been infected with the AIDS virus, the Board of Elders will be guided by current medical knowledge, the known behavior of Jesus Christ, and the principles of compassion and ministry established in the Bible.

An individual who has been diagnosed as being HIV-positive or having AIDS would be treated with the same compassion as any other individual attending FEFC. In general, FEFC will not reject or ostracize anyone who is HIV-positive or who has AIDS, as long as that individual presents no real threat to the safety of others in the congregation. The confidentiality of HIV-positive individuals will be determined case by case based on the risk of potential exposure to others within the church.

In the case of infants or small children who are HIV positive, U.S. Public Health Service guidelines are being followed. Nursery and children's workers will be trained accordingly.

We acknowledge that there are innocent victims who contract AIDS and other diseases through no fault of their own, such as health care workers, those who contract HIV through blood transfusions, rape, and babies born to HIV positive mothers. Due to the fact that AIDS has been spread in our nation and world primarily through behavior that is immoral and/or illegal (sexual immorality and drug abuse), we must affirm the biblical teaching that sexual intimacy is to be experienced only in the committed relationship of heterosexual marriage. Other kinds of sexual be-

havior are not only dishonoring to God but bear specific consequences of spiritual guilt and physical disease. The only "safe sex"
is sex that is according to the plan of God. The abuse of drugs in-
vites a variety of tragic consequences.

Source: First Evangelical Free Church, Wichita, Kansas. Used
by permission.

General Index

Moody Press, a ministry of the Moody Bible Institute, is designed for education, evangelization, and edification. If we may assist you in knowing more about Christ and the Christian life, please write us without obligation: Moody Press, c/o MLM, Chicago, IL 60610.